The OFFICIAL DSA THEORY TEST for Drivers of Large Vehicles

London: TSO

Written and compiled by the Learning Materials section of the Driving Standards Agency (DSA).

Questions and answers are compiled by the Question Development Team of the DSA.

Published with the permission of the Driving Standards Agency on behalf of the Controller of Her Majesty's Stationery Office.

First published 1996
Tenth edition 2008

ISBN 978 0 11 552903 0

A CIP catalogue record for this book is available from the British Library.

Other titles in the official DSA series

The Official DSA Theory Test for Car Drivers
The Official DSA Theory Test Revision Papers for Car Drivers
The Official DSA Guide to Learning to Drive
Helping Learners to Practise - the official DSA guide
The Official DSA Guide to Driving - the essential skills
The Official DSA Theory Test for Motorcyclists
The Official DSA Guide to Learning to Ride
The Official DSA Guide to Riding - the essential skills
The Official DSA Guide to Driving Buses and Coaches
The Official DSA Guide to Driving Goods Vehicles
The Official DSA Guide to Tractor and Specialist Vehicle Driving Tests
The Official DSA Theory Test for Car Drivers (CD-Rom)
Prepare for your Practical Driving Test (DVD)
The Official DSA Theory Test for Motorcyclists (CD-Rom)
The Official DSA Theory Test for Drivers of Large Vehicles (CD-Rom)
The Official DSA Guide to Hazard Perception (DVD)
DSA Driving Theory DVD Game
The Official Highway Code Interactive CD-Rom
Driver CPC – The Official DSA Guide for Professional Bus and Coach Drivers

Every effort has been made to ensure that the information contained in this publication is accurate at the time of going to press. The Stationery Office cannot be held responsible for any inaccuracies. Information in this book is for guidance only.

All metric and imperial conversions in this book are approximate.

Directgov

Directgov is the place to find all government motoring information and services. From logbooks to licensing, from driving tests to road tax, go to:

www.direct.gov.uk/motoring

Transportoffice

For all government motoring information relating to drivers of large vehicles, Approved Driving Instructors, trainers and taxi drivers, go to:

www.transportoffice.gov.uk

Theory and practical tests

DSA bookings and enquiries

Online **www.transportoffice.gov.uk**

Practical & Theory Tests
Enquiries & Bookings **0300 200 1122**
Welsh Speakers **0300 200 1133**

Practical Tests
Minicom **0300 200 1144**
Fax **0300 200 1155**

Theory Tests
Minicom **0300 200 1166**
Fax **0300 200 1177**
Customer Enquiry Unit **0300 200 1188**

DVA (Northern Ireland)

Theory test **0845 600 6700**
Practical test **0845 247 2471**

Driving Standards Agency

(Headquarters)

www.dsa.gov.uk

The Axis Building
112 Upper Parliament Street
Nottingham NG1 6LP

Tel **0115 936 6666**
Fax **0115 936 6570**

Driver & Vehicle Agency (Testing) in Northern Ireland

www.dvani.gov.uk

Balmoral Road, Belfast BT12 6QL

Tel **02890 681 831**
Fax **02890 665 520**

Driver & Vehicle Licensing Agency

(GB Licence Enquiries)

www.dvla.gov.uk

Longview Road, Swansea SA6 7JL

Tel **0870 240 0009**
Fax **01792 783 071**
Minicom **01792 782 787**

Driver & Vehicle Agency (Licensing) in Northern Ireland

www.dvani.gov.uk

County Hall, Castlerock Road,
Coleraine BT51 3TB

Tel **02870 341 469**
24 hour tel **0345 111 222**
Minicom **02870 341 380**

The Driving Standards Agency (DSA) is an executive agency of the Department for Transport. You'll see the DSA logo at theory and practical test centres.

DSA aims to promote road safety through the advancement of driving standards, by

- establishing and developing high standards and best practice in driving and riding on the road; before people start to drive, as they learn, and after they pass their test
- ensuring high standards of instruction for different types of driver and rider
- conducting the statutory theory and practical tests efficiently, fairly and consistently across the country
- providing a centre of excellence for driver training and driving standards
- developing a range of publications and other publicity material designed to promote safe driving for life.

www.dsa.gov.uk

The Driver and Vehicle Agency (DVA) is an executive agency within the Department of the Environment for Northern Ireland.

Its primary aim is to promote and improve road safety through the advancement of driving standards and implementation of the Government's policies for improving the mechanical standards of vehicles.

www.dvani.gov.uk/dvta

CONTENTS

introduction

ABOUT THE THEORY TEST

This section covers

- Getting started
- The Theory Test
- After the Theory Test
- Using the questions and answers section

A message from the Chief Driving Examiner

As the driver of a large goods vehicle (LGV) or passenger carrying vehicle (PCV) you have added responsibility. Consequently you must have knowledge and a clear understanding of the principles of safe driving and the ability to apply them.

Whether you're responsible for the safe transportation of goods or passengers, the need for comprehensive knowledge is recognised by the requirement to pass a bespoke theory test. Passing the theory test is an important step towards becoming a professional driver. The knowledge you've acquired should be put into practice on the road.

When you drive a large vehicle you should demonstrate your ability to drive safely and set a good example to others. Your attitude and approach should be courteous and considerate. The safety of the goods or passengers you carry, as well as other road users could depend on it.

This book will help you to prepare for the multiple choice part of the theory test. It contains all the questions from which the test papers are constructed, set out in an easy-to-read style. It also includes explanations as to why the answers are correct along with advice about good driving practice. The Official Guide to Hazard Perception DVD is recommended to help you prepare for the hazard perception part of the theory test.

You'll never know all the answers. Throughout your driving career there will always be more to learn. Remember, the passengers or goods you carry are your responsibility as is the safety of the vehicle and all other road users. By applying and developing the knowledge and skills you have gained during your training, adopting a responsible attitude whilst behind the wheel and driving in a fuel efficient and safe manner, you'll be well on your way to becoming a good professional driver.

Trevor Wedge

Trevor Wedge
Chief Driving Examiner and
Director of Safer Driving

Getting started

Applying for your licence

To obtain your provisional licence you should apply to the Driver and Vehicle Licensing Agency (DVLA) or, in Northern Ireland, Driver and Vehicle Agency (Licensing) (DVA). Application forms (D2) and information leaflets (D100) are available from Traffic Area Offices or DVLA.

To drive a large vehicle you must

- have a full car driving licence
- hold a provisional licence for the category of vehicle you want to drive
- meet the eyesight and medical requirements
- normally be over 21 years of age.

In Northern Ireland you must also complete a criminal records check if you want to drive a PCV.

You can get full details from the DVLA enquiry line on 0870 240 0009 (in Northern Ireland the DVA enquiry line is 02870 341 469).

Medical requirements

You'll be responsible for goods or passengers, so it's vital that you meet exacting medical standards. The medical requirements apply to both LGV and PCV licences.

You can't hold an LGV or a PCV licence unless your eyesight meets the high standard required.

You must be fit and free from any condition that affects your ability to retain control of a large vehicle. If you're disabled, you may drive a vehicle that has been specially adapted for you.

You must have a medical, carried out by a doctor. The doctor has to complete a medical report form, D4 (DLM1 in Northern Ireland) and then this has to be sent in with your licence application.

On the road

When you receive your provisional licence you should check all details are correct. You can then drive on the road as long as you

- drive under the supervision of a person who holds a current licence for the category of vehicle being driven (minimum licence requirements apply, check these with your trainer)
- display L-plates (or D-plates if you prefer when driving in Wales) at the front and back of the vehicle
- display LGV or PCV plates to the front and back of the vehicle when driving in Northern Ireland.

To help you choose an instructor, DSA has a Register of LGV Instructors. To be placed on this register, instructors have had to pass rigorous tests of their driving and instructional ability. You can obtain details from 0115 936 6502. There is no comparable register in Northern Ireland or for PCVs.

Driver Certificate of Professional Competence

A new qualification for professional bus, coach and lorry drivers – the Driver Certificate of Professional Competence (CPC) - is being introduced across the EU. From September 2008 bus and coach drivers, and from September 2009 lorry drivers, wishing to drive professionally will have to hold a Driver CPC.

As part of the initial qualification, they will have to pass a theory test based on case studies, in addition to the multiple choice and hazard perception theory test. There will also be an additional practical test. Further information can be found on www.transportoffice.gov.uk.

About the theory test

To become a professional driver you must have a thorough knowledge of the regulations that apply to your work. When you combine this with a high level of driving skill, it should help you to carry out your work safely.

If you're driving an LGV you have to make sure that your goods arrive at their destination safely. This will involve not only the safety of your load, but also your attitude to others on the road.

If you're driving a PCV you're providing a service to your customers.

Can I take the practical test first?

No. You have to pass both modules of your theory test before you can book a practical test.

Does everyone have to take the theory test?

Normally, if you upgrade your licence within the same category you won't have to sit the test. For example, if you upgrade from a rigid-bodied to an articulated lorry you won't have to take another theory test.However, if you have sub-category C1 and D1 entitlement from when you passed your car test, and you want to upgrade to C or D, you'll have to obtain the correct provisional entitlement and pass both modules of the theory test before booking a practical test.

If you have a full category C licence and wish to take a practical test for category D, you will have to obtain the correct provisional entitlement, and pass the appropriate theory test, before you can book a practical test, and vice versa.

These passengers have been entrusted to your care. You should be aware of the responsibility this carries.

From the start, you must be aware of the differences between driving smaller vehicles and driving large buses or lorries.

You must have a sound knowledge of *The Highway Code*, including the meaning of traffic signs and road markings. You must be particularly aware of those signs that show a restriction for lorries or buses.

Your knowledge of the above information is tested in the first part of the theory test, as a series of multiple choice questions. More information about this part of the test is given on p15 and the questions are given in the main part of the book, beginning on p21.

The second part of the theory test is called the hazard perception part, more information about this is given on p17.

Preparing for your tests

Although you have to pass your theory test before you can take your practical test, we recommend that you start studying for your theory test, but don't actually take it until you have some practical experience of driving larger vehicles.

To prepare for the multiple choice part of the theory test, we strongly recommend that you study the books from which the questions are taken as well as the questions themselves. These books are:

The Official Highway Code - 2007 Edition. Essential reading for all road users. This updated edition contains the very latest rules of the road, up-to-date legislation and provides advice on road safety and best practice.

Know Your Traffic Signs - this contains most of the signs and road markings that you are likely to come across.

Specialist publications - *The Official DSA Guide to Driving Goods Vehicles* and *The Official DSA Guide to Driving Buses and Coaches* cover all aspects of driving these vehicles, in particular the regulations and the way in which they differ from driving smaller vehicles.

They also contain the appropriate practical test syllabus.

The Official DSA Guide to Driving - the essential skills - this contains much general advice about driving which is not necessarily repeated in the specialist books detailed above.

These books will help you to answer the theory test questions correctly and will also help you with your practical test. The information in them will be relevant throughout your driving life so make sure you always have an up-to-date copy that you can refer to.

Why do the questions keep changing?

To make sure that all candidates are being tested fairly, questions and video clips are under continuous review.

Some questions may be changed as a result of customer feedback. They may also be changed to reflect revised legislation, and DSA publications are updated to reflect such changes.

Can I take a mock test?

You can take a mock test for the multiple choice part of the theory test online at **www.transportoffice.gov.uk.**

Other study aids

The Official DSA Theory Test for Drivers of Large Vehicles (CD-Rom) - this is an alternative way of preparing for the multiple choice part of the theory test. You can randomly test yourself against the complete range of theory test questions, create custom tests and take timed mock exams.

The Official DSA Guide to Hazard Perception (DVD) - will help you prepare for the hazard perception test. It includes interactive sample video clips which give you feedback on your performance. You should study and work through this, preferably with your trainer.

All these training materials are available online at **www.tsoshop.co.uk/dsa** or by mail order from **0870 243 0123**.

They are also available from good bookshops and selected computer software retailers.

The Theory Test

Booking your theory test

The easiest ways to book are online or by telephone. You can also book by post.

Booking online or by telephone - by using these methods you'll be given the date and time of your test immediately.

Book online at www.transportoffice.gov.uk (use www.dvani.gov.uk for Northern Ireland).

To book by telephone, call 0300 200 1122 (0845 600 6700 for Northern Ireland).

If you're deaf and use a minicom machine, call 0300 200 1166 and if you are a Welsh speaker, call 0300 200 1133.

You will need your

- DVLA or DVLNI driving licence number
- credit or debit card details (the card holder must book the test). We accept Mastercard, Visa, Delta, Switch/Maestro, Visa Electron and Solo.

You'll be given a booking number and should receive an appointment letter within ten days.

Where can I take the test?

There are over 150 theory test centres throughout England, Scotland and Wales, and six in Northern Ireland. Most people have a test centre within 20 miles of their home, but this will vary depending on the density of population in your area. You can find a list of test centres on page 428.

What if I don't receive an acknowledgement?

If you don't receive an acknowledgement within the time specified above, please telephone the booking office to check that an appointment has been made. We can't take responsibility for postal delays. If you miss your test appointment you will lose your fee.

When are test centres open?

Test centres are usually open on weekdays, some evenings and some Saturdays.

How do I cancel or postpone my test?

You can cancel or postpone your theory test online or by telephone. You should contact the booking office at least three clear working days before your test date, otherwise you'll lose your fee.

Only in exceptional circumstances, such as documented ill-health or family bereavement, can this rule be waived.

Booking by post - If you prefer to book by post, you'll need to fill in an application form. These are available from theory test centres or driving test centres, or your trainer may have one.

You should normally receive an appointment letter within ten days of posting your application form.

Taking your theory test

Arriving at the test centre - You must make sure that when you arrive at the test centre you have all the relevant documents with you, or you won't be able to take your test and you'll lose your fee.

You'll need

- your signed photocard licence and paper counterpart, or
- your signed driving licence and valid passport (your passport doesn't have to be British).

No other form of identification is acceptable.

All documents must be original. We can't accept photocopies.

The test centre staff will check your documents and make sure that you take the right category of test.

Make sure that you arrive in plenty of time so you aren't rushed. If you arrive after the session has started you may not be allowed to take the test.

Remember, if you don't bring your documents your test will be cancelled and you will lose your fee.

You'll then be ready to start your test. The Theory Test is a screen-based test and is made up of two modules. Module 1a is the multiple choice part of the test, and module 1b is the hazard perception part.

Modules 1a and 1b can be taken in any order, and at different sittings, but you must pass both modules to enable you to move onto the next stage of your driving

development, involving taking your practical test. Should you be required to take the new case studies test, you may sit this test either before or after completing both theory test modules as described above.

Languages other than English

In Wales, and at theory test centres on the Welsh borders, you can take your theory test with Welsh text on screen. A voiceover can also be provided in Welsh.

To take your test in any other language, you may bring a translator with you to certain theory test centres. The translator must be approved by DSA and you must make arrangements when you book your test. You have to arrange and pay for the services of the translator yourself.

Tests with translators can be taken at the following test centres: Aldershot, Birkenhead, Birmingham, Cardiff, Derby, Edinburgh, Glasgow, Ipswich, Leeds, Milton Keynes, Preston, Southgate and all test centres in Northern Ireland.

Provision for special needs

Every effort is made to ensure that the theory test can be taken by all candidates.

It's important that you state your needs when you book your test so that the necessary arrangements can be made.

Reading difficulties - There's an English language voiceover, on a headset, to help you if you have reading difficulties or dyslexia.

You can ask for up to twice the normal time to take the multiple choice part of the test. You will be asked to provide a letter from a suitable independent person who knows about your reading ability (such as a teacher or employer). Please check with the Special Needs section (on the normal booking number, see p12) if you're unsure who to ask.

We can't guarantee to return any original documents, so please send copies only.

Hearing difficulties - If you're deaf or have other hearing difficulties, the multiple choice part and the introduction to the hazard perception part of the test can be delivered in British Sign Language (BSL) by an on-screen signer.

A BSL interpreter, signer or lip speaker can be provided if requested at the time of booking. If you have any other requirements then please call the Special Needs section on the normal booking number (see p12).

Physical disabilities - If you have a physical disability which would make it difficult for you to use a mouse button to respond to the clips in the hazard perception part of the test, we may be able to make special arrangements for you to use a different method if you let us know when you book your test.

Multiple choice questions

Module 1a of the theory test consists of 100 multiple choice questions.

You select your answers for this part of the test by simply touching the screen. This 'touch screen' has been carefully designed to make it easy to use.

Before you start you'll be given the chance to work through a practice session for up to 15 minutes to get used to the system. Staff at the test centre will be available to help you if you have any difficulties.

The questions will cover a variety of topics relating to road safety, the environment and documentation. Only one question will appear on the screen at a time.

Most questions will ask you to mark one correct answer from four possible answers given. Some questions may ask for two or more correct answers from a selection, but this is shown clearly on the screen. If you try to move on without marking the correct number of answers you'll be reminded that more answers are needed.

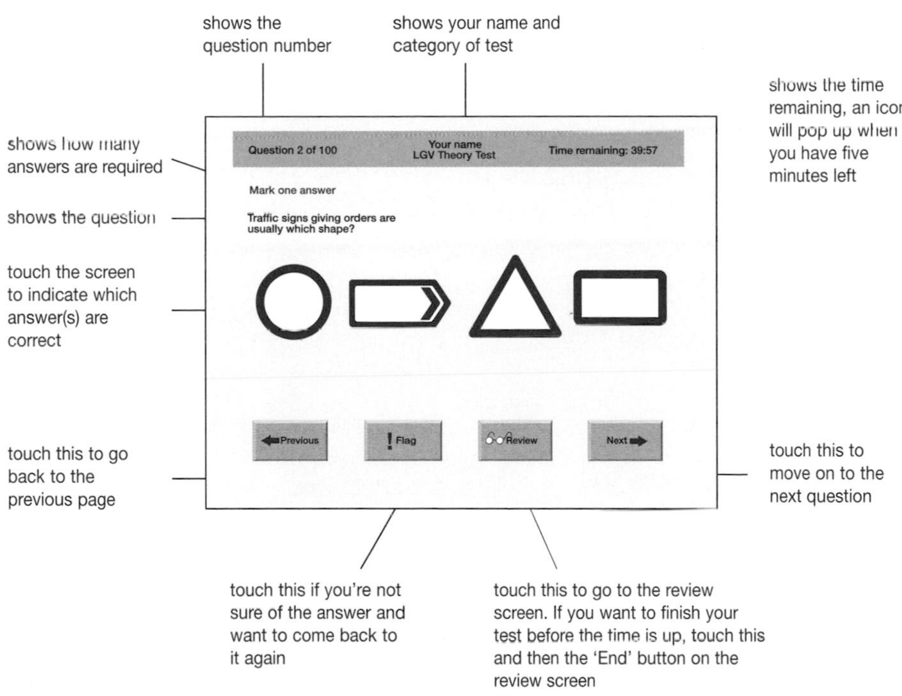

To answer, you need to touch the box alongside the answer or answers you think are correct. If you change your mind and don't want that answer to be selected, touch it again. You can then choose another answer.

Take your time and read the questions carefully. You're given 115 minutes for this part of the test, so relax and don't rush.

Extra time can be provided if you have special needs and you let us know when you book your test.

Some questions will take longer to answer than others, but there are no trick questions. The time remaining is displayed on screen.

You'll be able to move backwards and forwards through the questions and you can also 'flag' questions that you'd like to look at again. It's easy to change your answer if you want to.

Try to answer all the questions. If you're well prepared you shouldn't find them difficult.

Before you finish, if you have time, you can use the 'review' feature to check your answers. If you want to finish your test before the full time has elapsed, touch the 'review' button and then the 'end' button on the review screen. When you touch the review button you will see the following screen.

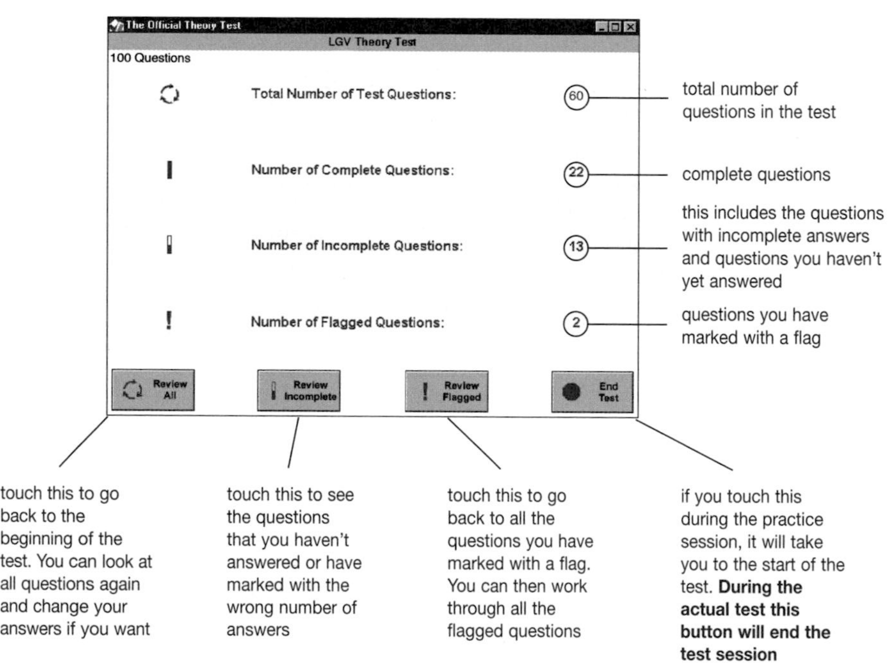

Hazard perception

Module 1b of the test will consist of a series of film clips, shown from a driver's point of view.

Before you start this test you'll be shown a short tutorial video that explains how the test works and gives you a chance to see a sample film clip. This will help you to understand what you need to do. You can run this video a second time if you want to.

During the test you'll be shown 19 film clips. Each clip contains one or more developing hazards. You should respond by pressing the mouse button **as soon as you see** a hazard developing that may result in you, the driver, having to take some action, such as changing speed or direction. The earlier you notice a developing hazard and make a response, the higher your score. There are 20 scoreable hazards in total.

Your response will not cause the scene in the video to change in any way. However, a red flag will appear on the bottom of the screen to show that your response has been noted.

Before each clip starts, there will be a 10-second pause to allow you to see the new road situation.

This test lasts about 25 minutes. For this part of the test there is no extra time available, and you can't repeat any of the clips - you don't get a second chance to see a hazard when you're driving on the road.

Trial questions

We're constantly checking the questions and clips to help us decide whether to use them in future tests. After your test, you may be asked to try a few trial questions or clips. You don't have to do these if you don't want to, and if you do answer them they won't count towards your final score.

Customer satisfaction survey

We want to ensure our customers are completely satisfied with the service they receive. At the end of your test you'll be shown some questions designed to give us information about you and how happy you are with the service you received from us.

Your answers will be treated in the strictest confidence. They are not part of the test and they won't be used in determining your final score or for marketing purposes. You'll be asked if you want to complete the survey, there's no obligation to do so.

The result

You should receive your result at the test centre within 10 minutes of completing the test. This result will also include the score you have obtained for this module.

Modules 1a and 1b can be taken in any order, and at different sittings, but you must pass both modules to pass the theory test. Should you be required to take the new case studies test, you may sit this test either before or after completing both theory test modules. You must have passed both the theory test and, if applicable, the new case studies test to enable you to take the practical test.

Why do I have to pass both theory test modules before i can take my practical test?

As the theory test is one test made up of two modules, you will still be required to pass both modules to pass the theory test. These modules are made up of either multiple choice questions or hazard perception cips, and can be taken at different times.

What's the pass mark?

To pass the multiple choice part of the theory test you must answer at least 85 questions correctly.

To pass the hazard perception part of the test, you must reach the required pass mark of 67 out of a possible 100. There are 19 clips with 20 scoreable hazards.

If I don't pass, when can I take the test again?

If you fail your test, you've shown that you're not fully prepared. You'll have to wait at least three clear working days before you take the theory test again. Good preparation will save you time and money.

After your theory test

The theory test is made up of two parts - the Multiple Choice part and the Hazard Perception part. You must pass both parts to pass the Driving Theory test. When you pass either of the parts, you will be given a result and feedback letter before you leave the test centre. Once you have passed both parts, a pass letter wll be sent to you in the post. Keep this carefully, as it contains the pass certificate number that you will need to book your practical test.

This pass certificate number has a life of two years from the date that you passed the first part of the Theory Test. This means that you have to take and pass the practical test for the category of vehicle you wish to drive within this two year period. If you don't, you'll have to take and pass the theory test again before you can book your practical test.

Your practical driving test

Your next step is to take a practical driving test. To help you prepare for this DSA has produced *The Official DSA Guide to Driving Goods Vehicles* and *The Official DSA Guide to Driving Buses and Coaches,* which contain the official syllabusses for the LGV and PCV practical test.

Both books include valuable advice about taking the practical test, outline the skills you need to show and the faults you should avoid. They also cover legal requirements, different types of vehicle and general driving techniques.

Passing the theory test is an important step to becoming a professional driver.

Using the questions and answers section

The following part of the book contains all the questions that could be used in the multiple choice part of the theory test.

For easy reference, and to help you to study, the questions have been divided into topics and put into sections. Although this isn't how you'll find them in your test, it's helpful if you want to refer to particular subjects.

The questions are in the left-hand column with a choice of answers beneath. On the right-hand side of the page you'll find the correct answers and a brief explanation of why they are correct. There will also be some advice on correct driving procedures.

Don't just learn the answers. It's important that you know why the answers are correct. This will help you with your practical skills and prepare you to become a safe and confident driver..

Taking exams or tests is rarely a pleasant experience, but you can make your test less stressful by being confident that you have the knowledge to answer the questions correctly.

Make studying more enjoyable by involving friends and relations. Take part in a question-and-answer game. Test those 'experienced' drivers who've had their licence a while: they might learn something too!

Some of the questions in this book will not be used in Northern Ireland theory tests. These questions are marked as follows: ***NI EXEMPT***

Questions specific to a single catagory

Most of the questions refer to drivers of all large vehicles, indicated by two icons - a bus and a lorry - beside the question numbers. However there are some questions that are only relevant to a specific group of vehicles.

Questions specifically for PCV drivers are marked with a bus icon only, just to the right of the question number.

Questions specifically for LGV drivers are marked with a lorry icon only, just to the right of the question number.

section **one**

VEHICLE WEIGHTS AND DIMENSIONS

This section covers

- Vehicle size
- Stowage and loading
- Vehicle markings
- Speed limiters

1.1 Mark **one** answer

Fifteen passengers on your vehicle would increase the weight by about

- 0.5 tonnes
- 1 tonne
- 2.5 tonnes
- 3 tonnes

1 tonne

You must be aware of the maximum authorised mass (MAM), which refers to the weight of your vehicle with both passengers and luggage. Fifteen passengers would add approximately one tonne to the weight of your vehicle. You should also allow for any luggage that they may be carrying.

1.2 Mark **one** answer

As a guide, how many passengers equal about one tonne?

- 15
- 20
- 25
- 30

15

Your bus will move away more slowly and handle differently when fully laden with passengers and their luggage. You'll have to make allowances for this, especially when moving off uphill.

1.3 Mark **one** answer

Certain weight limit signs do not apply to buses. How would the driver know?

- By a plate fitted beneath the weight limit sign
- By the colour of the weight limit sign
- By a plate attached to the vehicle
- By a certificate carried by the driver

By a plate fitted beneath the weight limit sign

Some weight restrictions apply to large goods vehicles (LGVs) only and not to passenger carrying vehicles (PCVs). Look out for a plate beneath a restriction sign that indicates this.

Road signs show weight restrictions in various ways, and you should make yourself familiar with all of them, so that you're in no doubt about their meaning and relevance.

1.4  *Mark **one** answer*

You are driving a bus on a local service. You can use this lane

- between 4 pm and 6.30 pm only
- before 4 pm and after 6.30 pm only
- at any time of the day
- any time except Saturdays

at any time of the day

As a local service bus driver you may use the bus lane at any time. The restrictions apply to other road users to keep it clear for you at peak times. Don't be tempted to speed when driving up the inside of slow-moving or stationary traffic. Be alert for pedestrians who may be trying to cross the road.

1.5 *Mark **one** answer*

The national speed limit for buses and coaches on a dual carriageway is

- 55 mph
- 60 mph
- 65 mph
- 70 mph

60 mph

Don't be tempted to drive on the limiter when using dual carriageway roads. The speed limit for passenger carrying vehicles is 60 mph. Be considerate to faster moving traffic by not using the middle or outside lanes unnecessarily.

1.6 *Mark **one** answer*

The D1 category licence allows you to drive buses with a maximum of

- 16 passenger seats
- 24 passenger seats
- 32 passenger seats
- 48 passenger seats

16 passenger seats

The D1 category allows any bus with 9 to 16 passenger seats to be driven for hire or reward.

1.7 *Mark **one** answer*

A driver should know the vehicle's unladen weight. Where can this information be found?

- On the dashboard of the vehicle
- On the driver's duty roster
- On the side of the vehicle
- On the depot noticeboard

On the side of the vehicle

As a driver of a passenger carrying vehicle (PCV) you'll need to know about the vehicles

- weight (for restrictions)
- height (for clearances)
- width (for restrictions)
- length and ground clearance (for humpback bridges, grass verges, kerbs etc).

1.8 *Mark **one** answer*

What category of licence is required to drive an articulated bus?

- D
- D + E
- D1
- D1 + E

D

A full category D licence entitles you to drive all buses and coaches including the increasingly common articulated type.

A full category D licence on its own does not cover you to drive buses or coaches drawing detachable trailers of more than 750 kg; for this you will need a D+E licence.

1.9 *Mark **one** answer*

The front of your bus overhangs well past the front wheels. Why should you allow for this when cornering?

- The steering will become much heavier
- Your speed will become more difficult to control
- You might hit a post or fence
- You will need to brake much sooner

You might hit a post or fence

The front of a bus or coach often extends well beyond the front wheels. Make allowances for this when turning. Try to avoid overhanging the pavement where possible but if you have to do this look out for fences, posts, traffic signs etc. Be especially careful where pedestrians are present, for example in bus stations.

1.10 *Mark **one** answer*

Your bus has a speed limiter fitted. What other related item must it have?

- An audible warning device for the driver
- A plate in the cab showing the limited speed
- A warning sign on the back of the bus
- A manual over-ride switch for emergencies

A plate in the cab showing the limited speed

You need to know if your bus is fitted with a speed limiter. A quick look inside the cab should tell you this. A plate must be fitted in an obvious position with the speed setting printed on it.

1.11 *Mark **one** answer*

You are the driver of a 1996 bus, which must be fitted with a speed limiter. At what speed is the limiter set?

- 60 mph (96 kph)
- 62 mph (100 kph)
- 70 mph (112 kph)
- 75 mph (120 kph)

62 mph (100 kph)

A speed limiter is designed to prevent the vehicle from exceeding a set limit.

1.12 *Mark **one** answer*

When a speed limiter is fitted to a bus, where must the setting be displayed clearly?

- In the driver's cab
- On the nearside of the vehicle
- On the rear of the vehicle
- On the driver's side at the front of the vehicle

In the driver's cab

If there's a speed limiter fitted to the vehicle, there should be a notice clearly displayed in the driver's cab, showing the speed at which it's set.

1.13 *Mark **one** answer*

Maximum authorised mass refers to the weight of

- your vehicle with passengers but no luggage
- your vehicle without passengers or luggage
- your vehicle with luggage but no passengers
- your vehicle with both luggage and passengers

your vehicle with both luggage and passengers

Weight limits are imposed on roads and bridges for two reasons, the structure may not be capable of carrying heavier loads and to divert larger vehicles to more suitable routes.

You're responsible for knowing the weight of your vehicle. Be aware of and understand the limits relating to any vehicle you drive. The unladen weight can be found on the side of your vehicle.

1.14 *Mark **one** answer*

Speed limiters are fitted to most modern buses and coaches. They normally work by

- applying the service brake
- applying the secondary brake
- reducing fuel supplied to the engine
- changing to a lower or higher gear

reducing fuel supplied to the engine

Most speed limiters work by taking a speed signal from the tachograph and transmitting it to the engine management system. This reduces the fuel supply to the engine, and allows the speed of the vehicle to be controlled to specific limits.

The speed at which a limiter is set must be shown on a plate clearly displayed in the cab. You should be aware of the effect a speed limiter will have on your vehicle, especially when overtaking.

1.15 *Mark **one** answer*

The 'turning circle' is the

- number of turns of the steering wheel between locks
- amount of space needed for the vehicle to turn
- amount by which the vehicle overhangs kerbs
- amount by which a vehicle cuts corners

amount of space needed for the vehicle to turn

You should be familiar with the room that your vehicle requires to make turns or carry out a manoeuvre. You'll need to consider this as you approach junctions and road layouts. If you're driving a new or temporary vehicle, familiarise yourself with its characteristics before you drive on public roads.

1.16 Mark **one** answer

What does this sign mean?

- ⊙ No entry for two-axled trailers
- ⊙ No entry for vehicles with two-speed axles
- ⊙ Maximum gross weight of 2 tonnes
- ⊙ Axle weight limit of 2 tonnes

⊙ **Axle weight limit of 2 tonnes**

Always look out for road signs, but be especially aware of those that refer to large or heavy vehicles. Get into the habit of checking for signs at junctions. There might be an indication on the junction layout sign. Before you turn, ensure that the road you're using doesn't have any restrictions for the vehicle you're driving.

1.17 Mark **one** answer

What does this sign mean?

- ⊙ Slippery road
- ⊙ Double bend
- ⊙ Overhead electrified cable
- ⊙ Cable laying ahead

⊙ **Overhead electrified cable**

Look out for restrictions that you may not have seen on a map. These may be temporary or permanent. It is essential to know how high your vehicle is before setting off. The height of your vehicle, and load when applicable, should be clearly marked, usually in the cab, and visible from the driving position.

1.18 *Mark **one** answer*

This sign means

- no vehicles over 14 feet 6 inches wide
- no vehicles over 14 feet 6 inches high
- road humps 14 feet 6 inches apart
- weight limit of 14.6 tonnes

no vehicles over 14 feet 6 inches high

Always be aware of the height of the vehicle you're driving, particularly if you drive different vehicles.

Special maps are published that show weight and height limits on roads in the UK.

1.19 *Mark **one** answer*

This sign warns of

- low bridge ahead
- accident ahead
- tunnel ahead
- accident blackspot ahead

tunnel ahead

There may also be additional signs showing height and width restrictions. If you're driving a high vehicle, make sure that there's enough headroom available for you to proceed through the tunnel.

1.20   *Mark one answer*

This sign means

- ⊙ length of tunnel
- ⊙ length of low bridge
- ⊙ distance to tunnel
- ⊙ distance to low bridge

⊙ **distance to tunnel**

In addition to height restrictions the tunnel may have restrictions with regard to the available width of headroom for high vehicles. The advance warning gives you the opportunity to find another route if your vehicle is too high or wide to proceed through the tunnel.

1.21 *Mark three answers*

You are driving a vehicle higher than 3.0 metres (10 feet). Extra care must be taken when driving

- ⊙ through arched bridges
- ⊙ through road tunnels
- ⊙ near airports
- ⊙ near overhead cables
- ⊙ up steep hills
- ⊙ over narrow bridges

⊙ **through arched bridges**

⊙ **through road tunnels**

⊙ **near overhead cables**

You must take care when approaching any hazard where height is limited. Know the height of your vehicle, and don't take any risks. Stop if you're in any doubt, and if you're not sure that it's safe, take another route.

1.22   *Mark one answer*

What is the minimum height of an unmarked bridge?

- ⊙ 4.5 metres (15 feet)
- ⊙ 4.7 metres (15 feet 6 inches)
- ⊙ 4.8 metres (16 feet)
- ⊙ 5.0 metres (16 feet 6 inches)

⊙ **5.0 metres (16 feet 6 inches)**

If a minimum height isn't shown on the bridge the headroom (in the UK) will be at least 5 metres (16 feet 6 inches).

1.23 *Mark one answer* NI EXEMPT

Your vehicle collides with a bridge. You must report it to

- the police
- the local authority
- your local garage
- the fire brigade

the police

Hitting a bridge with your vehicle can obviously have serious consequences for road and rail traffic. If the bridge is a railway bridge, immediately call the railway authority as well as the police to report the incident.

1.24 *Mark three answers*

Your vehicle has collided with a railway bridge. You must telephone the railway authority to inform them of the

- damage caused
- type of bridge
- vehicle height
- bridge number
- vehicle number
- bridge location

damage caused

bridge number

bridge location

It's vital that the railway authority are given this information promptly, so that they can take action to prevent railway passengers being put at risk.

1.25 *Mark one answer*

Bells hanging across the road warn of

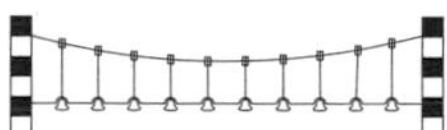

- a weight restriction
- trams crossing ahead
- overhead electric cables
- a railway level crossing

overhead electric cables

If your vehicle exceeds the safe travelling height beneath electrified overhead cables, bells suspended over the road will give you an audible warning. If your vehicle disturbs the bells you must stop immediately and seek advice.

1.26 Mark **one** answer

What does this sign mean?

- The width of the road is 6 feet 6 inches (2 metres)
- No vehicles over 6 feet 6 inches (2 metres) wide
- No vehicles over 6 feet 6 inches (2 metres) high
- Trailer length must not exceed 6 feet 6 inches (2 metres)

No vehicles over 6 feet 6 inches (2 metres) wide

You must always be aware of the size of your vehicle. Look out for road signs that show a width restriction. There should be an indication of this at the entrance to the road.

Don't get into a situation where you have to reverse out of a narrow road because you haven't seen a sign.

1.27 Mark **one** answer

This sign on a motorway means

- 11 tonnes weight limit
- stop, all lanes ahead closed
- leave the motorway at the next exit
- lane ahead closed

lane ahead closed

Warning lights show when there are dangers ahead, such as

- lane closures
- accidents
- fog
- icy roads.

1.28 *Mark **one** answer*

You are driving on a motorway. You see this sign. It means end of

- restriction
- crawler lane
- weight limit
- hard shoulder

restriction

Look out for variable-message warning signs advising you of

- lane closures
- speed limits
- hazards.

1.29 *Mark **one** answer*

You are driving a long vehicle. Your main concern at this hazard is your vehicle's

- height
- width
- weight
- length

length

Always be alert for situations where the size of your vehicle can get you into difficulties. You should know the weight, width, length, height and ground clearance of your vehicle. If in doubt, don't attempt to go where you may have to reverse an unreasonable distance.

1.30 Mark three answers

In which of the following places might vehicles over a certain length be restricted?

- On ferries
- At freight terminals
- In road tunnels
- On dual carriageways
- On motorways
- On level crossings

- **On ferries**
- **In road tunnels**
- **On level crossings**

Look out for restrictions for long vehicles. There are few, compared to width or height restrictions, but they're found where turning facilities are restricted or there's a risk of grounding.

1.31 Mark one answer

At this roundabout you intend to take the fourth exit. On this road there is a limit on

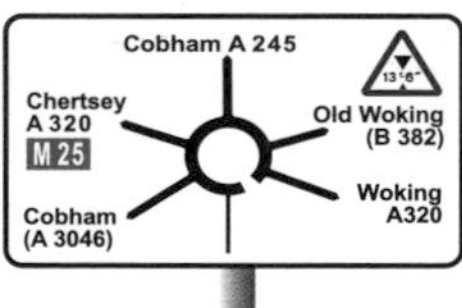

- height
- weight
- width
- length

- **height**

Be alert for signs giving you advance warning of height restrictions. As a professional driver you should always know the height of your vehicle or load. If you aren't sure of the safe height, STOP and check. Don't take chances.

1.32 Mark one answer

When using passing places on narrow roads you will MOST need to be aware of your vehicle's

- length
- roof height
- ground clearance
- weight

- **length**

On single track roads, if your vehicle is too long to get completely into a passing place you may need to wait opposite it to allow a following or approaching road user to pass. When you use this type of road you need to plan and look well ahead so as to avoid meeting another road user at an inappropriate place.

1.33 *Mark **one** answer*

You are driving on a motorway. Your stopping distance can increase by up to ten times if the road surface is

- bumpy
- icy
- worn
- wet

icy

Winter weather conditions affect all types of roads. Don't be misled by other drivers who are driving too fast. All but the gentlest braking will lock your wheels on ice. If your front wheels lock, you can't steer. If you can't steer, you can't keep out of trouble.

1.34 *Mark **one** answer*

You are driving on the motorway in icy conditions. Your stopping distance can increase by up to

- 2 times
- 4 times
- 10 times
- 20 times

10 times

Adequate separation distances are vital when driving on icy roads. You can never have too much safe space around your vehicle in these conditions. Motorways that appear wet may in fact be frozen.

Remember, all braking should be carried out gently to reduce the risk of losing control.

1.35 *Mark **one** answer*

When towing a trailer the maximum speed allowed on a motorway is

- 40 mph
- 50 mph
- 60 mph
- 70 mph

60 mph

On motorways with more than two lanes, caravans or trailers must not be towed in the outside lane unless other lanes are closed.

1.36 Mark **one** answer

Having just overtaken a motorcyclist on a motorway you MUST always check the

- speedometer
- left mirror
- right mirror
- road ahead

left mirror

When overtaking with a long vehicle it is very important to be aware of the position of the road user you are overtaking. You must carefully check the nearside mirror to ensure that you have passed safely before returning to the left.

Motorcyclists require special attention as they are more vulnerable and may be affected by buffeting from your vehicle.

1.37 Mark **one** answer

A large vehicle is most stable when driven in a straight line under

- harsh acceleration
- gentle braking
- gentle acceleration
- harsh braking

gentle acceleration

A vehicle is most stable when travelling in a straight line under gentle acceleration. Sudden acceleration, steering or braking can cause severe loss of control. Your driving should be as smooth as possible.

1.38 Mark **one** answer

What does this sign mean?

- Warning of lorry crossing a one-way road
- No entry for vehicles over 32 feet 6 inches (10 metres) long
- No entry for vehicles over 32.6 tonnes
- Warning of lorry straight ahead

No entry for vehicles over 32 feet 6 inches (10 metres) long

You need to know the length of your vehicle as well as the height and width. Places where the length of your vehicle will be relevant are

- road tunnels
- level crossings
- ferries
- bridges.

1.39 *Mark **one** answer*

You are driving a long vehicle. You want to turn right. There is a painted mini-roundabout. What should you do?

- Make sure none of your wheels touch the roundabout
- Avoid going over the roundabout if possible
- Go ahead, and turn right at the next junction
- Carefully mount the left-hand kerb to make more room

- **Avoid going over the roundabout if possible**

When turning at a small roundabout, it is unlikely that you will be able to avoid going over the marked area. You should, however, avoid going over the roundabout where possible.

1.40 *Mark **three** answers*

When planning your route which of the following should be taken into consideration?

- Any weight restrictions
- Any height restrictions
- Any speed restrictions
- Any parking restrictions
- Any width restrictions

- **Any weight restrictions**
- **Any height restrictions**
- **Any width restrictions**

You should plan your route very carefully to avoid vehicle restrictions which may prevent your access. Width, height, and weight restrictions are particularly important.

1.41 *Mark **one** answer*

Your vehicle is more than 3 metres (9 feet 10 inches) high. Where is this information usually displayed?

- On the tax disc
- On the weight plate
- In the driver's cab
- In the engine bay

- **In the driver's cab**

This information is usually displayed in the cab. It is a legal requirement that it can be read by the driver, when in the driving position.

It is important to know the height of your vehicle so that you can avoid low bridges or obstacles such as overhead electrical cables.

1.42 Mark **one** answer

The height of your vehicle is 4.2 metres (14 feet). What action should you take on the approach to this bridge?

- Keep to the centre of the arch and give way to oncoming traffic
- Drive through slowly, keeping to the left of the marked limits
- Keep to the centre of the arch and take priority over oncoming traffic
- Drive through quickly, keeping to the left of the marked limits

Keep to the centre of the arch and give way to oncoming traffic

The headroom under bridges in the UK is at least 5 metres (16 feet 6 inches) unless marked otherwise. But remember, this might mean the maximum height at only the highest point of an arch.

If your vehicle hits a bridge, you must report the incident to the police. If a railway bridge is involved, you must also report it to the railway authorities.

1.43 Mark **one** answer

Unless otherwise shown, the headroom under bridges in the UK is at least

- 4.0 metres (13 feet)
- 4.1 metres (13 feet 4 inches)
- 5.0 metres (16 feet 6 inches)
- 5.5 metres (18 feet)

5.0 metres (16 feet 6 inches)

Every year there are about 800 accidents where vehicles hit railway or motorway bridges. Most involve buses, coaches and lorries. Don't let one of them be yours. Not only can it cause major disruption, but if you're carrying passengers it could injure or kill them. There are also the costs involved in making the bridge safe, realigning railway tracks and ensuring the safety of rail passengers.

1.44 Mark **one** answer

In which one of these places may you park large vehicles at night without lights on?

- In an off-road parking area
- On a road with a 20 mph speed limit
- At least 10 metres (32 feet) away from any junction
- In most lay-bys

In an off-road parking area

Off-road lorry and coach parks are often well lit and patrolled by police or security firms. Never leave your vehicle unlit on a public road or in a lay-by after dark.

1.45 Mark **one** answer

You are driving a vehicle fitted with a speed limiter. You should allow for its effects when

- cornering
- braking
- overtaking
- changing gear

overtaking

Forward planning is important whenever you consider overtaking another road user. You should carefully assess the speed of the vehicle you intend to overtake. Remember that your vehicle's speed is limited and this could considerably increase the distance and time needed to complete overtaking safely.

1.46 Mark **one** answer

You must be aware of the effect a speed limiter has on your vehicle, especially when you intend to

- brake
- change gear
- overtake
- reverse

overtake

Plan well ahead before overtaking. Your vehicle's speed limiter may cause you difficulties if you attempt to pass another vehicle when climbing a hill.

1.47 Mark **one** answer

You are driving on a motorway in a vehicle fitted with a speed limiter. You should be aware of

- the lower running costs
- the smoother ride
- the limited power available when overtaking
- the increased fuel consumption

the limited power available when overtaking

When driving on a motorway, the speed difference between two large vehicles can be extremely small. If you wish to overtake, plan well ahead to avoid causing a long tailback of frustrated drivers.

1.48 Mark **one** answer

What does this sign mean?

- Hump-back bridge
- Risk of grounding
- Uneven road
- Road liable to subsidence

Risk of grounding

If you see this sign, you must be alert to the danger of grounding. This can happen where there's a pronounced bump in the road, such as at a level crossing or a hump-back bridge.

1.49 Mark **one** answer

As you approach this sign your main concern should be your vehicle's

- height
- width
- weight
- length

length

At humpback bridges there is a risk of long vehicles grounding. If you're not sure whether the floor of your vehicle will clear the bridge find another route.

1.50 *Mark **one** answer*

You are driving a long vehicle on a two-lane road. You want to turn left into a narrow road. What should you do?

- Keep well to the left on the approach
- Move out to the right immediately before turning
- Keep to the left and turn later than normal
- Straddle the lanes to make more room for the turn

Straddle the lanes to make more room for the turn

As the driver of a long vehicle you will often need to straddle lanes to turn into narrow roads. You need to watch out for smaller vehicles, especially motorcycles and cycles, trying to squeeze past on your inside.

1.51 *Mark **one** answer*

The repair of a speed limiter must be carried out at

- an authorised Speed Limiter centre
- any Vehicle Inspectorate site
- your nearest Service Centre
- the depot by a mechanic

an authorised Speed Limiter centre

Repair of speed limiters can only be entrusted to authorised Speed Limiter centres. They will ensure that all connections are sealed and that the system is tamper-proof.

1.52 *Mark **one** answer*

The information for the legal axle weight limits can be found on the

- vehicle plate
- operator's licence
- tax disc
- weighbridge printout

vehicle plate

Individual axle weights are shown on the vehicle plate. This can be found in a prominent place on the vehicle and any trailer.

1.53 Mark **one** answer

This sign means no entry for goods vehicles

- under 7.5 tonnes maximum authorised mass
- over 7.5 tonnes maximum authorised mass
- over 7.5 metres overall height
- under 7.5 metres overall height

over 7.5 tonnes maximum authorised mass

It's essential that all limits are complied with to avoid breaking the law and facing possible prosecution. Weight restrictions normally apply to the plated weight of a vehicle, often referred to as the maximum authorised mass (MAM).

1.54 Mark **one** answer

Your lorry is over 7.5 tonnes maximum authorised mass. This sign means you may use

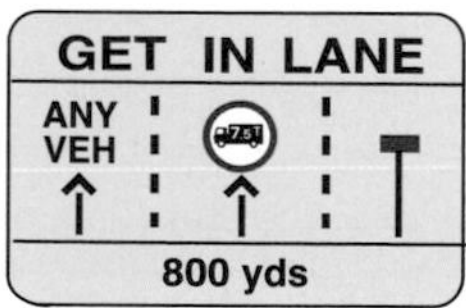

- either the left-hand or middle lane
- only the left-hand lane
- only the middle lane
- any of the lanes

only the left-hand lane

Lanes at roadworks often carry weight restrictions to keep larger vehicles in the left-hand lane. The width of the lanes through the roadworks are very often narrow and therefore not wide enough for large vehicles to pass each other safely.

Always look for restriction signs at roadworks. They are usually placed well in advance to give you time to move safely into the correct lane in good time.

1.55 *Mark **one** answer*

What is the national speed limit on a single carriageway road for a rigid lorry weighing more than 7.5 tonnes maximum authorised mass?

- 30 mph
- 40 mph
- 50 mph
- 60 mph

40 mph

Vehicles exceeding 7.5 tonnes MAM are restricted to a maximum of 40 mph on single carriageway roads.

1.56 *Mark **one** answer*

You are driving a lorry over 7.5 tonnes maximum authorised mass. On a three-lane motorway you can only use the right-hand lane

- to overtake slower lorries
- when the left-hand lane is closed
- if you do not go faster than 60 mph
- if you are not towing a trailer

when the left-hand lane is closed

Use of the right-hand lane on motorways with three or more lanes is NOT normally permissible for vehicles over 7.5 tonnes MAM, vehicles required to be fitted with speed limiters and vehicles towing trailers. In special circumstances such as the left-hand lane being closed this rule does not apply.

1.57 *Mark **three** answers*

When driving a low loader you should be aware of grounding on

- level crossings
- traffic calming humps
- yellow rumble strips
- hatched road markings
- hump-back bridges

level crossings

traffic calming humps

hump-back bridges

Traffic calming measures are becoming more common. You should know the size of your vehicle and plan well ahead.

Look out for signs informing you of hazards that will affect your vehicle. Change your route if necessary rather than take risks.

1.58 Mark **one** answer

You are driving a low loader. You see this sign. Your main concern is

- the ground clearance
- the weight limit
- the height limit
- the load

the ground clearance

As the driver of a low loader you have a special responsibility to be aware of the dimensions, including ground clearance, of your vehicle. When planning your route you will have to consider the following

- weight
- length
- height
- ground clearance.

1.59  Mark **one** answer

You are driving a vehicle that is over 17 metres (55 feet) long. What should you do at a level crossing?

- Cross over using your horn and hazard warning lights
- Stop before the crossing and phone the signal operator
- Increase your speed to clear the crossing quickly
- Stop before the crossing and look both ways before going on

Stop before the crossing and phone the signal operator

If your vehicle is over 17 metres (55 feet) long and you wish to cross a level crossing, you must stop before the level crossing and telephone the signal operator.

1.60 *Mark **one** answer*

What types of fastenings or restraints should you use when carrying a heavy load of steel?

- Chains
- Straps
- Ropes
- Sheeting

Chains

YOU are responsible for the safety of the load you're carrying. At no time should the load endanger other road users. It's therefore vital that you ensure your load is secure and safely distributed on your vehicle. The method to ensure this will differ according to

- bulk
- weight
- the type of vehicle you're driving (flat bed, curtain side, etc.)
- the nature of the load.

1.61 *Mark **one** answer*

You are driving a lorry carrying a load which is 4.5 metres (14 feet 9 inches) wide. What is your maximum allowed speed on a motorway?

- 10 mph
- 20 mph
- 30 mph
- 40 mph

30 mph

Speed limits imposed on vehicles carrying abnormal loads can be frustrating for other drivers, but don't be tempted to exceed the speed limit. Remember, the more weight you are carrying, the longer it will take you to stop safely.

1.62 *Mark **one** answer*

What is the maximum speed limit on a dual carriageway for a lorry carrying a load which is 4.5 metres (14 feet 9 inches) wide?

- 15 mph
- 25 mph
- 35 mph
- 45 mph

25 mph

Crossing traffic can be a danger on dual carriageways. Don't exceed the speed limits imposed on your loaded vehicle. The distance you need to stop will increase significantly with each extra mile per hour.

1.63 *Mark* ***one*** *answer*

Markings are required on the rear of lorries over 7.5 tonnes maximum authorised mass. What colour are these?

- Red/white
- Red/yellow
- Black/yellow
- Black/white

- **Red/yellow**

All vehicles over 7.5 tonnes must have markings on the rear of the vehicle. These are to inform other road users of the different characteristics of your vehicle. These markings are rectangular and coloured red and yellow. They should be kept clean so that they can be seen clearly at all times, especially at night and in poor visibility.

1.64  *Mark* ***one*** *answer*

When this vehicle turns, the overhang of the top deck will swing through

- a greater arc than the cab
- a lower arc than the cab
- a smaller arc than the cab
- the same arc as the cab

- **a greater arc than the cab**

As the top deck is longer than the cab and trailer, it will take up more room as the vehicle turns. You must make sure before turning that you've allowed for the wider swing of the deck. Even though your cab is well clear, the overhanging deck could hit telegraph poles or traffic signs as you go round the corner.

1.65 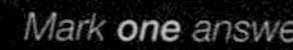 *Mark* ***one*** *answer*

You are the driver of an articulated car transporter. When turning corners, you should be aware that the overhang of the top deck swings through a

- smaller arc than the cab
- shorter arc than the cab
- lower arc than the cab
- greater arc than the cab

- **greater arc than the cab**

The longer top deck needs a wider turning circle than the cab below it. To avoid hitting lamp posts or telegraph poles etc., you must be careful to allow for this overhang when turning.

1.66 *Mark **one** answer*

The driver of a car transporter must be most aware of the trailer front-overhang when

- overtaking
- turning
- loading
- braking

turning

The long overhang at the front of a car transporter can cause problems where street furniture, such as lamp posts and traffic signs, is sited close to junctions. Particular problems may be encountered when there are 'Keep left' bollards in the middle of the road you are turning right into. Plan your route carefully to avoid such hazards.

1.67 *Mark **one** answer*

You are scheduled to make a delivery. You arrive at your destination during the morning rush hour. The road is edged with double red lines. You should

- unload only within a 'white box' area
- unload only within a 'red box' area
- delay your delivery until after the rush hour
- limit your stop to a maximum of 30 minutes

unload only within a 'white box' area

White boxes allow you to unload at any time, but during the day the length of stay is restricted. You should check nearby signs for specific times. At other times, when it's not so busy, there may not be any restrictions on parking.

1.68 *Mark **one** answer*

You are driving a lorry with a maximum authorised mass of more than 7.5 tonnes. What is the national speed limit on a dual carriageway?

- 40 mph
- 50 mph
- 60 mph
- 70 mph

50 mph

Be considerate to other road users who may be travelling faster than you are. Don't hog the middle or outside lane unnecessarily. Make effective use of your mirrors well before signalling your intention to change lanes.

1.69 *Mark* ***one*** *answer*

You are driving a petrol tanker. 'Roll-over' is least likely to occur on vehicles fitted with

- ⊙ tandem axles with double wheels
- ⊙ tandem axles with air suspension
- ⊙ tri-axles with single wheels
- ⊙ tri-axles with double wheels

⊙ **tri-axles with single wheels**

The type of suspension fitted to a vehicle will influence its resistance to 'roll-over'. Modern tri-axle semi-trailers fitted with single wheels on each side extend the tracking width available, compared to twin-wheeled units, and are more stable.

1.70 *Mark* ***one*** *answer*

You are driving a petrol tanker. The change from 'rear wheel lift' to 'roll-over' occurs

- ⊙ only at roundabouts
- ⊙ with very little warning
- ⊙ with plenty of warning
- ⊙ only when fully loaded

⊙ **with very little warning**

The transition from 'rear wheel lift' to 'roll-over' is more rapid on vehicles equipped with air suspension systems. Make sure you take advantage of any extra training that may be available to drivers of this type of vehicle.

1.71 *Mark* ***one*** *answer*

You are the driver of a refrigerated vehicle loaded with hanging meat carcasses. You should be especially careful when turning corners because of the

- ⊙ wave effect
- ⊙ camber effect
- ⊙ gravity effect
- ⊙ pendulum effect

⊙ **pendulum effect**

As you turn a corner, the hanging meat carcasses will all swing to one side of your vehicle adding extra pulling forces towards the outside of the curve. The faster you turn a corner, the greater this force will be. Even after taking the corner the carcasses will continue to swing back and forth, like pendulums, making the vehicle unstable. Keeping your speed down while cornering will help prevent your vehicle from being in danger of turning over.

1.72 *Mark **one** answer*

At overnight stops many drivers park with their rear doors close to another lorry. This is to

- keep the load safe
- ensure a clear path
- keep 'same company' lorries together
- stop the theft of their fuel

keep the load safe

Load security is extremely important. Make sure you park legally and, preferably, in a well lit area. Some lorry parks are patrolled regularly by the police or security services.

1.73 *Mark **one** answer*

Which of these should be fitted to a lorry with a maximum authorised mass of more than 7500 kg?

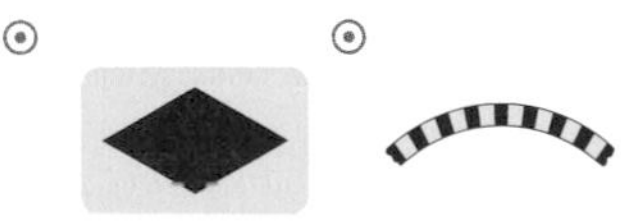

Motor vehicles over 7500 kg maximum authorised mass (MAM) and trailers over 3500 kg MAM should have these markings fitted to the rear of the vehicle.

1.74 *Mark **one** answer*

How far can a load overhang at the rear before you must use triangular projection markers?

- 1 metre (3 feet 3 inches)
- 1.5 metres (5 feet 0 inches)
- 2 metres (6 feet 6 inches)
- 2.9 metres (9 feet 6 inches)

2 metres (6 feet 6 inches)

It's not only important that you're aware of the length of your vehicle, but other road users should also be informed. This is to enable them to understand the reason why you might take up certain positions before turning. Marker boards must be fitted if the load on your vehicle overhangs by more than 2 metres (6 feet 6 inches).

1.75 Mark **one** answer

You are driving a lorry with a high load. Telephone companies on the route must be told if the height is more than

- 4.00 metres (13 feet)
- 4.30 metres (14 feet 2 inches)
- 5.00 metres (16 feet 6 inches)
- 5.25 metres (17 feet 6 inches)

5.25 metres (17 feet 6 inches)

You should tell telephone companies of your intended route when planning the movement of loads over 5.25 metres (17 feet 6 inches) high. You should tell them in plenty of time prior to making the journey.

1.76 Mark **one** answer

How wide can a load be before you must have side markers?

- 2.0 metres (6 feet 6 inches)
- 2.9 metres (9 feet 5 inches)
- 3.5 metres (11 feet 5 inches)
- 4.3 metres (14 feet 2 inches)

2.9 metres (9 feet 5 inches)

Side markers must be displayed if your load is over 2.9 metres (9 feet 5 inches) wide. Make sure that they're clearly visible, at both the front and rear, and that they indicate the actual width projection.

1.77 Mark **one** answer

Triangular projection markers are required when your load is wider than 2.9 metres (9 feet 5 inches). What colour are these?

- Black/yellow
- Red/yellow
- Black/white
- Red/white

Red/white

The marker boards should be red and white. To ensure that they can be seen clearly by other road users they must be kept clean and independently lit at night and in poor visibility.

1.78 *Mark one answer*

How should you secure an ISO steel cargo container onto your vehicle or trailer?

- Using battens and chocks
- Using straps
- Using twist locks
- Using ropes

Using twist locks

If you're carrying a steel ISO (International Standards Organisation) cargo container, ropes or straps won't be strong enough to take the strain. This type of load requires a special type of restraint using twist locks.

1.79 *Mark one answer*

You are driving an articulated lorry on a narrow road. There is a left-hand bend ahead. Why may you need to move out before going through the bend?

- To leave more room for braking
- To prevent anyone from overtaking
- To make room for the trailer cutting in
- To make sure oncoming drivers see you

To make room for the trailer cutting in

You should always be aware of the amount of room your trailer needs when going through bends and corners. If you need to go onto the other side of the road, make sure there is no oncoming traffic before you negotiate the bend.

section **two**

DRIVERS' HOURS AND REST PERIODS

This section covers

- Driving limits
- Keeping records
- Tachograph rules
- Tiredness
- Vehicle security
- Loads and load restraint

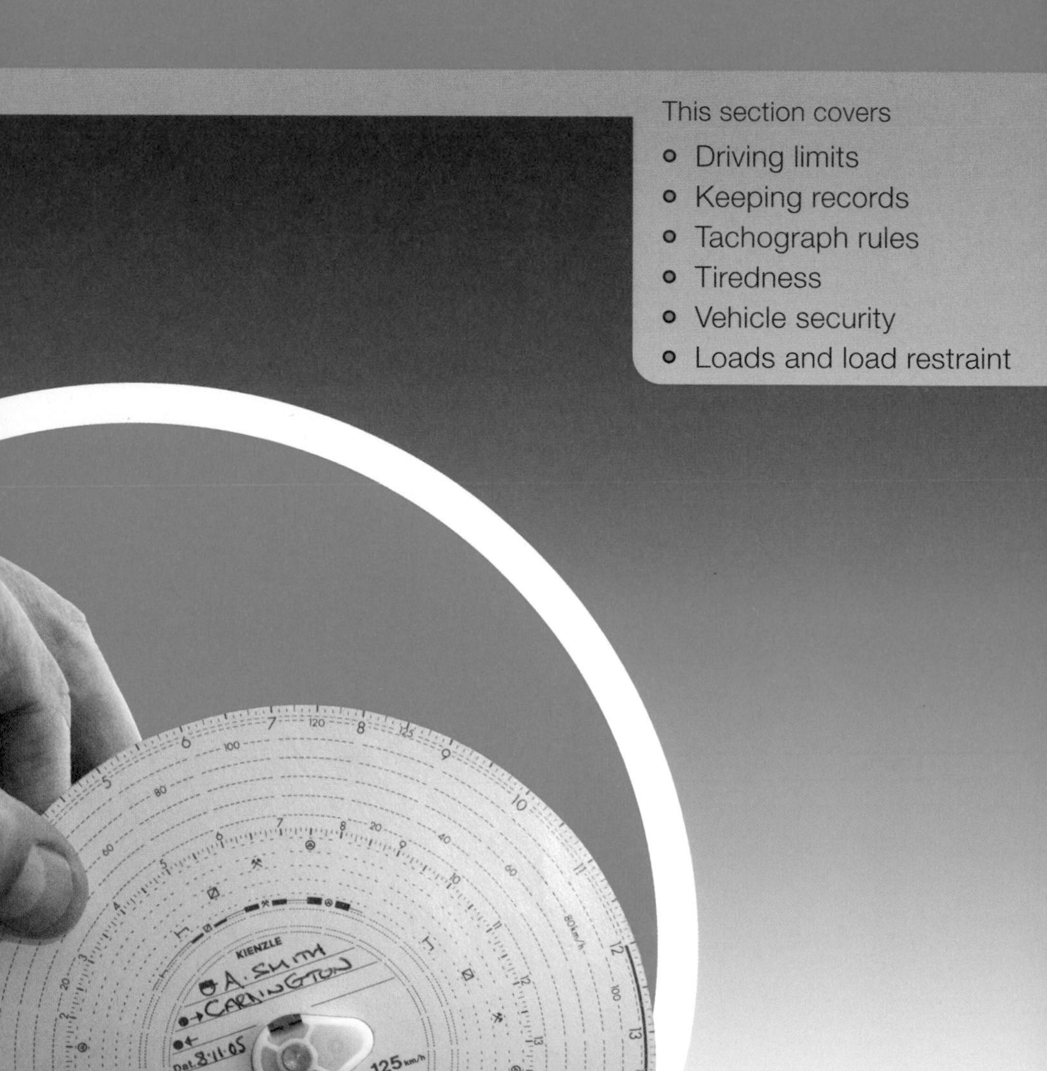

2.1 *Mark **one** answer*

The driver of a bus with 18 seats on an excursion journey from London to Scotland should abide by which drivers' hours rules?

- AETR only
- Domestic
- EC only
- EC and AETR

EC only

If you're driving a bus on an excursion journey (that is, not a regular journey) and your vehicle has 18 or more seats you must use EC rules and record the details.

2.2 *Mark **one** answer*

EC rules require that after driving continuously for the maximum period a bus driver must take a break. This must be at least

- 15 minutes
- 30 minutes
- 45 minutes
- 60 minutes

45 minutes

Always park your vehicle in a safe place off the road. Try to find somewhere you can get out of your vehicle for refreshment. This will help to ensure that you're fully refreshed. If you're carrying passengers, they'll also be grateful for a break. Taking breaks at the correct time will ensure that your passengers are safe and comfortable.

2.3 *Mark **one** answer*

A driver's daily rest period may be taken in a parked vehicle if

- it is fitted with a bunk
- there is a smoke alarm fitted
- the vehicle is in an authorised coach park
- there are no passengers on the vehicle

it is fitted with a bunk

Some vehicles are fitted with sleeping accommodation for the driver. If your vehicle is fitted with this facility you're permitted to take your daily rest period there, provided your vehicle is stationary.

2.4 *Mark **one** answer*

What should you do if asked to leave your bus by an official who is not in uniform?

- Comply with the request
- Ask to see a warrant card
- Refuse to leave the vehicle
- Invite the official aboard

Ask to see a warrant card

If you are asked to leave your vehicle by an official who's not in uniform, ask to see their warrant card. The official is likely to be an enforcement or police officer, but don't presume this.

2.5 *Mark **one** answer*

When a bus is left unattended the driver MUST ensure that

- the tachograph chart is removed
- the gear lever is in reverse
- the gear lever is in first
- the parking brake is applied

the parking brake is applied

Always ensure that your vehicle is safe when you leave it unattended. Always apply the parking brake and stop the engine.

2.6 *Mark **one** answer*

Bus operators are required to use tachographs for regular journeys. Beyond what distance does this apply?

- 10 km
- 20 km
- 50 km
- 80 km

50 km

Operators of buses used for regular journeys of more than 50 km must use tachographs.

2.7 Mark **three** answers

Why are drivers' hours under close control?

- To keep to a delivery schedule
- For fuel economy
- To save wear and tear
- For fair competition
- For road safety
- For safe working conditions

- **For fair competition**
- **For road safety**
- **For safe working conditions**

Altering drivers' hours records with intent to deceive, or tampering with the tachograph, is against the law and could lead to a prison sentence.

2.8 Mark **two** answers

Drivers who break EC tachograph regulations

- are allowed three warnings
- may lose their licence
- will be heavily fined
- are let off if they are not used to tachographs

- **may lose their licence**
- **will be heavily fined**

You, the driver, must take responsibility to ensure that you comply with the drivers' hours and tachograph rules.

2.9 Mark **two** answers

When using a tachograph which of the following apply?

- You must carry enough approved charts
- Damaged charts can be used if they are clean
- Dirty charts can be used if they are undamaged
- All charts must be clean and undamaged

- **You must carry enough approved charts**
- **All charts must be clean and undamaged**

Make sure you carry enough approved tachograph charts for your journey. Keep your spare charts in a plastic wallet to ensure they remain clean and undamaged.

2.10 Mark **one** answer

The tachograph on your vehicle becomes faulty. It can be repaired on return to base, if this is within

- one day
- three days
- one week
- two weeks

one week

If the tachograph on your vehicle becomes faulty you should take it to an approved tachograph repairer as soon as possible. If your vehicle can't return to your base within a week of discovery of the fault, the repair must be carried out while you're away on the journey. While the tachograph is faulty or broken you must keep a manual record of your activities.

2.11 Mark **one** answer

Tachograph records must be available for inspection. An enforcement officer keeps one of your charts. Who should sign the back of the replacement chart?

- You, the driver
- Your transport manager
- The vehicle owner
- The officer

The officer

If an enforcement officer retains a record chart, the driver should ask the officer to sign the back of the replacement chart with their name, telephone number and the number of charts retained.

This replacement chart must be used to continue the journey. You should always carry more blank charts than you need to use.

2.12 Mark **two** answers

When an enforcement officer keeps your tachograph records, the officer should sign the replacement chart with their

- name
- telephone number
- home address
- date of birth

name

telephone number

The enforcement officer should also record the number of charts retained. Alternatively, a receipt may be issued.

2.13 Mark **one** answer

Why should you carry spare tachograph charts?

- As a defence against a speeding prosecution
- To record when you have been in a traffic delay
- For recording extra loading duties and overtime
- To replace the original chart if it gets dirty

To replace the original chart if it gets dirty

Your employer should supply sufficient approved charts for your journey, plus some spares in case any get damaged, or are taken by an authorised inspecting officer.

2.14 Mark **one** answer

Under EC rules a driver must take a break after a continuous driving period of

- 3 hours
- 4 hours
- 4.5 hours
- 5.5 hours

4.5 hours

It's essential that you don't become drowsy through driving for excessively long periods. EC rules are in place to prevent this. You must follow these rules and ensure that the details of your journey and other work are recorded. Your work details must be available for inspection by enforcement staff. Make sure that you know the rules for the journey and the type of vehicle you're driving.

2.15 Mark **one** answer

You have been driving non-stop since 5 am. The time is now 9.30 am. Under EC rules you must have a break of at least

- 15 minutes
- 30 minutes
- 45 minutes
- 60 minutes

45 minutes

You must ensure that you take an uninterrupted break of 45 minutes after four and a half hours of driving. This break may be replaced by two shorter breaks of 15 and 30 minutes, taken in either order, and distributed over the period. During any break you must not drive or undertake any other work.

2.16 Mark **one** answer

Under EC rules what is the maximum daily driving time allowed?

- Nine hours extended to 11 hours on three days of the week
- Ten hours extended to 11 hours on two days of the week
- Nine hours extended to ten hours on two days of the week
- Ten hours extended to 11 hours on three days of the week

Nine hours extended to ten hours on two days of the week

You are allowed to extend your daily driving time twice a week to ten hours a day. A 'day' is generally any 24-hour period beginning with the resumption of driving or other work after the last daily or weekly rest period.

2.17 Mark **one** answer

Under EC rules your minimum daily rest is 11 hours. On three days of the week this may be reduced to

- seven hours
- eight hours
- nine hours
- ten hours

nine hours

Under EC rules you must have a minimum daily rest of 11 consecutive hours. A reduced daily rest period is any period of rest of at least 9 hours but less than 11 hours.

2.18 Mark **one** answer

Under EC rules your daily rest can be reduced to 9 hours but NOT more often than

- 1 day per week
- 2 days per week
- 3 days per week
- 4 days per week

3 days per week

It's vital that you are fit and well before starting any journey. Make sure you get enough sleep. Accidents are often caused by tired drivers' falling asleep at the wheel.

2.19 *Mark **one** answer*

Under EC rules your normal daily rest period should be at least

- 8 hours
- 11 hours
- 13 hours
- 14 hours

11 hours

Drivers' hours and rest periods are controlled in the interests of road safety. It's a serious offence to break these rules and anyone doing so is liable to a heavy fine and even imprisonment.

2.20 *Mark **one** answer*

Under EC rules what is the normal weekly rest that must be taken?

- 40 hours
- 41 hours
- 42 hours
- 45 hours

45 hours

The working week is defined as from 0.00 hours on Monday to 24.00 hours on the following Sunday. When taking the weekly rest period, a daily rest period must normally be extended to at least 45 consecutive hours.

2.21 *Mark **one** answer*

When a vehicle has two drivers each driver should

- share the same tachograph chart
- use a separate tachograph chart for every driving period
- use their own tachograph chart
- not use the tachograph for such duties

use their own tachograph chart

Your tachograph chart is your personal work record and, as such, should reflect the hours that you drive or carry out other work. The law requires these charts to be held on file by your employer for a period of at least one year. Enforcement officers can require charts to be handed over for inspection.

2.22 Mark **one** answer

You are making a journey with a co-driver. When the other person is driving you may show some of this time as

- a daily rest period
- a weekly rest period
- a break in daily driving
- driving time

a break in daily driving

You may only record a break when you are not engaged in any other type of work. It is permissible to take a break on a double-manned vehicle while the vehicle is driven by the other crew member. Any break must be a minimum of 15 minutes, otherwise it doesn't count.

2.23 Mark **three** answers

A tachograph will record

- load weight
- driving time
- fuel consumption
- rest periods
- engine temperature
- vehicle speed

driving time

rest periods

vehicle speed

The tachograph is designed to be used as a tool to help you be a safe and responsible driver.

2.24 Mark **one** answer

Which one of the following symbols on your tachograph indicates your break/rest period?

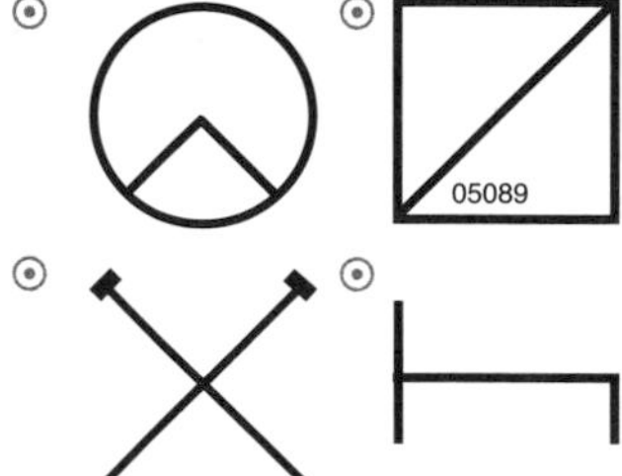

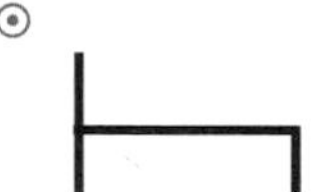

A tachograph allows you to select the mode or task that you're undertaking. Time spent on that task is then recorded automatically. Each task has a different symbol. You need to know the meaning of each so that your records are correct. The modes are, driving, doing other work, on duty and available for work, taking a break or rest.

2.25 *Mark **one** answer*

What does this tachograph chart symbol mean?

- Driver at rest
- Chart not required
- Other work
- Driving

Driving

Each activity has a different symbol. You should know what they mean so that you can select the correct one. You are responsible for recording all your activities correctly. Some tachographs don't have a 'driving' mode switch. These tachographs will automatically record driving time whenever the vehicle is moved, whatever mode the switch is set to.

2.26 *Mark **three** answers*

The 'mode' switch on a tachograph is used to record

- driving
- illness
- taking a weekly rest period
- other work
- resting

driving

other work

resting

It is important to change the mode switch to record your activities as they change during the working day. Failure to operate the mode switch could lead to a reprimand from your employer, or prosecution by the authorities.

2.27 *Mark **one** answer*

At the end of your working week you have driven a total of 56 hours. What is the maximum number of hours that you can drive in the following week under EC rules?

- 34
- 36
- 38
- 40

34

If you've driven a total of 56 hours in any one week you can only drive for 34 hours in the following week. If your hours add up to a total of 56 in any one week you must make sure that you don't exceed the permitted hours the following week. Keep your own record to make sure that you don't exceed these hours.

2.28 Mark one answer

An emergency situation has arisen. For safety reasons you will need to exceed the normal drivers' hours under EC rules. You should

- continue with the same tachograph chart and write an explanation on the back
- remove the tachograph chart and make a manual record of the rest of the journey
- continue; there is no need to give an explanation
- remove the tachograph chart and inform your employer of the reason

- **continue with the same tachograph chart and write an explanation on the back**

As long as road safety is not put at risk, you may depart from the drivers' hours rules just enough to ensure the safety of passengers, your vehicle, or its load. In these circumstances you should note all the reasons on the back of your tachograph chart.

2.29 Mark one answer

In an emergency situation you need to go over your normal drivers' hours. Under EC rules you should

- take no action, the tachograph chart will record this
- note the reasons on the back of the tachograph chart
- remove the chart from the tachograph before going over the hours
- note the reasons on the front of the tachograph chart

- **note the reasons on the back of the tachograph chart**

In an emergency, as long as road safety is not put at risk, a driver may depart from the drivers' hours rules just enough to get their load or passengers to a suitable stopping place.

2.30 Mark two answers

Which TWO of the following are most likely to cause tiredness?

- Making frequent and regular stops
- Driving breaks taken on board the vehicle
- Insufficient breaks from driving
- Modern vehicles with automatic gearboxes
- The cab becoming too warm

- **Insufficient breaks from driving**
- **The cab becoming too warm**

Tiredness will affect your concentration. Don't allow yourself to become weary through not taking proper breaks or rest periods. As a professional driver you have a responsibility either for goods or for passengers, as well as overall road safety. Ensure your vehicle is well ventilated. Open a window or turn down the heating to prevent yourself becoming drowsy.

2.31 Mark one answer

When driving, you start to feel tired or unable to concentrate. You should

- stop as soon as it is safe to do so
- wind down a window and carry on
- switch on the radio and complete your journey
- speed up to get to your destination sooner

- **stop as soon as it is safe to do so**

If you start to feel tired you should stop as soon as it's safe to do so, even if you aren't due a break.

Make sure that you get enough sleep before you're due to work, especially if you're on an early shift.

2.32 Mark one answer

You feel tired after driving for two and a half hours. What should you do?

- Slow down to a safer speed
- Reduce your planned driving time to three and a half hours
- Stop as soon as it is safe to do so
- Take a less busy route

- **Stop as soon as it is safe to do so**

Most accidents happen as a result of a lapse in concentration. Don't let this happen to you. If you start to feel tired you won't perform as well as you should. Your reactions will slow down and your anticipation and judgement of hazards will become flawed. It will be better for you, and for the safety of other road users, if you stop and rest as soon as it's safe to do so.

2.33 Mark **one** answer

You are driving on a motorway and suddenly become tired. What should you do?

- Stop on the hard shoulder and rest
- Leave by the next exit and find a place to stop
- Stop on the next slip road and rest
- Stop on the verge of the motorway and rest

Leave by the next exit and find a place to stop

If you're driving for long distances on a motorway take plenty of rest stops. Many accidents have been blamed on drivers falling asleep at the wheel. If you feel yourself becoming tired, stop at the next service area.

2.34 Mark **one** answer

You are feeling tired when driving on a motorway. Where can you stop?

- On the hard shoulder
- At a service station
- On a slip road
- In a deceleration lane

At a service station

Travelling long distances on a motorway can have a mesmerising effect. Any lack of concentration, however brief, could lead to an accident. If you start to feel tired leave the motorway by the next exit and pull over in a safe place to rest. Ideally you should use a service area, where you can have a rest and refreshment before you restart your journey.

2.35 Mark **one** answer

You have to leave your vehicle unattended for a very short time. You should

- avoid having to stop the engine
- leave keys available in case of obstruction
- keep the engine running but lock the doors
- be aware of the risks of theft or damage

be aware of the risks of theft or damage

Take all the precautions you can to eliminate opportunities for theft. Lock your vehicle, especially when making deliveries and leaving the vehicle unattended.

2.36 *Mark **one** answer*

The time is 10 am. You have been driving non-stop since 6 am. Under EC rules what is the longest you may now drive without a break?

- 15 minutes
- 30 minutes
- 40 minutes
- 45 minutes

30 minutes

The maximum driving period under EC rules is 4 hours 30 minutes, after which you must have a minimum break of 45 minutes.

Planning your route will allow you to take your statutory rest periods in a safe place, such as a service area, where you can get food, drink and a rest.

2.37 *Mark **one** answer*

Under EC rules you may drive for up to nine hours daily. On two days of the week this may be increased to a maximum of

- 9.5 hours
- 10 hours
- 11 hours
- 11.5 hours

10 hours

Don't drive for more than the maximum hours allowed. You're permitted to extend the daily nine hours to ten hours twice a week.

2.38 *Mark **one** answer*

Under EC rules you can drive for a maximum of nine hours daily. On how many days of the week can this be extended to ten hours?

- One
- Two
- Three
- Four

Two

Under EC rules your normal daily driving must not exceed nine hours. This nine-hour period must be the time between

- any two daily rest periods
- a daily rest period and a weekly rest period.

It's permitted to extend these hours to ten hours twice a week.

2.39 Mark **one** answer

How many days does a drivers smart card normally cover?

- 7
- 14
- 21
- 28

28

The smart card will record information covering a period of about 28 days. When used beyond this period some recorded information will be overwritten.

2.40 Mark **one** answer

Under EU driver's hours regulations a 45 minute break must be taken after 4.5 hours driving. This can be split into shorter breaks of

- one of 10 minutes plus one of 35
- one of 15 minutes plus one of 30
- one of 20 minutes plus one of 25
- one of 40 minutes plus one of 5

one of 15 minutes plus one of 30

Under EU regulations you must take a break of at least 45 minutes after four and a half hours driving. You may choose to take this break during the driving period. In this case it can be split into two breaks of 15 and 30 minutes, taken in either order.

2.41 Mark **one** answer

You are driving under EU tachograph regulations and lose your smart card. You must inform the relevant authority within a maximum of

- 5 days
- 7 days
- 14 days
- 28 days

7 days

As a professional driver you have a responsibility to report any loss or theft of your digital smart card. You must inform the nearest relevant authority within seven days.

2.42 Mark **one** answer

You have a digital tachograph driver smart card. It is valid for a maximum of

- One year
- Three years
- Five years
- Ten years

Five years

Digital tachograph driver cards are valid for a maximum period of five years. You should receive a reminder about three months before the expiry date. However it is your responsibility to make sure that you apply for a new card at least 15 days before the old one expires.

2.43 Mark **one** answer NI EXEMPT

Your driver tachograph card has been lost or stolen. Which authority MUST you contact?

- The police
- DVLA
- A tachograph centre
- VOSA

DVLA

Driver cards for digital tachographs are issued by the Driver and Vehicle Licensing Agency (DVLA) Swansea. In Northern Ireland the cards are issued by the Driver and Vehicle Agency (DVA).

2.44 Mark **one** answer NI EXEMPT

Where can you collect a replacement driver tachograph card from?

- DVLA local office
- Driving Standards Agency
- Any MOT test centre
- A tachograph centre

DVLA local office

Driver cards for digital tachographs are issued by the Driver and Vehicle Licensing Agency (DVLA), Swansea. Replacement cards can be collected from a DVLA local office or a VOSA testing station. In Northern Ireland the cards are issued by the Driver and Vehicle Agency (DVA).

2.45 Mark **one** answer

A driver is convicted of obstructing an enforcement officer during the course of their duties. Under EC drivers hours regulations what is the maximum fine they may receive?

- £2000
- £3000
- £4000
- £5000

£5000

EC drivers hours regulations state that any driver who fails to comply with, or obstructs an enforcement officer during the course of their duties, can be fined up to a maximum of £5000.

2.46 Mark **one** answer

When are you allowed to alter your tachograph record?

- If there are two or more drivers
- If your journey will exceed 50 miles
- At no time
- When you have no spare charts

At no time

Altering drivers' hours records or tampering with tachographs with intent to deceive, can lead to prison sentences. You could also lose your licence.

2.47 Mark **one** answer

You are driving under EU drivers hours. Under the rules governed by these, how is a week defined?

- A period between 0.00 hours on Monday and 24.00 hours the following Sunday
- Any seven day period
- Any period between 0.00 hours and 24.00 hours 6 days later
- A working period of 56 hours

A period between 0.00 hours on Monday and 24.00 hours the following Sunday

The rules define a week as a period between 0.00 hours on Monday and 24.00 hours the following Sunday. You must always make sure that any weekly driving limit is not exceeded.

2.48 Mark **one** answer

There are various types of Digital Tachograph Cards. Which is used by an approved calibration centre when recalibrating the tachograph?

- Control card
- Company card
- Driver card
- Workshop card

Workshop card

The workshop card is available only to approved calibration centres. There are three other types of Digital Tachograph Card.

Driver card, used by driver. Company card, used by operator. Control card, used by enforcement authorities.

2.49 Mark **one** answer

There are four types of Digital Tachograph Cards. What is the card known as that is only available to enforcement authorities ?

- Control card
- CPC card
- Company card
- Workshop card

Control card

There are various types of cards (known as Digital Tachograph Cards) used by the digital tachograph system. Driver card,

used by drivers. Company card, for use by the operator. Workshop card, available only to approved calibration centres. Control card, available only to Vehicle and Operators Services Agency (VOSA), and the police for carrying out enforcement.

2.50 Mark **one** answer NI EXEMPT

Drivers must have a driver smart card for use in digital tachographs. Where can you collect replacement smart cards from in Great Britain?

- VOSA testing station
- Highways Agency office
- DSA test centre
- Local Post Office

VOSA testing station

Replacement smart cards can only be collected from either a DVLA local office or a VOSA testing station. In Northern Ireland they are available from the Driver and Vehicle Agency (DVA).

2.51 Mark **one** answer

Who is responsible for the issue of tachograph charts to a bus or lorry driver?

- The driver's employer
- The local vehicle licensing office
- The authorised calibration centre
- The local MOT testing centre

The driver's employer

Your employer is responsible for the issue of tachograph charts. You, the driver, must ensure that the correct information is recorded on the tachograph chart.

2.52 Mark **one** answer

You can find out when an analogue tachograph was last recalibrated by

- a date on the tachograph chart
- contacting the vehicle's manufacturer
- checking the vehicle's service record
- a plaque on or near the tachograph

a plaque on or near the tachograph

An analogue tachograph must be checked every two years and recalibrated every six years. A plaque on or near the tachograph will say when these checks were last done.

2.53 Mark **one** answer

Under EC rules an analogue tachograph must be recalibrated every

- 2 years
- 4 years
- 6 years
- 8 years

6 years

When an analogue tachograph is installed and calibrated, an installation plaque is fixed near the tachograph. This shows the date of the most recent tachograph calibration.

2.54 Mark **one** answer

Your vehicle breaks down during a journey. You continue by driving in another vehicle with the same type of tachograph. What must you do with your tachograph chart?

- Leave it in the broken down vehicle
- Take it with you for security, but use a new chart in the new vehicle
- Telephone the testing authority for permission to drive without a chart
- Take it with you, using it in the new vehicle

Take it with you, using it in the new vehicle

When changing vehicles, you should also record certain information including the, closing odometer reading, registration number of the new vehicle, odometer start reading and time of the vehicle change.

2.55 Mark **one** answer

Under EC rules what is the maximum driving time allowed in any two consecutive weeks?

- 85 hours
- 90 hours
- 100 hours
- 105 hours

90 hours

The maximum number of hours that you can drive in any two consecutive weeks is 90 hours. These don't have to be split evenly, but the total amount of driving time in any one week should not exceed 56 hours. Don't exceed your driving hours. Learn the rules and stick to them. Heavy fines can be given to drivers who break the law.

2.56 Mark **one** answer

Under EC rules an analogue tachograph must be checked at an approved calibration centre every

- 1 year
- 2 years
- 5 years
- 6 years

2 years

An analogue tachograph must be checked every two years and recalibrated and sealed every six years. This must be done at an approved calibration centre. Digital tachographs, unlike analogue ones, must be recalibrated every two years.

2.57  *Mark **three** answers*

Goods vehicle drivers' hours of work are controlled for three reasons. They are

- vehicle sympathy
- fair competition
- fair road use
- vehicle security
- road safety
- working conditions

- **fair competition**
- **road safety**
- **working conditions**

Working conditions are governed by EC regulations. These set the maximum driving time and the minimum requirements for rest and break periods.

2.58  *Mark **two** answers*

Goods vehicle drivers' hours are controlled in the interests of

- fuel economy
- road safety
- traffic calming
- fair competition

- **road safety**
- **fair competition**

Drivers who break the rules are subject to heavy fines and could lose their licence to drive lorries.

2.59  *Mark **one** answer*

Under the rules for domestic drivers' hours you must

- keep a written record of hours worked
- only record any driving off public roads
- keep a written record of driving time only
- always use a vehicle fitted with a tachograph

- **keep a written record of hours worked**

Domestic rules apply to certain journeys within Great Britain which are not subject to EC rules. Under domestic rules you must keep written records of your hours of duty when driving goods vehicles.

2.60 *Mark **one** answer*

You must have enough tachograph charts with you for your journey. You will need at least one for every

- 10 hours
- 24 hours
- 36 hours
- 48 hours

24 hours

Your employer should supply you with enough tachograph charts for the entire journey. You'll need at least one for every 24 hours.

2.61 *Mark **one** answer*

One tachograph chart covers a period of

- 24 hours
- 48 hours
- 5 days
- 7 days

24 hours

Your tachograph is a legal document; it is a record of your work covering a rolling 24-hour period. Drivers who break the rules are subject to heavy fines and could lose their vocational licence entitlement. Altering your tachograph chart with intent to deceive is against the law and could lead to a prison sentence. Similar penalties exist for those who permit such offences.

2.62 *Mark **one** answer*

Your tachograph chart becomes dirty or damaged. What should you do?

- Continue with the same chart and enter the details in writing
- Use a spare chart and destroy the damaged chart
- Use a spare chart and attach it to the damaged one
- Continue to use the chart

Use a spare chart and attach it to the damaged one

If your current tachograph chart becomes damaged you should start another and then attach it to the damaged one. Your records must be clear and up to date at all times. It's sensible to carry more tachograph charts than you think you'll need for your journey. Then you'll be able to use a spare if one becomes dirty or damaged.

2.63 Mark **one** answer

During your break your vehicle will be moved by another person. What should you do with the tachograph chart?

- Leave the chart in the vehicle and record the changes on the back
- Put in a new chart on your return to the vehicle
- Switch to rest mode to record the break
- Remove the chart and make a manual record of the break period

Remove the chart and make a manual record of the break period

If your vehicle is likely to be used by another person while you're away from it, you should take your tachograph chart with you. Your break from driving should be entered on the reverse of the chart.

2.64  Mark **one** answer

You have been driving a lorry without a break for four and a half hours. Under EC rules a break must be taken. How long must it be?

- 30 minutes
- 35 minutes
- 40 minutes
- 45 minutes

45 minutes

If you're driving under EC rules you must not drive continuously for more than four and a half hours without taking a break. If you've driven continually for four and a half hours you must take a break of at least 45 minutes. Include your stops in the timetable when planning your journey.

2.65  Mark **one** answer

You are driving a lorry on a motorway and you are getting drowsy. There are no service areas or exits for some distance. What should you do?

- Stop on the hard shoulder and rest
- Open the window and turn the heating down
- Slow down and use the hazard warning lights
- Increase your speed to get to the next service area sooner

Open the window and turn the heating down

During very cold weather it's tempting to have the heating in the cab turned on full. Try to be aware of the effect this can have on your reactions and anticipation. It may dull them by making you feel drowsy and tired.

2.66 Mark **one** answer

You are driving a lorry. During the journey you are feeling ill and unable to concentrate. What should you do?

- Stop in a safe place and seek help
- Continue your journey and keep your windows open
- Increase your speed to finish your work earlier
- Keep stopping at regular intervals for rest

- **Stop in a safe place and seek help**

If you become unwell it will affect your concentration. You must be fully alert and ready for any hazards that might occur while you drive. Stop in a safe place and seek assistance. You may have to call out a relief driver to complete the journey for you.

2.67 Mark **two** answers

Which two of the following would NOT be helpful when trying to keep your load from being stolen?

- Giving a lift to a stranger
- Making sure all doors and windows are locked
- Discussing your load with members of the public
- Having a kingpin or drawbar lock fitted
- Parking in secure well-lit places when possible

- **Giving a lift to a stranger**
- **Discussing your load with members of the public**

Be careful of giving lifts to strangers. Some employers actively discourage this for very good reasons. Allowing strangers in your cab or letting slip information about your load could put the security of your vehicle and load at risk and may put you in danger.

2.68 Mark **one** answer

When leaving your vehicle for an overnight stop, it is good practice to park with the

- rear doors close up to another vehicle
- rear doors well away from another vehicle
- front doors well away from another vehicle
- front doors close up to another vehicle

- **rear doors close up to another vehicle**

Being responsible for the safety of your vehicle is very important. It is your responsibility.

2.69 — *Mark **three** answers*

You are parking overnight with a high-value load and intend sleeping in the cab. You should

- lock doors but leave a window open for ventilation
- ensure doors and windows will be secure
- be in a reputable, lit lorry park
- be in a quiet, unlit, non-residential area
- stay at the same location regularly
- block access to the rear door if possible

- **ensure doors and windows will be secure**
- **be in a reputable, lit lorry park**
- **block access to the rear door if possible**

Taking a few simple precautions will help to ensure your lorry and load are safe.

2.70  

*Mark **three** answers*

You are often involved in the carrying of high-value goods. What security measures can you adopt?

- Vary your routes and rest stops
- Always discuss details of your load
- Give lifts to anyone for added security
- Park overnight in well-lit areas
- Remove keys when not in attendance
- Keep your journeys to a strict routine

- **Vary your routes and rest stops**
- **Park overnight in well-lit areas**
- **Remove keys when not in attendance**

Use your common sense to plan your journeys. Avoid developing a set routine or pattern by using different routes whenever possible.

2.71  *Mark **one** answer*

It is necessary to leave your trailer unattended. It should be parked

- in a public car park
- on the public highway
- on secure premises
- in a quiet residential area

- **on secure premises**

Instances of theft of vehicles and trailers are unfortunately common. You are responsible for the safety and security of your vehicle and trailer. Try to avoid leaving any trailer unattended unless on approved secure premises.

2.72 Mark **one** answer

Your trailer should be fitted with a kingpin or drawbar lock when

- driving on motorways
- being driven abroad
- partly loaded
- left unattended

left unattended

Instances of theft are unfortunately common. You are responsible for your vehicle. You should ensure that a kingpin or drawbar lock is fitted to any trailer that has to be left unattended.

2.73 Mark **one** answer

Only lorries above a specific maximum authorised mass need a tachograph. That weight is

- 3.5 tonnes
- 5 tonnes
- 7.5 tonnes
- 10 tonnes

3.5 tonnes

Normally, a tachograph should be fitted and in full working order if your vehicle is over 3.5 tonnes. You should be aware of how it works and the regulations that govern its use.

2.74 Mark **one** answer

Before starting driving, which of the following should you complete on the centre field of your tachograph chart?

- The place from which you start your days journey
- Details of the goods carried
- The name and address of your employer
- The amount of daily rest taken prior to starting the shift

The place from which you start your days journey

Before starting on your journey there are a number of items that must be recorded on your tachograph chart. One of these is where the journey begins.

2.75 *Mark **one** answer*

During your working day you are changing to another vehicle with the same type of tachograph. What should you do with your tachograph chart?

- Use the chart that is already in the other vehicle
- Take the chart with you and use it in the other vehicle
- Record your driving hours in a record book
- Install a new chart in the other vehicle

- **Take the chart with you and use it in the other vehicle**

If you're changing vehicles during the working day, you should take your chart with you and use it in the next vehicle. This isn't always possible, however, as charts produced by different manufacturers may not be interchangeable. In this case you should use another chart, ensuring that all the information for the day is recorded.

2.76 *Mark **one** answer*

A lorry driver must take care of the vehicle and load. Which of the following is NOT good practice?

- Always parking it in a quiet area out of sight
- Parking with the rear doors hard up against another vehicle
- Avoiding using the same route and stops too often
- Always asking to see the identity of any officer who may stop you

- **Always parking it in a quiet area out of sight**

Load security is one of the many responsibilities placed on the driver. When choosing a site to park your vehicle overnight, you should always look for a location which is legal and well lit. Many allocated lorry parks are patrolled by the police or security firms.

2.77 *Mark **three** answers*

You are driving a lorry at night. What can you do to help you keep alert?

- Eat a heavy meal before setting off
- Keep plenty of cool fresh air moving through the cab
- Keep the cab warm and comfortable
- Take proper rest periods at correct intervals
- Drive faster to get to your destination sooner
- Walk around in fresh air at a rest stop

Keep plenty of cool fresh air moving through the cab

Take proper rest periods at correct intervals

Walk around in fresh air at a rest stop

Driving at night can make you feel tired more quickly. If you're starting your shift at the end of the day, make sure that you have enough rest before you start work. You must be able to stay alert for the duration of your shift.

Make sure that you have good ventilation in the cab. Ensuring that there's enough fresh air will help you to stay alert. Stale, warm air can dull your senses and cause drowsiness.

2.78 *Mark **two** answers*

How can you reduce the risk of your lorry or trailer being stolen?

- Fit an alarm and immobiliser
- Fit a kingpin lock to your trailer
- Use the same route and rest periods
- Park in quiet areas away from other vehicles

Fit an alarm and immobiliser

Fit a kingpin lock to your trailer

Planning and taking sensible precautions can help to deter the most determined thief.

2.79 Mark **one** answer

You are planning to carry high-value goods on a regular basis. You should seek advice from

- other drivers in your area
- your local crime prevention officer
- other operators in your area
- your local road safety officer

your local crime prevention officer

Research has shown that more than 3000 lorries with an insured value of £30 million were stolen in the UK, in one year. To prevent their lorries becoming another statistic, operators are advised to seek advice from their local crime prevention officer.

2.80 Mark **one** answer

A driver's week is defined as

- 0.00 hours Monday to 24.00 hours the following Sunday
- 0.00 hours Sunday to 24.00 hours the following Saturday
- any seven consecutive days
- any 56 hours driven

0.00 hours Monday to 24.00 hours the following Sunday

A week is defined as a period from 0.00 hours on Monday to 24.00 hours the following Sunday.

2.81 Mark **one** answer

When driving you notice your tachograph is not working. What should you do?

- Stop immediately until it is repaired
- Report it to the nearest police station
- Telephone the vehicle testing authority and report the fault
- Continue your journey but make a manual record

Continue your journey but make a manual record

If you cannot return to base within a week of the tachograph becoming defective, it must be repaired during the journey. While it is broken you must keep a manual record.

section **three**

BRAKING SYSTEMS

This section covers

- Types of brake
- Maintenance and inspection
- Connection and proper use of the brakes
- Tailgating
- Freezing conditions
- Anti-lock brakes

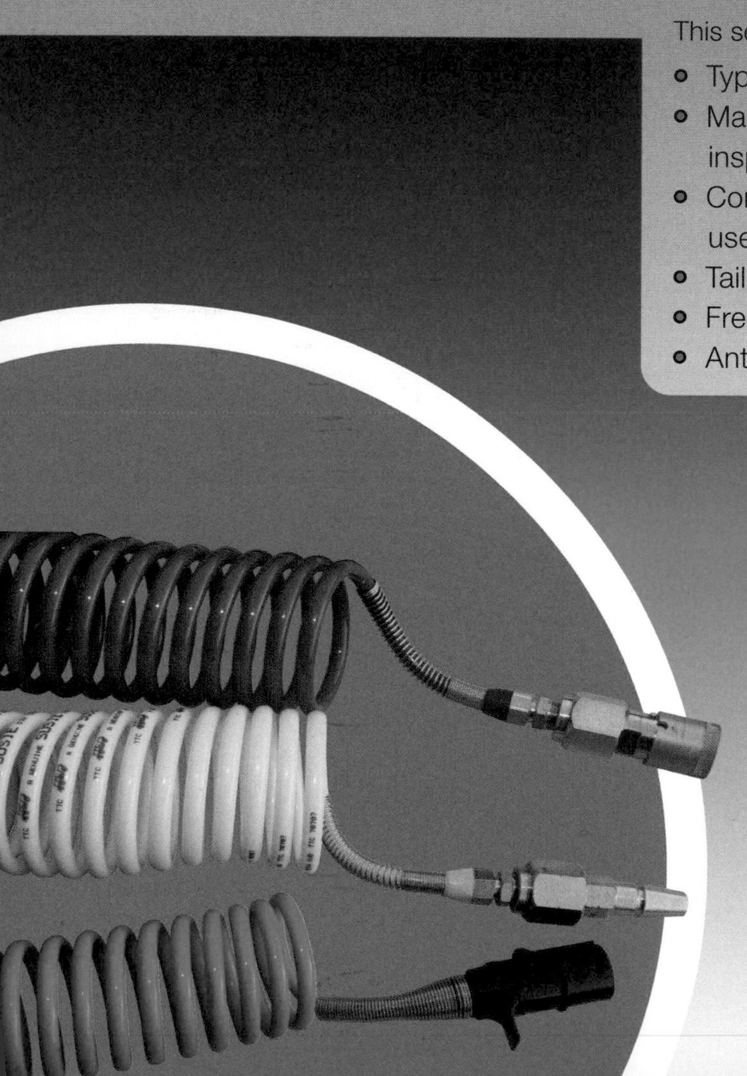

3.1 *Mark **one** answer*

You are about to set off in your bus in very frosty weather. You notice a lack of brake air pressure. What is the likely cause of this?

- Engine temperature too low
- Weak engine anti-freeze mixture
- Brake pedal needs adjustment
- Frozen moisture in the storage tanks

Frozen moisture in the storage tanks

Air braking systems use air from the atmosphere which contains moisture. All air braking systems are fitted with manual or automatic drain valves. Ensure the air tanks are drained daily to help prevent the system freezing in cold weather.

3.2 *Mark **one** answer*

What could prevent the build-up of brake air pressure on a bus in frosty weather?

- Lack of anti-freeze in storage tanks
- Insufficient lagging of tanks and pipes
- Low engine revolutions
- Moisture freezing in the system

Moisture freezing in the system

When the weather is frosty, any moisture in the storage tanks may freeze and prevent pressure building up properly.

3.3 *Mark **one** answer*

An anti lock braking system warning light fitted to a bus should go out

- when the brakes are used for the first time
- immediately after the anti-lock braking system comes into operation
- when road speed is 10 kph (6 mph) or more
- when the secondary braking system is used

when road speed is 10 kph (6 mph) or more

Every vehicle fitted with anti-lock brakes must have a warning light fitted in the cab of the vehicle. Check this as part of your routine. Driving with defective anti-lock brakes may constitute an offence.

Anti-lock warnings may differ between manufacturers, but all types should come on with the ignition and should go out when the vehicle reaches 6 mph (10 kph). Make yourself familiar with the warnings and gauges when you're driving a vehicle for the first time and don't carry on any further if the light fails to go out. The safety of your passengers and all other road users will be at risk.

3.4  *Mark **one** answer*

The MOST powerful brake on a bus is normally the

- secondary brake
- anti-lock braking system
- endurance brake (retarder)
- service brake

service brake

The most powerful and effective brakes on the vehicle are the service brakes, and these should be used in normal circumstances. Well-maintained brakes should apply an even pressure to all the wheels, providing an efficient, controlled stop.

3.5 *Mark **one** answer*

When making a short stop, facing uphill, you should

- hold the vehicle on the clutch
- hold the vehicle on the footbrake
- select neutral and apply the parking brake
- apply the parking brake after stopping

apply the parking brake after stopping

If you have to make a stop on an uphill gradient, wait until the vehicle has come to a stop before applying the parking brake, just as you would normally.

3.6 *Mark **one** answer*

You are about to move off. Your vehicle has automatic transmission. Before you select drive (D) you must

- put your foot on the footbrake
- signal to move off
- alter your seat position
- adjust your mirrors

put your foot on the footbrake

It is important to apply the footbrake before you engage 'D' or drive so your vehicle does not creep forward or roll back out of control when you are about to move away. This can be dangerous, for example if there's another road user close behind.

3.7 Mark *three* answers

Which THREE of the following are advantages of progressive braking when driving a bus?

- Passenger safety and comfort
- Increased air brake pressure
- Lower fuel consumption
- Reduced tyre wear
- Avoidance of 'brake fade'

Passenger safety and comfort

Lower fuel consumption

Reduced tyre wear

As the driver of a bus, the safety and comfort of the passengers is your first priority. If you have the correct attitude when you're driving, your passengers will be assured of a comfortable and pleasant journey.

Good forward planning and anticipation will enable you to avoid harsh braking and late, sharp steering.

Badly driven vehicles cost more to run and maintain.

3.8 Mark *one* answer

What does this simplified diagram show?

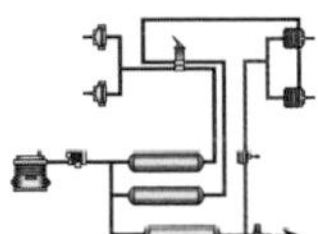

- Range change gearbox
- Air brake system
- Engine management system
- Two-speed axle

Air brake system

Check all warning systems before starting a journey. Never set off with a defective warning device or when a warning is showing.

3.9 Mark **one** answer

Your vehicle has anti-lock brakes. This allows you to

- follow vehicles more closely
- steer while braking
- drive faster on wet roads
- brake later than normal

steer while braking

Although anti-lock braking gives you the ability to brake and steer, it should not be relied on to keep you out of trouble. Good forward planning and anticipation will minimise the risk of skidding more effectively than relying on your braking system.

3.10 Mark **one** answer

What could prevent air pressure building up in an air brake system in cold frosty weather?

- Moisture in the air may form bubbles in the brake fluid
- The air will contract, reducing the pressure
- The dampness may cause valves to rust
- Moisture drawn in with the air may freeze and cause a blockage

Moisture drawn in with the air may freeze and cause a blockage

Large vehicles normally have braking systems that use compressed air to control the action of the brake shoes. The compressed air is built up by the vehicle's engine and stored in tanks on the chassis. This compressed air is vital to the effectiveness of the brakes. You must understand the system and know how to keep it in good condition, so that the brakes won't fail when you need them.

3.11 Mark **one** answer

The brake air pressure warning light comes on whilst driving. You should

- stop and seek help without delay
- report the fault on return to your depot
- boost the pressure through added acceleration
- drain air tanks and continue normally

stop and seek help without delay

If the warning light indicating a loss of brake pressure comes on, you must stop and get the fault put right immediately. Your safety, the safety of your load or your passengers, and that of all other road users will be at risk.

3.12 Mark **one** answer

When the brake air pressure warning light is operating, you should NEVER

- leave your vehicle
- release the parking brake
- switch your engine off
- engage the clutch

release the parking brake

Even though the warning device is operating, there may be sufficient pressure to release the parking brake, but you must not do this as the service brake may be ineffective.

3.13 Mark **one** answer

Your vehicle is fitted with an anti-lock braking system. Its main purpose is to help you to

- drive at faster speeds
- brake much later than normal
- apply the brakes more quickly
- stop safely in an emergency

stop safely in an emergency

Anti-lock braking systems work in a similar manner to cadence braking. Just as the wheels are about to lock, the sensor control releases the brakes and immediately applies them again.

3.14 Mark **one** answer

As the driver of a vehicle fitted with an anti-lock braking system, you should check it is working before each

- service
- day's work
- week's work
- journey

journey

Modern anti-lock braking systems rely on electrical power for their operation. The satisfactory operation of the system can be checked from the warning signal on the dashboard. The warning signal should go out by the time the vehicle has reached a speed of about 10 kph (6 mph).

3.15 Mark **one** answer

'Pumping' the brake pedal in a vehicle fitted with anti-lock brakes will cause

- increased effectiveness
- reduced effectiveness
- reduced brake wear
- increased brake wear

reduced effectiveness

Always refer to the owner's handbook for details of the manufacturer's recommended method of use. Remember, anti-lock brakes will enhance your skills, NOT replace them.

3.16 Mark **one** answer

You are driving a vehicle fitted with anti-lock brakes. When braking in an emergency, you should

- 'pump' the brake pedal harshly
- apply minimum force to the brake pedal
- use the exhaust brake (retarder) then the footbrake
- apply firm continuous pressure to the brake pedal

apply firm continuous pressure to the brake pedal

Always check with the vehicle manufacturer for details of their recommended method of use. Plan well ahead to avoid emergency situations developing.

3.17 Mark **one** answer

You are driving a vehicle not fitted with anti-lock brakes. How can 'wheel lock' be controlled during heavy braking?

- By using engine braking
- By cadence braking
- By braking suddenly
- By using clutch and brake together

By cadence braking

Cadence braking is a special braking technique for slowing or stopping a vehicle without anti-lock brakes in slippery conditions. It is not a substitute for lack of proper care and anticipation.

3.18 *Mark **one** answer*

You have to stop quickly in an emergency. Which of the following are most likely to prevent 'wheel lock'?

- Using the parking brake
- Selecting neutral
- Cadence braking
- Changing up a gear

Cadence braking

The principle of cadence braking is to brake using maximum pressure, to the point where the wheels are about to lock; you momentarily release the brake pressure and then quickly reapply it again. You will need to do this rapidly a number of times.

3.19 *Mark **one** answer*

What is 'brake fade'?

- Reduction of air pressure
- Smooth progressive braking
- Reduction of braking effectiveness
- Low hydraulic brake fluid level

Reduction of braking effectiveness

Continually using the brakes could cause them to 'fade'. This will mean that they are less effective.

Make sure that you're in the correct gear before you negotiate downhill stretches of road. A low gear will assist with braking and help prevent the vehicle gaining momentum as you negotiate the hill. Look out for road signs and 'dead ground', which indicate a dip or a hill.

3.20 *Mark **one** answer*

'Brake fade' is a loss of effectiveness of the brakes, caused by their continuous use. When would this be most likely to happen?

- On a long journey
- On a long downhill gradient
- On the approach to hazards
- On a long uphill gradient

On a long downhill gradient

Continuous use of the brakes will cause them to overheat, and in extreme cases they'll become ineffective. When you're going downhill, the momentum of your vehicle will cause you to gather speed very quickly. Don't underestimate the importance of the correct use of your brakes.

3.21   *Mark **two** answers*

When driving down a steep hill the driver of a large vehicle should

- partly apply the parking brake
- have changed to a lower gear
- use an endurance brake (retarder)
- put the gear lever into neutral
- use as high a gear as possible

- **have changed to a lower gear**
- **use an endurance brake (retarder)**

Forward planning to deal with hazards is important at all times. When approaching a long hill you should take note of any early warning signs. Reduce your speed and select the appropriate gear in good time. Using an endurance brake (retarder), if fitted, will help control your speed.

3.22   *Mark **one** answer*

Your vehicle has anti-lock brakes. When stopping in an emergency this should allow you to

- brake more gently
- brake much later
- maintain steering control
- stop over a long distance

- **maintain steering control**

Anti-lock brakes are a driver aid; they shouldn't be used to get you out of trouble. Don't rely on being able to make sudden direction changes when braking.

3.23  *Mark **one** answer*

Your vehicle is fitted with an anti-lock braking system. When braking normally you should press the brake pedal

- in the usual way
- on and off rapidly
- quickly and firmly
- later than usual

- **in the usual way**

Anti-lock brakes don't remove the need for good driving practices, such as anticipating hazards and assessing road and weather conditions.

3.24 Mark **one** answer

Your vehicle has anti-lock brakes. This means that when you brake normally you will

- not need to alter the way you brake
- be able to brake much later
- need to brake more firmly
- not need to brake so early

not need to alter the way you brake

Plan well ahead to enable you to brake normally. You shouldn't rely on anti-lock brakes to make up for deficiencies in your driving.

3.25 Mark **one** answer

You would see an escape lane

- outside a fire station
- alongside a bus lane
- before a motorway exit
- down a steep hill

down a steep hill

The sign shows you the direction of the road. A chequered area, usually straight ahead, defines the escape route, which is for use in emergencies such as brake failure.

3.26 Mark **one** answer

You would use an escape lane

- where motorways merge
- when carrying a dangerous cargo
- when your brakes have failed
- for emergency vehicle repairs

when your brakes have failed

On steep downhill sections of road you will sometimes see an escape lane. This is designed to give a 'run-off' area, usually straight ahead, to allow you to stop your vehicle in the event of an emergency.

3.27  *Mark **one** answer*

On steep hills an emergency area to be used only when your brakes have failed is called

- a buffer lane
- an escape lane
- a rumble strip
- the hard shoulder

an escape lane

Do not park in the area designated as an escape lane; this would put yourself and others in danger if a vehicle needed to use the 'run-off' area in an emergency.
Do NOT use it as a viewing area or for taking a rest period. Find an appropriate place to stop where you will not endanger other road users.

3.28  *Mark **one** answer*

An endurance brake (retarder) can be especially useful

- when driving down long hills
- when driving on steep cambers
- to reduce gear changes
- to improve fuel consumption

when driving down long hills

Plan ahead and use your endurance brake (retarder) to help hold your speed in check on long downhill gradients. This can help prevent your brakes from overheating.

3.29   *Mark **one** answer*

You are driving down a long hill and want to avoid the brakes overheating. The vehicle's speed should be controlled by using the

- anti-lock braking system
- footbrake
- secondary brake
- endurance brake (retarder)

endurance brake (retarder)

Systems that assist in controlling a vehicle's speed without using the wheel brakes are called endurance brakes or 'retarders'. Retarders operate by applying resistance via the transmission to the rotation of the vehicle's driven wheels. This may be achieved by

- increased engine braking
- exhaust braking
- transmission-mounted electromagnetic or hydraulic devices.

3.30 *Mark **one** answer*

A system for controlling the vehicle's speed without using the footbrake is

- a secondary brake
- an endurance brake (retarder)
- a differential lock
- an emergency air system

an endurance brake (retarder)

If your vehicle is fitted with any of these devices, you must become familiar with them before you make your journey. Don't be afraid to ask a colleague to show you. Don't risk an accident through ignorance.

3.31 *Mark **two** answers*

An endurance brake (retarder) may work in which TWO of the following ways?

- Increasing engine braking
- Using an extra transmission device
- Sensing wheel speed
- Using the parking brake
- Using the secondary brake

Increasing engine braking

Using an extra transmission device

These systems provide a way of controlling a vehicle's speed without using the wheel-mounted brakes. When descending long hills the vehicle speed can be stabilised without using the service brakes.

3.32 *Mark **one** answer*

An endurance brake (retarder), when not combined with the footbrake, should be used

- on motorways only
- on long downhill slopes
- when braking quickly
- all the time when stopping

on long downhill slopes

Mechanically operated endurance brakes (retarders) alter the engine exhaust gas flow. They are usually operated by a floor-mounted switch. Electrically operated endurance brakes (retarders) can be combined with the use of the footbrake. Alternatively, they may be operated via a multi-position dashboard-mounted lever which offers predefined stages of retardation.

3.33 Mark **one** answer

An endurance brake (retarder) should be used

- ⊙ on motorways only
- ⊙ when braking quickly
- ⊙ when you stop or park
- ⊙ on long downhill slopes

⊙ **on long downhill slopes**

Using an endurance brake on long downhill slopes will help control your speed, without using the service brake. Reducing the demand on the service brake helps prevent the brakes overheating and so reduces the risk of brake fade.

3.34 Mark **one** answer

An electromagnetic endurance brake (retarder) operates by applying resistance to the

- ⊙ hydraulic lines
- ⊙ starter motor
- ⊙ air lines
- ⊙ transmission

⊙ **transmission**

Electromagnetic retarders work by applying a magnetic resistance to the prop shaft which, in turn, slows down the wheels. This allows the service brake to stay cool for optimum performance when required. Retarders are particularly useful when going down long steep hills.

3.35 Mark **two** answers

Your vehicle is fully loaded. When dealing with bends all braking should be done

- ⊙ as close to the bend as possible
- ⊙ smoothly and in good time
- ⊙ when driving in a straight line
- ⊙ as you start to turn the wheel
- ⊙ when halfway round the bend

⊙ **smoothly and in good time**

⊙ **when driving in a straight line**

Braking should always be

- progressive
- correctly timed
- smooth
- sensitive.

When a vehicle changes direction, forces are applied to it and its load. Sudden, excessive or badly timed braking can result in loss of control.

3.36 *Mark **one** answer*

A lorry is overtaking you on a two-lane motorway. It does not have the speed to get past. What should you do?

- Continue at the same speed
- Be prepared to reduce your speed
- Increase your speed and force the lorry to drop back
- Brake hard to allow the other driver to cut in

Be prepared to reduce your speed

Always be prepared to give way to overtaking lorries or buses. Maintaining your speed will only block the motorway to other traffic unnecessarily. Remember, you may find yourself in a similar situation if the limiter on your vehicle does not allow you enough speed to complete an overtaking manoeuvre.

3.37 *Mark **one** answer*

After driving through a flood what should you do?

- Carry out an emergency stop
- Drive in low gear with the footbrake lightly applied
- Avoid braking until the brakes are dried out
- Pump the footbrake when approaching hazards

Drive in low gear with the footbrake lightly applied

If you have to drive through a flood, do so with caution.

Once out of the flood you need to test the brakes on your vehicle to make sure that they are working properly. To do this drive in a low gear with the brakes gently applied. Don't forget to check what's behind you before you do this.

3.38 *Mark **one** answer*

Coasting downhill could seriously affect the correct working of the

- air brakes
- cooling system
- tachograph
- electrical systems

air brakes

Air brake systems rely on an engine-driven compressor to replenish the air in the brake reservoir tanks. Coasting downhill and relying on the brakes to control your speed could result in loss of sufficient air pressure to operate the brakes effectively, particularly if the compressor is worn.

3.39 Mark **one** answer

'Brake fade' happens when the brakes get too

- hot
- cold
- dry
- wet

hot

'Brake fade' occurs when the brakes become too hot. Continuous use of the brakes can result in them becoming overheated and losing their effectiveness, especially on long downhill gradients.

3.40 Mark **two** answers

To prevent 'brake fade' you should

- use the endurance brake (retarder)
- apply the parking brake
- select a lower gear
- repeatedly pump the brake pedal
- select neutral for a short distance

use the endurance brake (retarder)

select a lower gear

Brake fade occurs due to the brakes overheating. Good forward planning and correct use of the gears to descend long hills, combined with proper use of the endurance brake (retarder), can help eliminate brake fade.

3.41 Mark **one** answer

What causes 'brake fade'?

- Continuous use of the brakes
- Repeated pumping of the brakes
- Loss of air pressure in the system
- Badly worn brake pads

Continuous use of the brakes

The continuous use of the brakes on a long downhill gradient can cause them to overheat and could result in them becoming ineffective. You should engage a low gear to enable the engine's braking effect to assist with controlling your speed. This also allows air pressure to be maintained in the tanks.

3.42 *Mark **one** answer*

The main cause of 'brake fade' is

- the brakes overheating
- moisture in the air tanks
- oil on the brake linings
- the brakes out of adjustment

the brakes overheating

Planning ahead will enable you to select an appropriate gear and use your endurance brake (retarder) to control the speed of your vehicle when travelling downhill. This will help prevent your brakes overheating on long downhill gradients.

3.43 *Mark **one** answer*

When using an endurance brake (retarder), extra care must be taken on

- uneven roads
- slippery roads
- downhill gradients
- uphill gradients

slippery roads

The endurance brake (retarder) is usually a mechanical device. It works by either altering the engine exhaust gas flow or amending the valve timing to create a 'compressor' effect. The result is enhanced engine braking which helps to slow your vehicle.

3.44 *Mark **one** answer*

You are stationary. The air brake pressure warning light comes on. Why should you NOT release the parking brake?

- Because the vehicle will suddenly roll backwards
- Because it will cause the air pressure to rise
- Because the service brake may not stop you
- Because the warning light will go out

Because the service brake may not stop you

Even though a warning device indicates low air brake pressure you may still be able to release the parking brake. If you do this and start moving the service brake may be ineffective and you may not be able to stop.

3.45 Mark **one** answer

You are about to drive a vehicle fitted with air-assisted hydraulic brakes. The brake pedal feels hard when pressed. What could this mean?

- The vacuum pump is not working
- The pedal movement requires adjustment
- The brakes are locked on fully
- The brake fluid reservoir is empty

The vacuum pump is not working

If the brake pedal is hard to press, this could mean a loss of vacuum or a fault in the vacuum pump. You should not drive the vehicle until the fault has been fixed by a qualified person.

3.46 Mark **one** answer

Your vehicle is fitted with an air-assisted hydraulic braking system. What would warn you that the vacuum pump is not working?

- The brake pedal feels spongy when pressed
- The brake pedal has little resistance
- The brake pedal feels hard when pressed
- The brake pedal travels a long way

The brake pedal feels hard when pressed

The pump creates the vacuum in the servo unit. This reduces the amount of pressure you need to apply to the brake pedal. Without this vacuum it would be extremely difficult to press the brake pedal down.

3.47 Mark **one** answer

Your vehicle is fitted with hydraulic brakes. The brake pedal goes down too far when pressed. What could this mean?

- There is too much fluid in the braking system
- The pedal travel requires adjustment
- The vacuum exhauster is not working
- There is not enough fluid in the braking system

There is not enough fluid in the braking system

A fault like this would suggest a serious loss of fluid from the hydraulic system. This must be checked and fixed by a qualified person. Do not drive it until this has been done.

3.48 *Mark **one** answer*

You are driving a vehicle fitted with a hydraulic brake system. What is it important to check, specific to this, before driving away?

- The hydraulic brake fluid level
- The power steering fluid level
- The cooling system fluid level
- The windscreen washer fluid level

The hydraulic brake fluid level

It is important to check all fluid levels during your daily checks, but it is especially important to remember the hydraulic fluid reservoir. A loss of fluid could lead to brake failure.

3.49 *Mark **one** answer*

Your vehicle is fitted with air-assisted hydraulic brakes. What would warn you that there is insufficient air in the system?

- An increase of pressure in the air gauge
- A buzzer or light
- The exhaust brake will not work
- Brake fade

A buzzer or light

If a warning buzzer or light alerts you to a loss of air pressure you should pull over without delay. You should have sufficient air in reserve to allow you to stop safely. Do not start or continue your journey until the fault has been repaired.

3.50 *Mark **one** answer*

You are driving down a long steep hill. You will make best use of engine braking by keeping the rev counter in which coloured band?

- Blue
- Red
- Amber
- Green

Blue

When going down a steep hill you should try to keep your rev counter in the blue band. This will allow you to make best use of engine braking.

3.51 Mark **one** answer

Your vehicle is fitted with air brakes. As you start the engine a brake warning light shows. What does this mean?

- Low air pressure
- Increased air pressure
- The parking brake is not working
- The air reservoirs are fully charged

Low air pressure

It is dangerous to drive a vehicle with low air pressure. To alert you to this, all vehicles are fitted with a warning light and/or buzzer. Do NOT attempt to move your vehicle.

3.52 Mark **one** answer

Your vehicle is fitted with air-assisted hydraulic brakes. The brake pedal becomes hard to press. What does this mean?

- The brake system has a loss of vacuum
- The brake linings are worn
- The brake linings need adjusting
- The brake system requires more fluid

The brake system has a loss of vacuum

A fault on the vacuum pump could be the cause of this. It could also be a leaking connection allowing air into the vacuum system.

3.53 Mark **one** answer

Your vehicle is fitted with a retarder. This has been activated. On which of these would wear be minimized?

- The brake linings
- The catalytic converter
- The exhaust system
- The transmission

The brake linings

By using a retarder the life of the brake linings is extended. This is because a retarder usually works by acting on the transmission or by applying engine braking.

3.54 *Mark **one** answer*

What action would you take if a brake air pressure warning device comes on?

- Continue to drive the vehicle
- Drain the air tanks
- Stop and get the fault put right
- Pump the brake pedal repeatedly

Stop and get the fault put right

Air brake systems are fitted with a warning device that operates if the air pressure in the tanks drops below a safe level. This may be a warning buzzer and/or pressure gauges. You must be aware of the function of all gauges on your vehicle, and check them as you drive.

3.55 *Mark **one** answer*

You are driving down a snow-covered hill. You should take extra care when using an independent endurance brake (retarder) because

- your brakes could overheat
- your speed could increase
- compressed air could escape
- the drive-wheels could lock

the drive-wheels could lock

Select an appropriate gear in good time and, if your vehicle has a dashboard mounted lever, apply the endurance brake (retarder) in stages. Careful use is necessary when driving on extremely slippery surfaces to avoid braking too much too soon with the result that you lock your drive-wheels.

3.56 *Mark **one** answer*

When using an independent endurance brake (retarder) on slippery roads, you should take care to avoid

- the front wheels spinning
- the drive-wheels locking
- brake pad wear
- anti-skid road surfaces

the drive-wheels locking

The endurance brake (retarder) usually operates by applying resistance via the transmission to the rotation of the vehicle's driven wheels.

3.57 Mark **one** answer

You are about to drive an unfamiliar vehicle. There may be moisture in the air brake reservoir. What should you do?

- Assume the system has automatic drain valves
- Find out whether you need to drain the system manually
- Nothing, it is the vehicle owner's responsibility
- Leave the engine running for a while before driving

- **Find out whether you need to drain the system manually**

Moisture left in the braking system can cause serious problems, especially in cold weather when it could freeze, causing the brakes to fail. Most modern vehicles have a system which drains automatically, but make sure you know which system is fitted to any vehicle that you drive.

3.58 Mark **one** answer

Your lorry does not have an anti-lock braking system fitted. You may prevent the wheels from locking under heavy braking by

- pushing the brake pedal harder until you stop
- depressing the clutch pedal as you brake
- rapid pumping of the brake pedal
- changing down through the gears as you brake

- **rapid pumping of the brake pedal**

Use maximum pressure to the point where the wheels are about to lock, momentarily release the brake pressure, then quickly apply it again. This technique is known as cadence braking. Only use this method when the vehicle is NOT fitted with an anti-lock braking system. It should only be used in an emergency situation to avoid skidding.

3.59 Mark **three** answers

Trailer swing is more likely to occur on a lorry and draw bar combination when

- braking on a bend
- oversteering at speed
- the brakes are out of adjustment
- braking lightly several times
- steering at slow speed and fully loaded
- an endurance brake (retarder) is fitted

- **braking on a bend**
- **oversteering at speed**
- **the brakes are out of adjustment**

All braking and changes of direction should be carried out smoothly and under full control. Make sure all the brakes are properly adjusted.

3.60 *Mark **one** answer*

Your vehicle is fitted with a 'diff-lock'. You would normally use it when

- driving on straight roads
- towing an empty trailer
- driving on muddy construction sites
- uncoupling a trailer

driving on muddy construction sites

The differential gears in the drive axle allow the drive wheels to rotate at different speeds, which is very important to enable you to negotiate corners and bends safely. The 'diff-lock' effectively locks the driven wheels together, so that power is transmitted equally to both. This is very useful in slippery or muddy conditions where otherwise the drive wheels can spin at different speeds and result in a loss of traction.

3.61 *Mark **one** answer*

On a three-line braking system to the trailer of a lorry what colour is the auxiliary line?

- Red
- Blue
- Green
- Yellow

Blue

If you're driving an articulated vehicle or a trailer combination it's vital that you understand the rules that apply to coupling and uncoupling the brake lines. If you're taking a test with a trailer, you'll be expected to demonstrate this during your practical test. The lines must be connected strictly in accordance with the correct procedure. Study the information in the publication The Official DSA Guide to Driving Goods Vehicles (published by the Stationery Office), to ensure that you know and understand the way this should be done.

3.62 *Mark **one** answer*

The emergency line is common to both two and three-line brake systems. What is its colour?

- Red
- Blue
- Black
- Yellow

Red

The red emergency line is common to both two- and three-line braking systems. ALWAYS set the parking brake before disconnecting any brake lines.

3.63 Mark **one** answer

Air brake systems usually have two lines. What additional line is fitted on a three-line system?

- Emergency
- Service
- Electrical
- Auxiliary

- **Auxiliary**

The blue (auxiliary) line is not used when connecting to a two-line system. Follow the manufacturer's instructions about what to do with the third (blue) line.

3.64 Mark **one** answer

In frosty weather, what precaution could a lorry driver take to prevent moisture freezing in brake air storage tanks?

- Drain the tanks daily
- Cover the tanks with a blanket
- Keep the engine at high revs when starting
- Pump the brakes

- **Drain the tanks daily**

You should make sure that you drain the tanks daily to avoid moisture freezing in the system. Most modern vehicles have an automatic draining system, which should be checked regularly.

3.65 Mark **one** answer

To help to avoid 'brake fade' lorry drivers should ensure that

- the air tanks are drained before journeys
- the air pressure is correct
- the handbrake is applied before stopping
- the appropriate gears are engaged before downhill gradients

- **the appropriate gears are engaged before downhill gradients**

It's important that you engage a low gear as you approach the hill to ensure the engine is building up air and can assist with braking. If the road has a long downhill gradient this is doubly important. You should be anticipating hazards like this as you drive. Good planning and preparation will ensure that you are always in the correct gear for the situation.

3.66 *Mark **one** answer*

Exhaust brakes give greatest efficiency when used

- at high engine speed in low gears
- at low engine speed in high gears
- on stop-start town work
- on high-speed motorway runs

- **at high engine speed in low gears**

Because excessive braking can have serious effects on the brakes, some vehicles are fitted with exhaust brakes. These brakes alter the engine's exhaust flow, using it to assist with the braking. They're most efficient when the engine is at high speed and in a low gear, such as when descending a long hill. Using the exhaust brakes can relieve the service brakes, preventing them from becoming hot and failing through over-use.

3.67 *Mark **one** answer*

The principal braking system on a lorry is called the

- endurance brake (retarder)
- service brake
- parking brake
- handbrake

- **service brake**

The service brake is usually operated by the foot control. It is used to control the speed of the vehicle and to bring it to a halt safely. It may also incorporate an anti-lock braking system.

3.68 *Mark **three** answers*

The three main braking systems fitted to lorries are known as

- over-run
- cadence
- exhaust
- service
- secondary
- parking

- **service**
- **secondary**
- **parking**

The service brake performs the primary function of stopping the vehicle when you depress the footbrake. The secondary brake system is for use in the event of failure of the service brake. The parking brake should normally only be used when the vehicle is stationary.

3.69 *Mark **one** answer*

You are driving a lorry and trailer. You change to a lower gear when going too fast. This could cause the

- vehicle to jack-knife
- engine to stall
- brakes to fail
- trailer to uncouple

vehicle to jack-knife

Jack-knifing is usually more likely to occur with an unladen vehicle, particularly when not travelling in a straight line. Severe braking or selection of a gear too low for your road speed can cause the tractor unit to be pushed by the semi-trailer pivoting around the coupling (fifth wheel).

3.70  *Mark **three** answers*

An articulated vehicle is more likely to jack-knife when

- unladen
- manoeuvring slowly
- braking sharply
- fully loaded
- on a bend
- fitted with an endurance brake (retarder)

unladen

braking sharply

on a bend

A combination of sharp braking and excessive steering can cause your vehicle to become unstable. Jack-knifing is more likely to occur when the vehicle is empty.

3.71  *Mark **one** answer*

Your lorry is stuck in snow. You use the diff-lock to move off. When should you switch the diff-lock off?

- Only after selecting top gear
- Once the engine has warmed up
- As soon as the vehicle is moving
- As soon as the snow has cleared

As soon as the vehicle is moving

You must always disengage the diff-lock as soon as the vehicle is moving. The differential allows the rear wheels to revolve at different speeds, which allows the vehicle to be steered. Attempting to turn with the diff-lock engaged could have disastrous consequences, as your vehicle will try to go straight on.

3.72 Mark **one** answer

Your tractor unit has three air lines. You are connecting to a trailer with two air lines. What colour is the line you should NOT connect to the trailer?

- Red
- Yellow
- Black
- Blue

Blue

When connecting three lines to a two-line trailer the third (blue) line is the one that should NOT be connected to the trailer. It is vitally important to follow the manufacturer's advice. It may be necessary to reconnect the extra line to the tractor unit.

3.73 Mark **one** answer

On an articulated lorry which has a three-line connection, the red line is the

- emergency line
- service line
- auxiliary line
- electrical line

emergency line

The red emergency line is common to both two-line and three-line brake systems. The other colours are

- blue – auxiliary
- yellow – service.

3.74 Mark **one** answer

You are driving a tractor unit fitted with two air lines. You want to couple up to a trailer with three air lines. How should this be done?

- The trailer auxiliary line should be left unconnected
- The trailer service line should be left unconnected
- Only the service line should be connected
- Only the auxiliary line should be connected

The trailer auxiliary line should be left unconnected

A two-line system consists of

- emergency – red line
- service – yellow line.

It is vitally important that you understand the rules that apply to safely connecting brake systems and mixing two- and three-line systems.

3.75 Mark **one** answer

The correct procedure for stopping a lorry equipped with an anti-lock braking system in an emergency is to

- apply the footbrake firmly in a pumping action until the vehicle has stopped
- apply the footbrake firmly and continuously until the vehicle has stopped
- apply the footbrake and handbrake until the vehicle has stopped
- apply the handbrake only

apply the footbrake firmly and continuously until the vehicle has stopped

If you're driving a vehicle with anti-lock brakes and you feel the vehicle beginning to skid, you should keep your foot firmly on the brake pedal until the vehicle stops. This will allow the system to work. Although anti-lock brakes on a vehicle contribute to safe braking, it doesn't take away the need to drive with good planning and anticipation, which should greatly reduce the need to brake harshly. Reliable and efficient equipment is essential, but it's your action that can prevent an accident.

3.76  Mark **one** answer

Changing to a lower gear can be useful in some circumstances. You should do this to help avoid

- brake fade
- clutch slip
- excessive engine revs
- tyre wear

brake fade

Engaging lower gears and using engine braking will assist you to slow down. This will help to prevent the brake linings from becoming overheated, and lessen the chance of brake fade occurring.

3.77 *Mark **one** answer*

What does this simplified diagram show?

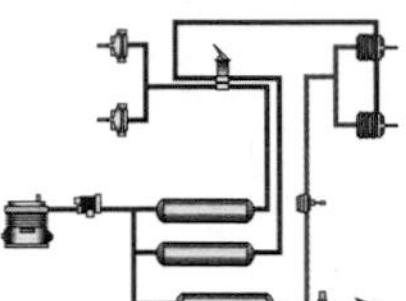

- Automatic gearbox unit
- Air conditioning unit
- Air brake system
- Fuel injection system

Air brake system

Large vehicles usually use air operated brakes. Gauges in the cab will show the air pressure in the system. If it drops too low a buzzer will usually sound to warn you.

3.78 *Mark **one** answer*

A Jake brake is an additional method of slowing a vehicle down. It works by

- altering the valve timing in the engine
- altering the number of axles in contact with the road
- operating automatically as you descend steep hills
- operating if you exceed the limit of your cruise control

altering the valve timing in the engine

A Jake brake is a long established system for retarding speed. It alters the valve timing in the engine. This then becomes a compressor and holds back the vehicle's speed.

3.79 *Mark **one** answer*

You have to drive onto a muddy building site. Why should you switch on your diff-lock?

- To make your steering lighter
- To improve your fuel consumption
- To increase your engine power
- To make the wheels less likely to spin

To make the wheels less likely to spin

Engaging the diff-lock means that power is shared between the driven wheels. This reduces the chances of wheelspin. Remember to switch off the diff-lock as soon as you are on firm ground again, otherwise you could damage the transmission.

section **four**
THE DRIVER

This section covers

- Consideration
- Courtesy
- Priority
- Vehicle safety equipment
- Tiredness
- Drugs and alcohol

4.1 Mark **two** answers

The driver of a bus should wear a seat belt if one is fitted UNLESS

- the seat belt is particularly uncomfortable
- the vehicle is being reversed
- a valid medical exemption certificate is held by the driver
- the belt is of the lap-only type
- the passengers carried are children

- **the vehicle is being reversed**
- **a valid medical exemption certificate is held by the driver**

If your vehicle is fitted with a seat belt you must wear it, unless you're exempt for medical reasons. You may also remove it before a reverse manoeuvre. Seat belts save lives. If the fitting of the belt is uncomfortable and it prevents you obtaining a safe driving position, report this to your employer. If it isn't right for you, it's likely that it won't be right for other drivers either.

4.2 Mark **four** answers

Which of the following MUST be clearly displayed on your bus?

- Seating and standing capacity
- Location of all bus stops
- Emergency exit location
- The route timetable
- Fuel cut-off switch
- Electrical isolator switch

- **Seating and standing capacity**
- **Emergency exit location**
- **Fuel cut-off switch**
- **Electrical isolator switch**

Ensure that all information required on the vehicle, by law referred to as the 'legal lettering', is displayed – seating/standing capacity, emergency exit location, fuel cut-off switch and electrical isolator.

4.3 Mark **one** answer

The nearside mirror is used for checking

- if the driver's door is closed properly
- for any vehicles moving up on the left
- if passengers are seated
- for any vehicles parking in front of you

- **for any vehicles moving up on the left**

Always be aware of any vehicles on your nearside, particularly on dual carriageways or motorways where, because of the limits on your vehicle, it can take some distance to overtake safely. When you think you are far enough ahead to move back to the left safely, check again, as other vehicles may accelerate up on the nearside.

4.4 Mark **one** answer

You are driving a bus in a built-up area. You should NOT

- block side road junctions
- leave a safe stopping distance
- anticipate traffic ahead
- use the MSM routine

block side road junctions

This is inconsiderate to other road users. You should look at the flow of traffic and be aware of side junctions when you are slowing down or stopping.

4.5 Mark **one** answer

You are driving on a motorway. A moving lorry just ahead of you switches on its hazard warning lights. What does this mean?

- There are speed cameras ahead
- The lorry is about to change lanes
- The lorry is leaving the motorway
- Traffic further ahead may be stopping

Traffic further ahead may be stopping

The driver ahead has spotted a hazard which you may not be able to see yet. Slow down and be ready to stop if necessary.

4.6 Mark **one** answer

You are driving in busy traffic. You lose your way. What should you do?

- Stop at traffic lights and ask pedestrians
- Shout to other drivers to ask them the way
- Drive on until you find a safe place to stop
- Check a map as you keep moving with the traffic

Drive on until you find a safe place to stop

Driving in busy traffic needs 100% concentration. If you become lost, find a safe place to stop before checking a map or asking directions. Don't risk losing concentration by glancing at a map while driving, even if you are in stop-start traffic.

4.7 Mark **three** answers

You should show extra consideration for pedestrians when driving past

- mobile shops
- open moorland
- shopping areas
- ice cream vans
- wooded areas
- suspension bridges

- **mobile shops**
- **shopping areas**
- **ice cream vans**

In all three of these situations, pedestrians may suddenly step out into the road. Vehicles such as mobile shops and ice cream vans require extra care, as there may be children hidden from view who could suddenly run into your path. Always keep your speed down when approaching these situations.

4.8 Mark **three** answers

Which of the following are most likely to cause danger to a group of horse riders?

- Powerful brake lights
- Size of your vehicle
- Noise of your vehicle
- The hiss of air brakes
- Leaving plenty of room
- Reacting in good time

- **Size of your vehicle**
- **Noise of your vehicle**
- **The hiss of air brakes**

The size of your vehicle can be intimidating, as well as reducing the amount of room left for other road users. Any noise can easily startle horses. You should take care to leave as much room as you can for riders. Keep the noise to a minimum by gentle use of the brakes and, if necessary, stopping and turning your engine off.

4.9 Mark **three** answers

Which of these should you do when passing sheep on a road?

- Pass quickly and quietly
- Tap your horn once
- Drive very slowly
- Allow plenty of room
- Be ready to stop

- **Drive very slowly**
- **Allow plenty of room**
- **Be ready to stop**

Animals can be very unpredictable. You should give them as much room as you can, keep speed and noise down to a minimum to avoid panicking them, and always be ready to stop if necessary.

4.10 Mark *one* answer

Your nearside mirror is most likely to endanger pedestrians when

- using a crawler lane
- braking hard on a bend
- driving close to the kerb
- passing a traffic sign

driving close to the kerb

You must be aware that a nearside mirror could strike the head of a pedestrian when you drive close to the kerb. This is a particular hazard in built-up areas and congested shopping centres.

4.11 Mark *one* answer

Which of the following can prevent you from obtaining a bus or lorry licence?

- heart disorders
- dyslexia
- skin problems
- stomach problems

heart disorders

A number of reasons can prevent you from obtaining, or keeping, a bus or lorry licence. If you develop any serious illness or disability that is likely to last more than three months, and which could affect your driving, you must tell the DVLA Drivers' Medical Group at Swansea immediately. Partial blindness and mental disorders can also prevent you from obtaining a bus or lorry licence.

4.12 Mark *three* answers

Before starting your engine your seat should be adjusted for

- height
- back support
- seat belt tension
- air ventilation
- distance from the controls
- leaving the cab

height

back support

distance from the controls

Being seated properly is very important when driving long distances. A poor driving position can quickly cause fatigue.

4.13 Mark **one** answer

A properly adjusted head restraint will

- ⊙ make you more comfortable
- ⊙ help you to avoid neck injury
- ⊙ help you to relax
- ⊙ help you to maintain your driving position

⊙ **help you to avoid neck injury**

The restraint should be adjusted so that it gives maximum protection to the head, in the event of a rear end collision.

4.14 Mark **one** answer

You may remove your seat belt when carrying out a manoeuvre that involves

- ⊙ reversing
- ⊙ a hill start
- ⊙ an emergency stop
- ⊙ driving slowly

⊙ **reversing**

Don't forget to put your seat belt back on when you've finished reversing.

4.15 Mark **one** answer

You are driving along this road. The red van cuts in close in front of you. What should you do?

- ⊙ Accelerate to get closer to the red van
- ⊙ Give a long blast on the horn
- ⊙ Drop back to leave the correct separation distance
- ⊙ Flash your headlights several times

⊙ **Drop back to leave the correct separation distance**

There are times when other drivers make incorrect or ill-judged decisions. Try to stay calm and don't retaliate or react aggressively. Always consider the safety of other road users, any passengers and yourself.

4.16 Mark **two** answers

While driving you approach a large puddle that is close to the left-hand kerb. Pedestrians are close to the water. You should

- ignore the puddle
- brake suddenly and sound your horn
- slow down before the puddle
- try to avoid splashing the pedestrians
- wave at the pedestrians to keep back

slow down before the puddle

try to avoid splashing the pedestrians

The effect of your vehicle driving through a puddle will be to throw water onto the pavement. If there are pedestrians close by they could be splashed with the water. Be considerate and, if it's safe to do so, avoid driving through it.

4.17 Mark **one** answer

A long, heavily laden lorry is taking a long time to overtake you. What should you do?

- Speed up
- Slow down
- Hold your speed
- Change direction

Slow down

A long lorry with a heavy load will need more time to pass you than a car. It won't be able to accelerate to pass you quickly, especially on an uphill stretch of road. Be considerate to the lorry driver – ease off the accelerator and allow the lorry to pass.

4.18 Mark **one** answer

You are driving a slow-moving vehicle on a narrow road. When traffic wishes to overtake you should

- take no action
- put your hazard warning lights on
- stop immediately and wave them on
- pull in safely as soon as you can do so

pull in safely as soon as you can do so

Try not to hold up a queue of traffic. This might lead to other road users becoming impatient. If you're driving a slow-moving vehicle and the road is narrow, look out for a safe place to pull in.

4.19 *Mark **one** answer*

You are driving a slow-moving vehicle on a narrow winding road. In order to let other vehicles overtake you should

- wave to them to pass
- pull in when you can
- show a left turn signal
- keep left and hold your speed

pull in when you can

Don't frustrate other road users by driving for long distances with a queue of traffic behind you. This could cause them to lose concentration or make ill-judged decisions.

4.20 *Mark **one** answer*

What should you use your horn for?

- To alert others to your presence
- To allow you right of way
- To greet other road users
- To signal your annoyance

To alert others to your presence

Don't use it to greet others, show impatience or to give or claim priority.

Your horn must not be used between 11.30 pm and 7 am in a built-up area, or when your vehicle is stationary, unless another vehicle poses a danger.

4.21 *Mark **two** answers*

You are following a car driven by a learner driver. You cannot overtake it. You should

- flash your lights so that the driver sees you
- be patient and stay well behind
- switch your hazard lights on and stay well behind
- be ready for mistakes made by the driver
- drive along the centre line of the road

be patient and stay well behind

be ready for mistakes made by the driver

Learner drivers are often nervous. If you stay well back this will reduce the risk of accidents occurring if mistakes are made by the learner driver. Remember, you were once in that situation yourself.

4.22 Mark **one** answer

You are signalled to stop by a police car. You should

- ⊙ brake harshly to a stop
- ⊙ drive on until you reach a side road
- ⊙ pull up on the left when it is safe to
- ⊙ stop immediately wherever you are

⊙ **pull up on the left when it is safe to**

If a police car signals for you to stop you should always find a safe place on the left and pull over.

4.23 Mark **one** answer

A police car is following you. The police would like you to stop. They will do this by flashing their headlights and

- ⊙ signalling with the right indicator
- ⊙ signalling with the left indicator
- ⊙ switching their hazard flashers on
- ⊙ switching their rear fog lights on

⊙ **signalling with the left indicator**

Indicating to the left shows that the police want you to pull in. You should find a safe place to stop before doing so.

4.24 Mark **one** answer

You are driving a vehicle fitted with a hand-held telephone. To answer it you should

- ⊙ find a safe place to stop
- ⊙ reduce your speed to less than 30 mph
- ⊙ steer your vehicle with one hand
- ⊙ be very careful when dealing with junctions

⊙ **find a safe place to stop**

Telephone calls can distract you, which means that you are not in proper control of your vehicle. You must have full control of your vehicle at all times. If you need to use any telecommunications equipment when driving, find a safe place to stop first.

4.25  *Mark **one** answer*

You have a mobile telephone fitted in your vehicle. It should only be used when you are

- stopped in a safe place
- travelling slowly
- on a motorway
- in light traffic

- **stopped in a safe place**

It's illegal to use a hand-held phone while driving. Once you have stopped your vehicle, you can concentrate on your call or message. If you use your phone while driving, you won't have full control of your vehicle. This could result in a collision with serious or even fatal consequences.

4.26  *Mark **one** answer*

A pelican crossing that crosses the road in a STRAIGHT line and has a central island must be treated as

- one crossing in daylight only
- one complete crossing
- two separate crossings
- two crossings during darkness

- **one complete crossing**

The lights that control the crossing show to both directions of traffic. If a pedestrian from either side is still crossing when the amber light is flashing, you must wait until they have finished crossing before moving off.

4.27  *Mark **one** answer*

At a pelican crossing the flashing amber light means you should

- stop, if you can do so safely
- give way to pedestrians already on the crossing
- stop and wait for the green light
- give way to pedestrians waiting to cross

- **give way to pedestrians already on the crossing**

Pelican crossings are light-controlled crossings where pedestrians use push-button controls to change the signals. Pelican crossings have no red-and-amber stage before green. Instead, they have a flashing amber light, which means you must give way to pedestrians on the crossing. If it's clear, you may proceed with caution.

4.28 *Mark **one** answer*

At a zebra crossing you should

- ⊙ rev your engine to encourage pedestrians to cross quickly
- ⊙ park only on the zigzag lines on the left
- ⊙ always leave it clear in traffic queues
- ⊙ wave pedestrians to cross if you intend to wait for them

⊙ **always leave it clear in traffic queues**

Look well ahead down the line of traffic so that you don't stop on the crossing and block it. Leave it clear so that pedestrians can cross safely.

4.29 *Mark **one** answer*

A coach is overtaking you. When it is safe for the coach to move back to the left you should

- ⊙ do nothing and let the driver decide
- ⊙ switch your sidelights on and off
- ⊙ flash your headlights once
- ⊙ flash your headlights twice

⊙ **do nothing and let the driver decide**

Allow the coach driver to make the decision to complete the manoeuvre.

4.30 *Mark **three** answers*

Which THREE of the following emergency vehicles will use blue flashing beacons?

- ⊙ Motorway maintenance
- ⊙ Bomb disposal team
- ⊙ Blood transfusion
- ⊙ Police vehicle
- ⊙ Breakdown recovery vehicle

⊙ **Bomb disposal team**

⊙ **Blood transfusion**

⊙ **Police vehicle**

Try to move out of the way of emergency vehicles with blue flashing beacons. Do so safely and without delay.

4.31 Mark **one** answer

When being followed by an ambulance showing a flashing blue beacon you should

- pull over as soon as safely possible to let it pass
- accelerate hard to get away from it
- ignore it if possible, let it pass if forced to
- brake harshly and immediately stop in the road

- **pull over as soon as safely possible to let it pass**

Pull over safely in a place where the ambulance can pass you. Check that there are no bollards or obstructions in the road that will prevent it doing so.

4.32 Mark **one** answer

You see a car showing a flashing green beacon. Should you give way to it?

- Yes, it is a doctor going to an emergency
- Yes, it is a fire crew support vehicle
- No, it is a slow-moving vehicle
- No, it is a breakdown vehicle

- **Yes, it is a doctor going to an emergency**

Give way by pulling over and letting the vehicle pass, but don't just stop suddenly. Choose a safe place as soon as you can to let the doctor's car pass safely.

4.33 Mark **one** answer

What type of emergency vehicle is fitted with a green flashing beacon?

- Fire engine
- Road gritter
- Ambulance
- Doctor's car

- **Doctor's car**

A green flashing light on a vehicle means the driver or passenger is a doctor on an emergency call. Give way to them if it's safe to do so. Be aware that the vehicle may be travelling quickly or may stop suddenly.

4.34 Mark **one** answer

You stop for pedestrians waiting to cross at a zebra crossing. They do not start to cross. What should you do?

- Be patient and wait
- Sound your horn
- Drive on
- Wave them to cross

Be patient and wait

If you stop for pedestrians and they don't start to cross, don't wave them across or sound your horn. This could be dangerous if an approaching vehicle is not aware of them. The driver may not have seen or heard your signal and it would be very dangerous for the pedestrians to start to cross.

4.35 Mark **one** answer

You should beckon pedestrians to cross the road at

- pedestrian crossings
- no time
- junctions
- school crossings

no time

Beckoning pedestrians to cross can be dangerous. Other road users may not have seen your signal and you might encourage the pedestrians to put themselves in danger.

4.36 Mark **one** answer

You should never wave people across at pedestrian crossings because

- there may be another vehicle coming
- they may not be looking
- it is safer for you to carry on
- they may not be ready to cross

there may be another vehicle coming

If it's safe you should always stop for pedestrians waiting at pedestrian crossings. Don't wave them to cross the road since another driver may not

- have seen them
- have seen your signal
- be able to stop safely.

4.37 Mark *three* answers

You are driving close to the kerb in a busy shopping area. What dangers should you be most aware of?

- ⊙ Traffic lights suddenly changing to green
- ⊙ The amount of fuel being used when driving slowly
- ⊙ Pedestrians stepping off the edge of the pavement
- ⊙ The nearside mirror striking the heads of pedestrians
- ⊙ Cyclists moving up the left side of your vehicle

- ⊙ **Pedestrians stepping off the edge of the pavement**
- ⊙ **The nearside mirror striking the heads of pedestrians**
- ⊙ **Cyclists moving up the left side of your vehicle**

When you need to drive close to the kerb, be aware of the dangers.

- Pedestrians may step off the kerb.
- The nearside mirror may be at a pedestrian's head height.
- Cyclists may be tempted to pass you on your left if you are driving slowly in congested conditions.

4.38 Mark *three* answers

You should NOT park your vehicle or trailer

- ⊙ at an overnight service area
- ⊙ near the brow of a hill
- ⊙ opposite a traffic island
- ⊙ in front of an entrance to a property
- ⊙ in a factory yard

- ⊙ **near the brow of a hill**
- ⊙ **opposite a traffic island**
- ⊙ **in front of an entrance to a property**

Do not park where you would endanger or inconvenience others. If your choice of parking place obstructs drivers, riders or pedestrians, move to a more suitable area.

4.39 Mark *two* answers

Mirrors fitted to your vehicle MUST be

- ⊙ clean
- ⊙ properly adjusted
- ⊙ convex
- ⊙ tinted
- ⊙ concave

- ⊙ **clean**
- ⊙ **properly adjusted**

It is important to know what is happening behind as well as ahead. Your mirrors must be clean and properly adjusted.

4.40 Mark **one** answer

As you drive past a group of school children standing close to the kerb you should

- check your offside mirror
- check your nearside mirror
- switch on your headlights
- switch on your hazard lights

check your nearside mirror

On approach you should consider if you need to use the horn as a warning (this may not be appropriate where animals are around). Always check your nearside mirror as you pass potential hazards on the left.

4.41 Mark **one** answer

You are driving at the legal speed limit. A vehicle comes up quickly behind, flashing its headlights. You should

- accelerate to maintain a gap behind you
- touch the brake pedal sharply to show your brake lights
- maintain your speed and prevent the vehicle from overtaking
- allow the vehicle to overtake

allow the vehicle to overtake

Don't enforce the speed limit by blocking another vehicle's progress. This is likely to cause the other driver to become more frustrated. Slow down or move over when it is safe to do so and allow the other vehicle to pass.

4.42 Mark **one** answer

A vehicle pulls out in front of you at a junction. What should you do?

- Swerve past it and sound your horn
- Flash your headlights and drive up close behind
- Slow down and be ready to stop
- Accelerate past it immediately

Slow down and be ready to stop

Try to be ready for the unexpected. Plan ahead and learn to anticipate hazards. You'll then give yourself more time to react to any problems that might occur. Be tolerant of other road users who don't behave correctly.

4.43 *Mark **three** answers*

Which THREE of these are likely effects of drinking alcohol on driving?

- Reduced coordination
- Increased confidence
- Poor judgement
- Increased concentration
- Faster reactions
- Colour blindness

- **Reduced coordination**
- **Increased confidence**
- **Poor judgement**

Alcohol can increase confidence to a point where a driver's behaviour might become 'out of character'. Someone who normally behaves sensibly suddenly takes risks and enjoys it. Never let yourself or your friends get into this situation.

4.44 *Mark **three** answers*

Drinking any amount of alcohol is likely to

- reduce your ability to react to hazards
- increase the speed of your reactions
- worsen your judgement of speed
- increase your awareness of danger
- give a false sense of confidence

- **reduce your ability to react to hazards**
- **worsen your judgement of speed**
- **give a false sense of confidence**

Never drink if you are going to drive. It's always the safest option not to drink at all.

If you are convicted of drink-driving you will certainly lose your job, so don't be tempted – it isn't worth it.

4.45 *Mark **three** answers*

What else can seriously affect your concentration when driving, other than alcoholic drinks?

- Drugs
- Tiredness
- Tinted windows
- Contact lenses
- Loud music

- **Drugs**
- **Tiredness**
- **Loud music**

The least distraction can allow your concentration to drift. Focus on your driving so you stay in full control of your vehicle at all times.

4.46 Mark **one** answer

How does alcohol affect your driving?

- It speeds up your reactions
- It increases your awareness
- It improves your coordination
- It reduces your concentration

It reduces your concentration

Concentration and good judgement at all times are needed to be a good, safe driver.

4.47 Mark **one** answer

You have been convicted of driving whilst unfit through drink or drugs. You will find this is likely to cause the cost of one of the following to rise considerably. Which one?

- Road fund licence
- Insurance premiums
- Vehicle test certificate
- Driving licence

Insurance premiums

You have proved yourself to be a risk to yourself and others on the road. For this reason insurance companies may charge you a high premium for the use of your own vehicle. You will certainly lose your job.

4.48 Mark **one** answer

What advice should you give to a driver who has had a few alcoholic drinks at a party?

- Have a strong cup of coffee and then drive home
- Drive home carefully and slowly
- Go home by public transport
- Wait a short while and then drive home

Go home by public transport

Drinking black coffee or waiting a few hours won't make any difference. Alcohol takes time to leave the body. You might even be unfit to drive the following morning.

4.49 Mark **one** answer

A driver attends a social event. What precaution should the driver take?

- Drink plenty of coffee after drinking alcohol
- Avoid busy roads after drinking alcohol
- Avoid drinking alcohol completely
- Avoid drinking alcohol on an empty stomach

Avoid drinking alcohol completely

This is always going to be the safest option. One drink could be too many.

4.50 Mark **two** answers

It is eight hours since you last had an alcoholic drink. Which of the following applies?

- You will certainly be under the legal limit
- You will have no alcohol in your system
- You may still be unfit to drive
- You may still be over the legal limit

You may still be unfit to drive

You may still be over the legal limit

Alcohol can take a long time to leave the body. You may feel all right to drive, but its effect will last for many hours.

4.51 Mark **one** answer

Your doctor has given you a course of medicine. Why should you ask if it is OK to drive?

- Drugs make you a better driver by quickening your reactions
- You will have to let your insurance company know about the medicine
- Some types of medicine can cause your reactions to slow down
- The medicine you take may affect your hearing

Some types of medicine can cause your reactions to slow down

Always check the label of any medication container. The contents might affect your driving. If you aren't sure, ask your doctor or pharmacist.

4.52 Mark **one** answer

You have been taking medicine for a few days which made you feel drowsy. Today you feel better, but still need to take the medicine. You should only drive

- if your journey is necessary
- at night on quiet roads
- if someone goes with you
- after checking with your doctor

- **after checking with your doctor**

Take care, it's not worth taking risks. Always check to be really sure. The medicine may have an effect on you later in the day.

4.53 Mark **two** answers

You are not sure if your cough medicine will affect your driving. What TWO things could you do?

- Ask your doctor
- Check the medicine label
- Drive if you feel all right
- Ask a friend or relative for advice

- **Ask your doctor**
- **Check the medicine label**

If you're taking medicine or drugs prescribed by your doctor, check to ensure that they won't make you drowsy. If you forget to ask at the time of your visit to the surgery, check with your pharmacist.

4.54 Mark **one** answer

You take some cough medicine given to you by a friend. What must you do before driving?

- Drink some strong coffee
- Ask your friend if taking the medicine affected their driving
- Check the label to see if the medicine will affect your driving
- Make a short journey to see if the medicine is affecting your driving

- **Check the label to see if the medicine will affect your driving**

Never drive having taken drugs you don't know about. They might affect your judgement and perception and, therefore, endanger lives.

4.55 Mark **two** answers

You are driving along a motorway and become tired. You should

- stop at the next service area and rest
- leave the motorway at the next exit and rest
- increase your speed and turn up the radio volume
- close all your windows and set heating to warm
- pull up on the hard shoulder and change drivers

- **stop at the next service area and rest**
- **leave the motorway at the next exit and rest**

If you have planned your journey properly to include rest stops, you will arrive at your destination in good time.

4.56 Mark **one** answer

You are about to drive home. You feel very tired and have a severe headache.
You should

- wait until you are fit and well before driving
- drive home, but take a tablet for headaches
- drive home if you can stay awake for the journey
- wait for a short time, then drive home slowly

- **wait until you are fit and well before driving**

All your concentration should be on your driving. Any pain you feel will distract you. Change your plans and be safe.

4.57 Mark **one** answer

If you are feeling tired it is best to stop as soon as you can. Until then you should

- increase your speed to find a stopping place quickly
- ensure a supply of fresh air
- gently tap the steering wheel
- keep changing speed to improve concentration

ensure a supply of fresh air

If you're travelling on a long journey, plan your route before you leave. This will help you to

- be decisive at intersections and junctions
- plan your rest stops
- know approximately how long the journey will take.

Make sure that the vehicle you're travelling in is well ventilated. A warm, stuffy atmosphere can make you drowsy, which will impair your judgement and perception.

4.58 Mark **one** answer

Your reactions will be much slower when driving

- if tired
- in fog
- too quickly
- in rain

if tired

Try to avoid becoming tired by taking plenty of rest stops and allowing fresh air into your vehicle.

4.59 Mark **one** answer

You are driving on a motorway. You feel tired. You should

- carry on but drive slowly
- leave the motorway at the next exit
- complete your journey as quickly as possible
- stop on the hard shoulder

leave the motorway at the next exit

If you do feel tired and there's no service station for many miles, leave the motorway at the next exit. Find a place off the motorway where you can pull up and stop safely for a rest.

4.60 Mark *one* answer

You are taking medication that could affect your driving. What should you do?

- ⊙ Seek medical advice
- ⊙ Make short journeys only
- ⊙ Drive only at night
- ⊙ Drink plenty of water

⊙ **Seek medical advice**

Check all medicines. Consult your doctor or pharmacist if you are not sure.

4.61 Mark *one* answer

You are driving on a motorway and feel tired. You should

- ⊙ stop on the hard shoulder for a rest
- ⊙ carry on, but drive slowly
- ⊙ leave at the next exit
- ⊙ try to complete your journey more quickly

⊙ **leave at the next exit**

Don't continue to drive without taking your proper rest periods. Walking around in the fresh air during your break will help before setting off again.

4.62 Mark *one* answer

You have driven a long distance and feel tired. Your tachograph shows that you have not exceeded your driving hours. What should you do?

- ⊙ Park in a suitable place and rest
- ⊙ Reduce your speed and drive more slowly
- ⊙ Carry on driving to use up your hours
- ⊙ Increase your speed and reduce your journey time

⊙ **Park in a suitable place and rest**

The smallest lapse in concentration can result in loss of control. If you feel that you may be losing concentration, pull up at the next safe place for a rest.

4.63 *Mark **one** answer*

Persistent misuse of drugs or alcohol may lead to

- better concentration
- better eyesight
- withdrawal of a driving licence
- faster reactions

withdrawal of a driving licence

Persistent misuse of drugs and or alcohol may lead to the withdrawal of your driving licence. Your insurance premiums will probably increase as well.

4.64 *Mark **one** answer*

You are driving a vehicle on a motorway. A front tyre bursts. You should

- loosen your grip on the steering wheel
- brake firmly to a stop
- hold the steering wheel firmly
- drive to the next service area

hold the steering wheel firmly

A front wheel blow-out can be a heart-stopping moment. Keep calm and resist the temptation to brake hard or swerve. Allow the vehicle to slow down gradually. Be aware of anything on your left. Try to get the vehicle onto the hard shoulder, as far to the left as possible. Switch on your hazard warning lights.

4.65 *Mark **one** answer*

Your mobile phone rings while you are driving. You should

- stop immediately
- answer it immediately
- pull up in a suitable place
- pull up at the nearest kerb

pull up in a suitable place

Never risk losing control of your vehicle through any distractions to your driving. It is not worth taking the risk of endangering other road users. Make sure that you pull up in a place that does not obstruct other road users. The safest option of all is to use a message service. This enables you to complete your journey without interruptions and you can catch up with your calls when you take your rest breaks.

4.66 Mark **one** answer

You break down on a motorway. You need to call for help. Why may it be better to use an emergency roadside telephone rather than a mobile phone?

- It connects you to a local garage
- Using a mobile phone will distract other drivers
- It allows easy location by the emergency services
- Mobile phones do not work on motorways

It allows easy location by the emergency services

On a motorway it is best to use a roadside emergency telephone so that the emergency services are able to locate you easily.

4.67 Mark **one** answer

You are most likely to lose concentration when driving if you

- use a mobile phone
- switch on the windscreen wipers
- switch on the heated rear window
- look at the door mirrors

use a mobile phone

Using a hand-held mobile phone while driving is illegal. It will distract you from your driving to the point where you are paying more attention to the phone call or message than you are to your driving.

4.68 Mark **one** answer

You should not use a mobile phone whilst driving

- until you are satisfied that no other traffic is near
- unless you are able to drive one handed
- because it might distract your attention from the road ahead
- because reception is poor when the engine is running

because it might distract your attention from the road ahead

Driving requires your total attention and concentration at all times. Don't be distracted by taking or making mobile phone calls. Be safe, switch it off and use the messaging facility. It is illegal to use a hand-held mobile phone whilst driving.

4.69 Mark **one** answer

You should ONLY use a mobile phone when

- receiving a call
- suitably parked
- driving at less than 30 mph
- driving an automatic vehicle

suitably parked

It's illegal to use a hand-held mobile phone while driving. Park in a suitable place before receiving or making a call or text. It's more convenient for you, and safer. You may need to take notes or refer to papers, this would not be possible while driving.

4.70 Mark **one** answer

Using a mobile phone while you are driving

- is acceptable in a vehicle with power steering
- will reduce your field of vision
- could distract your attention from the road
- will affect your vehicle's electronic systems

could distract your attention from the road

Driving today requires all of your attention, all of the time. Any distraction, however brief, is dangerous. This is why it's illegal to use a hand-held mobile phone while driving.

4.71 Mark **one** answer

Your vehicle breaks down on the hard shoulder of a motorway. You decide to use your mobile phone to call for help. You should

- stand at the rear of the vehicle while making the call
- try to repair the vehicle yourself
- get out of the vehicle by the right hand door
- check your location from the marker posts on the left

check your location from the marker posts on the left

In an emergency, time can be of the essence. The emergency services need to know your exact location. Look at the marker posts on the edge of the hard shoulder before you phone, there is a number on them. Tell this to the services as it will help them to locate you. Be ready to describe where you are, for example by reference to the last place or junction you passed.

4.72 Mark **one** answer

To answer a call on your mobile phone while driving you should

- reduce your speed wherever you are
- stop in a proper and convenient place
- keep the call time to a minimum
- slow down and allow others to overtake

stop in a proper and convenient place

No phone call is important enough to endanger someone's life. If you must be contactable when driving, plan your route to include breaks where you can catch up on telephone messages in safety. Always choose a proper and convenient place to take a break.

4.73 Mark **one** answer

You are overtaking a lorry. You see the driver flash their headlights. What should you do?

- Move back to the left when it is safe to do so
- Indicate left and move back slowly
- Act immediately on the other driver's signal
- Flash your rear lights on and off twice

Move back to the left when it is safe to do so

Never presume what someone means when they flash their headlights. Wait until it is safe to complete your manoeuvre.

4.74 Mark **one** answer

A bus has stopped at a bus stop ahead of you. Its right-hand indicator is flashing. You should

- flash your headlights and slow down
- slow down and give way if it is safe to do so
- sound your horn and keep going
- slow down and then sound your horn

slow down and give way if it is safe to do so

Give way to buses whenever you can do so safely, especially when they signal to pull away from bus stops. Look out for people leaving the bus and crossing the road without looking. They may run out from behind the bus. Also look out for people running to catch a bus who may be more concerned about catching it than watching for traffic.

4.75 *Mark **one** answer*

You have stopped for an elderly pedestrian who is slowly crossing the road. Traffic behind you is being held up. What should you do?

- Edge forward slowly and make them hurry
- Remain where you are and allow them to cross in their own time
- Steer slowly around them to ease the build up of traffic
- Get out of your vehicle and wave them across

Remain where you are and allow them to cross in their own time

Elderly pedestrians can be hesitant and may move slowly when crossing the road. Also, their awareness of traffic may be limited. Be patient and show courtesy and understanding.

4.76 *Mark **one** answer*

You are driving a slow-moving vehicle along a narrow road. You should let other vehicles overtake by

- maintaining a steady speed
- waving them past
- giving a left turn signal
- pulling in when you can

pulling in when you can

Drivers queuing behind you may make hasty or ill-judged decisions in an effort to overtake. If you see a queue of traffic building up behind give way as soon as you can do so safely by pulling in to the left.

4.77 *Mark **one** answer*

Your vehicle is fitted with a hands-free phone system. Using this equipment whilst driving

- is quite safe as long as you slow down
- could distract your attention from the road
- is recommended by The Highway Code
- could be very good for road safety

could distract your attention from the road

Using a hands-free system doesn't mean that you can safely drive and use a mobile phone. You may still be distracted, reducing your level of concentration. Your responsibility is to keep yourself and other road users safe at all times.

4.78 Mark *one* answer

Using a hands-free phone is likely to

- improve your safety
- increase your concentration
- reduce your view
- divert your attention

divert your attention

Unlike a passenger, the person speaking to you is unable to see the traffic situations you are dealing with. They will continue to speak to you even if you are approaching a hazardous situation. You need to be concentrating on your driving all of the time, and especially when dealing with a hazard.

4.79 Mark *one* answer

Your mobile phone rings while you are on the motorway. Before answering you should

- reduce your speed to 40 mph
- pull up on the hard shoulder
- move into the left-hand lane
- stop in a safe place when you can

stop in a safe place when you can

Plan your journey and take breaks to keep in touch if necessary. When driving on motorways, you can't just pull up to answer your mobile phone. You will need to turn off the motorway or wait until you get to the next service area. Be safe, switch it off while driving and use the message facility to listen to any calls when you are parked in a safe and proper place.

4.80 Mark *three* answers

Which THREE of these are likely effects of drinking alcohol on driving?

- Less control
- A false sense of confidence
- Faster reactions
- Poor judgement of speed
- Greater awareness of danger

Less control

A false sense of confidence

Poor judgement of speed

You must understand the dangers of mixing alcohol with driving. One drink is too many if you're going to drive. Alcohol will reduce your ability to drive safely.

4.81 Mark **one** answer

You are driving on a motorway. There has been an accident on the other side of the carriageway. You should take extra care as traffic in your lane may

- leave at the next exit
- slow down to have a look
- pull out to overtake
- stop on the hard shoulder

slow down to have a look

Most people cannot resist the temptation to slow down to look at a traffic incident, even if it is on the other side of the carriageway. Further collisions can sometimes occur as a direct result of this. Keeping a safe following distance and planning well ahead should enable you to keep out of trouble in situations like this.

4.82 Mark **one** answer

You are driving on a motorway. There has been an accident on the opposite carriageway. What should you do?

- Concentrate on your driving
- Slow down to look across
- Switch on your hazard lights
- Stop on the hard shoulder

Concentrate on your driving

Drivers slowing down to watch what's happening on the other carriageway can often cause further problems, and even collisions, by not concentrating on their driving. Don't allow yourself to be distracted, concentrate on what's happening on your own side of the motorway.

4.83 Mark **one** answer

You are driving on a motorway. There has been an accident on the opposite carriageway. Busy traffic ahead is slowing to look. You should

- concentrate on the road ahead
- slow down to take a look
- pull up on the hard shoulder
- overtake using the hard shoulder

concentrate on the road ahead

'Rubber-necking' drivers at accident scenes can often end up having collisions themselves, when they allow their vehicle to wander or fail to notice that the driver ahead has slowed right down or stopped. You need to keep your concentration in a situation like this and ignore what's happening on the other carriageway.

4.84 Mark **one** answer

Your vehicle has power-assisted steering. Its main purpose is to

- reduce tyre wear
- assist with braking
- reduce driver effort
- assist road holding

- **reduce driver effort**

The main purpose of power-assisted steering is to reduce driver effort. When cornering it is possible to oversteer and scrub the front tyres, resulting in excessive wear.

4.85 Mark **three** answers

Many vehicles are fitted with power-assisted steering. You need to be aware that this

- causes less tyre wear
- prevents you from oversteering
- makes it easier for you to steer
- senses when you start to turn the wheel
- only works at high speeds
- makes the steering seem light

- **makes it easier for you to steer**
- **senses when you start to turn the wheel**
- **makes the steering seem light**

Power-assisted steering only operates when the engine is running. If a fault develops, much greater effort is required to turn the steering wheel. Do not attempt to drive a vehicle if you are aware of a fault in the power steering system.

4.86 Mark **one** answer

A driver pulls out of a side road in front of you. You have to brake hard. You should

- ignore the error and stay calm
- flash your lights to show your annoyance
- sound your horn to show your annoyance
- overtake as soon as possible

- **ignore the error and stay calm**

If you're driving where there are a number of side roads, be alert. Drivers approaching or emerging from the side road might not be able to see you. Be especially careful if there are a lot of parked vehicles. If a vehicle does emerge and you have to stop quickly, try to be tolerant and learn from the experience.

4.87 Mark **one** answer

A car driver pulls out causing you to brake. You should

- keep calm and not retaliate
- overtake and sound your horn
- drive close behind and sound your horn
- flag the driver down and explain the mistake

keep calm and not retaliate

You have to understand that others on the road might disobey the rules or make an error of judgement at times. Try to accept this calmly and learn from other people's mistakes.

4.88 Mark **one** answer

Another driver's behaviour has upset you. It may help if you

- stop and take a break
- shout abusive language
- gesture to them with your hand
- follow their car, flashing your headlights

stop and take a break

Tiredness may make you more irritable than you would be normally. You might react differently to situations because of it. If you feel yourself becoming tense, take a break.

4.89 Mark **one** answer

Another driver does something that upsets you. You should

- try not to react
- let them know how you feel
- flash your headlights several times
- sound your horn

try not to react

There are occasions when other drivers or riders make a misjudgement or a mistake. If this happens, try not to let it worry you. Don't react by showing anger. Sounding the horn, flashing your headlights or shouting at the other driver won't help the situation. Good anticipation will help to prevent these incidents becoming collisions.

4.90 Mark **one** answer

You are driving in fast-moving traffic along a motorway. There is a stationary queue of traffic ahead. What should you do?

- ⊙ Move to the hard shoulder
- ⊙ Change lanes
- ⊙ Switch on your rear foglights
- ⊙ Switch on your hazard warning lights

⊙ **Switch on your hazard warning lights**

Traffic queues on the motorway are becoming more common, whether due to the sheer volume of traffic at peak times or to accidents. Keep well back from the vehicle in front so you'll be able to see the problems ahead on the road. If you see a queue of stationary traffic ahead, switching on your hazard warning lights for a short while will warn those behind you of the hazard ahead.

4.91 Mark **one** answer

You are turning right onto a dual carriageway from a side road. Your vehicle is too long for the central gap. How should you proceed?

- ⊙ Move forward and wait in the middle
- ⊙ Wait until it is clear from both directions
- ⊙ Move out blocking traffic from the right
- ⊙ Edge out slowly so other traffic will see you

⊙ **Wait until it is clear from both directions**

When turning right onto a dual carriageway don't stop in the middle, unless the gap is big enough for your vehicle to do so without impeding moving traffic. When it's busy consider turning left and using a roundabout further up the road. This will avoid you having to cross the central reservation.

4.92 Mark *three* answers

You want to turn left at a road junction. What is most important when deciding your position?

- ⊙ The length of the vehicle
- ⊙ The width of the roads
- ⊙ The camber of the road
- ⊙ The type of road surface
- ⊙ The angle of the corner

⊙ **The length of the vehicle**

⊙ **The width of the roads**

⊙ **The angle of the corner**

Where you position your vehicle on approach to a left turn will depend on several factors. You should be considering and deciding on the best position as you approach. If you need to take up part of any other lane, be extra-cautious. Other road users might not understand your reasons for doing this. They might try to pass on the left in the gap that you need to make the turn. Always check the left-hand mirror as you approach and just before you turn. It's better to take extra road space on the road that you're leaving than to expect there to be extra room on the road that you're entering. There might not be any.

4.93 Mark *one* answer

As well as planning your route before starting a journey, you should also plan an alternative route. Why is this?

- ⊙ To let another driver overtake
- ⊙ Your first route may be blocked
- ⊙ To avoid a railway level crossing
- ⊙ In case you have to avoid emergency vehicles

⊙ **Your first route may be blocked**

It's a good idea to plan an alternative route in case your original route is blocked for any reason. You're less likely to feel worried and stressed if you've got an alternative in mind. This will enable you to concentrate fully on your driving or riding. Always carry a map that covers the area you will travel in.

4.94 Mark **one** answer

You are making an appointment and will have to travel a long distance. You should

- allow plenty of time for your journey
- plan to go at busy times
- avoid all national speed limit roads
- prevent other drivers from overtaking

allow plenty of time for your journey

Always allow plenty of time for your journey in case of unforseen problems. Anything can happen, punctures, breakdowns, road closures, diversions etc. You will feel less stressed and less inclined to take risks if you are not 'pushed for time'.

4.95 Mark **one** answer

While driving you should remain alert at all times. How can you help yourself to maintain concentration?

- Eat sugary snacks when on duty
- Have regular meals and rest breaks
- Do not eat at all on duty
- Avoid meals containing bread and vegetables

Have regular meals and rest breaks

Try to base your meals around foods that contain slowly digested calories. Complex carbohydrates such as bread and vegetables, are good for slow energy release. They will keep you satisfied and prevent hunger for longer than those with a high sugar content.

4.96 Mark **one** answer

The amount of fluid you need to drink can vary. It is influenced by the temperature in your vehicle. What is the best type of fluid to drink?

- Bottled water
- Sugary canned drinks
- High caffeine drinks
- Hot chocolate

Bottled water

Water is the ideal drink because it quenches your thirst for longer periods than tea or coffee. It is good practice to carry water when driving especially in very hot weather. Nutritionists recommend you should drink 1.5 to 2 litres of water per day.

4.97 Mark **one** answer

You have to drive through the night. What should you do to help concentration?

- Have continual snacks whilst driving
- Not prepare your own food in advance
- Have a meal at the beginning of your shift
- Not eat anything during your period of work

Have a meal at the beginning of your shift

Concentration and safe driving will be improved by regular meals timed to fit in with your scheduled rest periods/breaks. This is better than continually snacking while on the move.

4.98 Mark **one** answer

A number of vehicle accidents are sleep-related. Between which times is there a particular risk?

- 2am and 7am
- 11pm and 2am
- 6pm and 11pm
- 7am and 2pm

2am and 7am

There is a particular risk when driving between 2am and 7am. This is when the 'body clock' is programmed for sleep in most people. There is another smaller dip between 2pm and 4pm.

4.99 Mark **one** answer

A number of sleep related vehicle incidents (SRVIs) are probably work related. What percentage involve commercial vehicles?

- 20%
- 40%
- 60%
- 80%

40%

Research into the effects of fatigue and sleep related incidents has been undertaken for the DfT. These incidents often result in serious injuries. Tired drivers have NOT used their brakes, and continued to drive in "automatic mode". This has caused them to run off the road or hit the vehicle in front.

4.100 *Mark **one** answer*

Commercial vehicles have been shown to be involved in sleep related vehicle incidents (SRVIs). Approximately what percentage of these incidents involve commercial vehicles?

- 40%
- 55%
- 70%
- 95%

40%

Research shows that approximately 40% of sleep related vehicle incidents involve commercial vehicles. A tired driver has probably not used the brakes. This often results in running off the road or into other vehicles, with serious consequences.

4.101 *Mark **one** answer*

Driving for long periods can cause fatigue. Tired drivers are normally

- aware of their sleepiness
- over their permitted hours
- not aware of their sleepiness
- able to judge hazards better

aware of their sleepiness

If you begin to feel tired, stop in a safe place. A short "nap or doze"of about 15 minutes can help to counter your sleepiness.

4.102 *Mark **three** answers*

Poor eating habits can increase your risk of long term health problems. Which THREE may result from a poor diet?

- Deafness
- Obesity
- Lung disease
- Diabetes
- Heart disease
- Epilepsy

Obesity

Diabetes

Heart disease

Obesity, diabetes and heart disease can increase your risk of sudden incapacity at the wheel. You could also develop a serious illness and ultimately suffer an early death. Smoking and a lack of exercise can also increase these risks.

4.103 *Mark **one** answer*

You have driven for a long time and are fighting sleep. What should you do?

- ⊙ Stop driving
- ⊙ Open a window
- ⊙ Play loud music
- ⊙ Stretch your arms

⊙ **Stop driving**

There is only one safe countermeasure to driver sleepiness, particularly when you start fighting sleep. Stop in a safe place and take a break.

4.104 *Mark **one** answer*

Driver sleepiness most often occurs on which type of road?

- ⊙ Motorway
- ⊙ One-way street
- ⊙ Rural road
- ⊙ Tourist route

⊙ **Motorway**

Falling asleep whilst driving accounts for a significant proportion of vehicle incidents under monotonous driving conditions. Driving at a constant speed for long periods can cause drowsiness. This often happens on motorways. Stop for regular breaks.

4.105 *Mark **one** answer*

Many sleep-related vehicle incidents (SRVIs) occur at work. Men are more likely than women to be involved. Between what ages are men most at risk?

- ⊙ 30 years and under
- ⊙ 31 - 45 years
- ⊙ 46 - 59 years
- ⊙ 60 years and over

⊙ **30 years and under**

Sleep-related vehicle incidents (SRVIs) are more evident in young male drivers. These usually happen during the early hours of the day. Many people believe this won't happen to them. Make sure you get enough sleep before starting work and take sufficient rest breaks.

4.106 *Mark one answer*

Your vehicle has a front wheel blow-out. What should you try to do?

- Hold the steering wheel firmly and slow down gradually
- Steer to the right-hand side and brake firmly
- Do not use your brakes in any circumstance
- Brake hard and steer towards the affected side

Hold the steering wheel firmly and slow down gradually

With a front wheel blow-out you will not be able to steer properly. Keep a firm hold of the steering wheel and slow down gradually to a stop. Don't brake hard or steer sharply.

4.107 *Mark one answer*

Your vehicle is fitted with seat belts. You must wear them unless

- you hold a medical exemption certificate
- the seat belt is too large for your use
- you are driving on a motorway
- the speed limit is 30 mph or less

you hold a medical exemption certificate

If seat belts are fitted to your vehicle, they must be worn unless you hold a valid medical exemption certificate. Those making deliveries or collections in goods vehicles when travelling less than 50 metres (162 feet) are also exempt.

4.108 *Mark one answer*

When you are driving between 2 am and 7 am there is a particular risk, in relation to your 'body clock'. You are more likely to

- fall asleep at the wheel
- face road rage
- meet traffic congestion
- have a vehicle breakdown

fall asleep at the wheel

A significant number of sleep-related vehicle incidents involve commercial vehicles. There is a particular risk when driving between 2 am and 7 am because this is when the 'body clock' is in a daily trough. It's important to take proper rest before, during, and between driving duties.

4.109 Mark one answer

Which of these is specifically provided to protect against neck and whiplash injuries?

- An air-sprung seat
- Anti-lock brakes
- A collapsible steering wheel
- A properly adjusted head restraint

A properly adjusted head restraint

Head restraints can help to reduce the risk of neck injury if you're in a collision. They must be properly adjusted. Make sure they aren't positioned too low because this could cause damage to the neck.

4.110 Mark one answer

You are approaching a green traffic light and going straight on. Traffic in front of you is stopped and queuing just beyond the junction. What should you do?

- Only go if your vehicle will clear the junction
- Drive slowly across the junction
- Maintain your speed and sound your horn
- Stop in the junction until the traffic clears

Only go if your vehicle will clear the junction

Look well ahead and plan your approach to all junctions. Even though the lights are on green, don't go forward if queuing traffic will cause you to block the junction. Be aware of the length of your vehicle and any inconvenience it may cause to other road users.

4.111 Mark one answer

In rural areas why should you avoid parking on the grass verge?

- When moving off you may leave mud on the road
- There may be sheep or cattle grazing in the area
- You will be blocking an entrance to premises or a driveway
- Your vehicle will probably be blown over by high winds

When moving off you may leave mud on the road

Parking on the grass verge in rural areas should be avoided. The weight of your vehicle may cause damage to the verge and as you drive away you might leave mud and debris on the road.

4.112 Mark **one** answer

Seat belts are fitted to your lorry. The wearing of them is

- not advisable
- advisable
- required by law
- not required by law

required by law

If seat belts are fitted in your lorry you must wear them unless you are exempt.

4.113 Mark **one** answer

You are waiting to turn right in this box van. Just before turning you should

- wave the pedestrian across
- check your left mirror and blind spot
- wave out the green car (arrowed)
- check your right mirror and blind spot

check your right mirror and blind spot

Always make a final check in your mirrors and blind spots before you turn. Another driver or a motorcyclist may have committed themselves to overtaking traffic behind you before they realised you intended to turn.

4.114 Mark **two** answers

Extra skills are needed when driving at night. The MAIN problems you will have to deal with are

- headlight dazzle
- other drivers speeding
- cold weather conditions
- dazzle from shop windows
- becoming tired

headlight dazzle

becoming tired

You must concentrate even harder than normal when driving at night. The slightest distraction or break in your concentration could result in an accident.

4.115 Mark **one** answer

You are driving a lorry in a busy town. A driver pulls out in front of you. You have to brake hard. What should you do?

- Overtake as quickly as possible
- Stay calm and accept the error
- Flash your lights to show your annoyance
- Sound your horn and speed up

Stay calm and accept the error

Some drivers might emerge from a junction when it is not safe to do so. Don't intimidate them by driving up too close or revving the engine. Understand that other drivers might make mistakes.

4.116 Mark **one** answer

Your lorry is fitted with a driver's seat belt. You MUST wear it at all times unless

- your deliveries are less than 50 metres apart
- you are towing at less than 50 mph
- you are working less than 50 hours in a week
- you are within 50 miles of your depot

your deliveries are less than 50 metres apart

It is compulsory for drivers and passengers to wear seat belts. If you are making deliveries of less than 50 metres apart you are exempt from wearing a seat belt. Over such short distances it could be impractical to keep putting your belt on and off.

4.117 Mark **one** answer

You have been issued with protective clothing. Whose responsibility is it to make sure it is worn?

- You, the driver
- The insurance company
- The Health and Safety Executive
- Your employer

You, the driver

It is your responsibility to ensure that you use any essential protective clothing properly. It will usually be provided by your company.

section **five**

CARRYING PASSENGERS

This section covers

- Passenger comfort
- Vehicle stability
- Driver attitude and responsibility
- Special passengers

5.1 Mark **one** answer

As a bus driver your first consideration is to your

- ⊙ timetable
- ⊙ passengers
- ⊙ employer
- ⊙ workmates

⊙ **passengers**

Consideration for your passengers can be shown in lots of ways. Be courteous at all times. Give people time to get seated before moving away. Some passengers have special needs: allow them to be independent, but be prepared to help if necessary. Look out for people by the side of the road who may not be able to see or hear your bus coming.

5.2  Mark **one** answer

As a bus driver your main responsibility is

- ⊙ the safety and comfort of your passengers
- ⊙ keeping to a strict timetable
- ⊙ the collecting of fares
- ⊙ the issuing of tickets

⊙ **the safety and comfort of your passengers**

You should deliver them to their destination

- safely
- on time
- efficiently
- courteously.

5.3  Mark **two** answers

As a bus driver you should show care to your passengers. You can do this by

- ⊙ stopping close to the kerb
- ⊙ reaching destinations early
- ⊙ not speaking when taking fares
- ⊙ giving them time to get seated

⊙ **stopping close to the kerb**

⊙ **giving them time to get seated**

Ensure that you stop the vehicle where it is safe and convenient for your passengers to get on and off. Accelerating as you move off can easily unsteady a passenger; try to wait until all passengers are seated or settled before moving off.

5.4 Mark **one** answer

What is the MAIN reason for using smooth acceleration when driving your bus?

- To reduce wear on the tyres
- To reduce wear on the engine
- To improve fuel consumption
- To improve passenger comfort

To improve passenger comfort

Operators often publicise journeys as being

- comfortable
- convenient
- fast

You play an important part in delivering this standard of service.

5.5 Mark **two** answers

When driving a bus, your main priorities should be

- the safety of your passengers
- the comfort of your passengers
- keeping strictly to your timetable
- greeting all passengers with a smile
- making sure passengers take their luggage

the safety of your passengers

the comfort of your passengers

A bus driver should set a good example for others to follow. Adopting the correct attitude will help you fulfil your main priority, which is the safety and comfort of your passengers.

5.6 Mark **one** answer

For the comfort of your passengers harsh braking should be avoided. You should

- pump the brakes when approaching a bus stop or hazard
- use the gears to slow down
- use the parking brake just before stopping to avoid throwing passengers forward
- plan ahead and take early action on all stops and hazards

plan ahead and take early action on all stops and hazards

As the driver of a bus, your first duty is to your passengers. You are delivering a service to paying customers who wish to reach their destination comfortably and safely. Set yourself a high professional standard and take pride in your work. You must ensure that you have a thorough knowledge of The Highway Code and other matters relating to vehicle and passenger safety.

5.7 *Mark **one** answer*

A bus driver brakes harshly. Passengers may be thrown towards

- the front of the bus
- the rear of the bus
- the nearside
- the offside

the front of the bus

When approaching hazards or bus stops you should always be aware of what your passengers are doing. Late, harsh braking as they leave their seats can take passengers by surprise and cause them to fall over, possibly injuring themselves or others.

5.8 *Mark **one** answer*

How can you avoid harsh braking?

- Gently apply the parking brake
- Plan ahead and take early action
- Slow down by using your gears only
- Pump the brake pedal several times

Plan ahead and take early action

Always look well ahead. Early planning and anticipation will help you to avoid braking harshly. Your passengers won't want to be thrown around every time you deal with a hazard.

5.9 *Mark **two** answers*

On which TWO occasions would passengers be most likely to notice weight transfer?

- Braking
- Cornering
- Reversing
- Overtaking

Braking

Cornering

A smooth ride at all times is not always easy to achieve. However, scanning ahead for hazards will help you avoid such things as late braking and taking corners too fast.

5.10 Mark **one** answer

Well ahead of you are traffic lights on green. What should you do in case the lights change to red?

- Accelerate to make sure you can cross before they change
- Slow down to avoid the need to stop suddenly
- Accelerate, but warn your passengers you may have to stop
- Carry on at a constant speed, but be ready to sound your horn

Slow down to avoid the need to stop suddenly

If you're approaching a set of traffic lights and they've been on green for a while, be prepared for them to change. Ease off the accelerator and be ready to come to a gradual stop if you need to. Don't try to beat the red light; it may change as you come closer, causing you to brake late and harshly. Think of your passengers.

5.11 Mark **one** answer

A bus driver accelerates sharply. Passengers may be thrown towards

- the rear of the bus
- the front of the bus
- the nearside
- the offside

the rear of the bus

After passengers have boarded, avoid accelerating to build up speed while they are still in the aisle. This can cause them to lose their balance and sustain unnecessary injury. A few seconds delay to allow passengers time to be seated will make little difference to your overall journey time.

BE PROFESSIONAL – BE PATIENT.

5.12 Mark **one** answer

A bus driver should avoid stopping harshly MOSTLY for the benefit of the

- tyres
- brakes
- passengers
- suspension

passengers

Passengers are very vulnerable when they are standing in a moving vehicle. Inconsiderate use of the footbrake can easily cause injury to your passengers, especially the young or infirm, who may not wait until you have stopped before they leave their seat. If you seem to be in a hurry, they may even have left their seat early because they don't want to feel responsible for holding you up.

5.13 Mark *one* answer

If a bus takes a bend too fast passengers may be thrown towards

- the outside of the bend
- the inside of the bend
- the front of the bus
- the rear of the bus

the outside of the bend

Turning corners or travelling around bends too quickly will push passengers sideways. In addition, the weight of the passengers being transferred to one side of the vehicle will make it even more unstable. This in turn will make steering out of the bend more difficult.

5.14 Mark *three* answers

For the safety and comfort of your passengers you should

- brake smoothly
- think well ahead
- stop close to the kerb
- brake hard on a bend
- give change on the move
- drive with the door open

brake smoothly

think well ahead

stop close to the kerb

How well you look after your passengers and drive your bus is a measure of your professionalism. Dealing competently and safely with hazards and other road users is expected. A safe, comfortable ride, even when you are under pressure, will be appreciated by your passengers.

5.15 Mark *two* answers

Before moving off from a standstill, a bus driver should be especially aware of passengers who attempt to

- change seats
- smoke
- ask you questions
- get off
- get on
- refuse to pay

get off

get on

Check your nearside external and internal mirrors before you move away for anyone attempting to board or leave your vehicle. Always give passengers time to be seated safely before you move away.

5.16 Mark **one** answer

When seat belts are fitted in a bus your passengers SHOULD wear them

- on journeys over distances of 25 km (15.5 miles)
- only when travelling in EC countries
- only when travelling on motorways
- at all times

at all times

As the driver of a bus you may be responsible for several passengers at any given time. If a situation occurs where you have to brake or steer harshly in an emergency, your passengers could be thrown about the vehicle in different directions. Due to the necessary fittings on board, such as luggage racks, handrails and poles, there's a significant danger of injury. If seat belts are provided for passengers, they should wear them. In certain situations they must be worn by law.

Seat belts save lives.

5.17 Mark **one** answer

Which of the following is a legal requirement for every bus?

- A fire extinguisher
- A current timetable
- A mobile phone or radio
- A working tachograph

A fire extinguisher

Every bus must carry a fire extinguisher. Make sure that you know where it's located and how to use it, so that you're fully prepared in the event of a fire.

5.18 Mark **three** answers

The location of which of the following MUST be clearly labelled on a bus?

- Air vents
- First aid equipment
- Vehicle length
- Route timetables
- Fuel cut-off switch
- Fire extinguisher

First aid equipment

Fuel cut-off switch

Fire extinguisher

It is essential to know the location of first aid equipment, the fuel cut-off device and the fire extinguisher on every PCV that you drive. Take time to familiarise yourself with their location whenever you drive a different vehicle. When you take your PCV test you will be asked questions on safety.

5.19 Mark **one** answer

If a passenger carries a white stick with a red ring painted on it this shows the person is

- ⊙ blind and deaf
- ⊙ deaf only
- ⊙ unable to climb steps
- ⊙ blind only

⊙ **blind and deaf**

Give extra care to those passengers who require more time or help to get on or off the vehicle. Recognise their disability and help them as much as you can. There's a lot of competition these days and passengers often have a choice of how they travel. Take pride in your work and this will show through in the way that you deal with your passengers. They'll appreciate this and may travel with your company again.

5.20 Mark **one** answer

A passenger is boarding your bus. They are carrying a white stick with a red ring painted on it. What does this mean?

- ⊙ They have a learning difficulty
- ⊙ They have poor vision and hearing
- ⊙ They have a physical disability
- ⊙ They have a speech problem

⊙ **They have poor vision and hearing**

Be prepared to help if they appear to need it, or ask for it. Always do your best to provide a smooth and comfortable ride for your passengers.

5.21 Mark **one** answer

A disabled passenger is boarding your bus. They tell you that getting on board is not a problem to them. You should

- ⊙ let them board without help
- ⊙ ask a passenger to help them
- ⊙ leave your cab and help them
- ⊙ do nothing, you cannot leave your seat

⊙ **let them board without help**

Always be prepared to offer assistance if they ask for it, but allow them to show their independence, even if it delays you for a few seconds longer.

5.22  *Mark **three** answers*

As a bus driver, which of the following should you not do?

- ⊙ Signal if necessary when pulling in
- ⊙ Drive on before people are seated
- ⊙ Issue tickets without looking at customers' faces
- ⊙ Use smooth acceleration and anticipate braking needs
- ⊙ Give time to passengers and show consideration
- ⊙ Always rush to keep to a timetable

⊙ **Drive on before people are seated**

⊙ **Issue tickets without looking at customers' faces**

⊙ **Always rush to keep to a timetable**

Nobody likes to be late; but you should not let the pressure of your timetable make you feel you have to rush people. Being pleasant to your passengers and showing them some common courtesies will encourage them to use your service again.

5.23  *Mark **three** answers*

While you are collecting fares you should look at passengers when speaking to them. This will

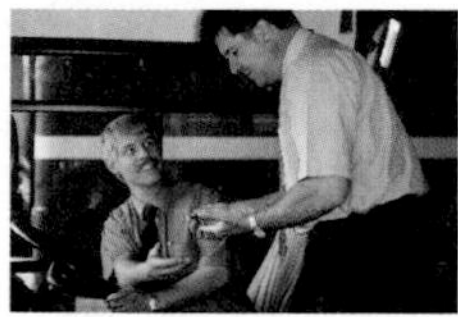

- ⊙ help you to recognise someone having difficulty
- ⊙ show people you are in a rush to keep to a timetable
- ⊙ show common courtesy and help the image of your company
- ⊙ help deaf and hearing-impaired people to understand you
- ⊙ help you decide whether people with a disability should get on the bus

⊙ **help you to recognise someone having difficulty**

⊙ **show common courtesy and help the image of your company**

⊙ **help deaf and hearing-impaired people to understand you**

You are a representative of your company, so showing passengers that their custom is appreciated will encourage them to travel with you again.

5.24 *Mark **two** answers*

When dealing with passengers who are hard of hearing it is important that you

- shout as loudly as you can
- look at them when speaking to them
- hurry them to get seated
- are as helpful as possible

- **look at them when speaking to them**
- **are as helpful as possible**

Hard-of-hearing passengers may want to lip read. Make sure that they are able to see your face clearly as you speak.

5.25 *Mark **one** answer*

The purpose of a 'kneeling bus' is to

- improve passenger comfort on bumpy roads
- help with access under low bridges
- allow the step height to be raised and lowered
- give more clearance over speed ramps

- **allow the step height to be raised and lowered**

This type of bus can be especially useful for disabled passengers. Using air suspension, the front entrance can be lowered for easier access. Make sure you are properly trained to operate this equipment. Only use it for the intended purpose, and make sure it is in the correct position before continuing your journey.

5.26 *Mark **one** answer*

This sign fitted to the front and rear of a bus means that

- the bus may be carrying children
- children must be accompanied by an adult
- the bus is carrying blind people
- the driver will help disabled people

- **the bus may be carrying children**

If you're carrying children on your vehicle and it isn't on a scheduled route used by the general public, it must have this sign displayed to the front and rear. When carrying children to and from school it's likely that you'll have to make several stops in places other than recognised bus stops. Think carefully before you stop. Don't cause unnecessary inconvenience to other road users.

5.27  *Mark **one** answer*

Hazard warning lights may only be used at certain times. In addition, a bus displaying this sign may use them when

- stopped at a pedestrian crossing
- stopped and children are getting on or off the vehicle
- approaching a school crossing patrol
- there is a sign warning of a school ahead

stopped and children are getting on or off the vehicle

You may be driving in the rush hour, when traffic is heavy, so when you stop you're permitted to show your hazard warning lights. This will show other road users that children are getting on and off the vehicle. Look out for passing traffic and try to ensure that all your passengers get on and off safely.

5.28 *Mark **one** answer*

You are driving a bus. The bell rings four times. This means

- continue past the next bus stop
- the bus is full
- move off when safe
- there is an emergency

there is an emergency

Four bell rings indicate that someone on the bus considers an emergency situation has occurred. As the driver, you must stop the vehicle safely, with consideration for your passengers, before investigating further.

5.29  *Mark **one** answer*

Your bus has broken down at night in heavy rain. Why should you move your passengers to the front of the bus?

- To keep the bus stable
- To help you see clearly out of the back window
- To limit injuries in case of a rear-end collision
- To keep them informed about the breakdown

To limit injuries in case of a rear-end collision

The safety of your passengers should be your first priority. You should take every possible precaution to ensure they are out of danger.

5.30 *Mark **one** answer*

You are driving a half-cab bus and have no contact with the passengers. This is only allowed if

- it is fitted with an interior mirror
- there is a chain or strap across the doorway
- a responsible person is in charge of them
- you make sure no one stands on the platform

a responsible person is in charge of them

It's essential that the passengers on the vehicle are able to report any problems to a responsible person. This person should be aware of the correct bell signals so that they are able to communicate with the driver.

5.31 *Mark **one** answer*

You are driving a coach at night with passengers on board. You should never

- stop at service stations
- switch the radio on
- leave the interior in darkness
- close any curtains

leave the interior in darkness

Passengers should be able to move about the vehicle in safety. You should ensure that all interior lights are in working order before you start your journey.

5.32 *Mark **three** answers*

There is a fire on the upper deck of your double-deck bus. You should

- stop safely and quickly
- get everyone off the bus
- contact emergency services
- open all the windows
- move the passengers into the lower deck
- make sure passengers have their belongings

- **stop safely and quickly**
- **get everyone off the bus**
- **contact emergency services**

Fire can spread extremely quickly. Your first priority is the safety of your passengers. If at all possible disconnect electrical lines and cut off the fuel supply. Fire can destroy a vehicle in an alarmingly short time.

5.33 *Mark **one** answer*

Kneeling buses are specifically designed to improve access for

- the driver
- extra luggage
- elderly passengers
- low bridges

- **elderly passengers**

Some buses are equipped with air or hydraulic systems that allow the step level to be lowered. They are known as kneeling buses. Don't forget to raise the step again before moving off.

5.34 *Mark **one** answer*

You are driving a bus carrying passengers at night. Why should you always put the interior lights on?

- It will help you see the road ahead
- So that passengers can see to move around
- It will help passengers to see outside
- So that you can see your controls

- **So that passengers can see to move around**

Passengers need a properly lit area so they can move around safely.

5.35 *Mark **one** answer*

As you move off watch out, in particular, for any passengers who attempt to

- smoke in the lower saloon
- stand in the upper saloon
- avoid paying the correct fare
- board the bus

- **board the bus**

Always check your nearside mirror before moving away as a passenger may be attempting to open the door to board the bus or running to jump aboard an open platform. Also check for passengers trying to get off the bus as you move away.

5.36 *Mark **one** answer*

A passenger finds walking difficult. What could you do to help?

- Drive quickly so that passengers will not be on for long
- Wait until the passenger is sitting down before moving away
- Make sure they have a window seat
- Suggest they stand near the door

- **Wait until the passenger is sitting down before moving away**

Try to wait until your passengers have sat down before you move off. This is even more important if they are elderly or have difficulty walking. Don't forget the personal touch. Offer help when you think it might be needed and remember, a smile goes a long way.

5.37  *Mark **two** answers*

You are the driver of a bus displaying reflective yellow signs. You are permitted to use hazard warning lights when

- ⊙ stationary and parked to take a rest period
- ⊙ stationary and children are boarding
- ⊙ stationary and children are getting off
- ⊙ slowing down to find a parking space
- ⊙ slowing down in town centre traffic queues
- ⊙ slowing down approaching a bus stop

⊙ **stationary and children are boarding**

⊙ **stationary and children are getting off**

Buses carrying children must display a distinctive yellow reflective sign on the front and rear, unless running a scheduled service for the general public. Buses displaying the sign are permitted to use hazard warning lights when they have stopped for children to get on or off.

5.38 *Mark **two** answers*

You are parking your coach at a coastal resort. Your passengers will still have access. You should make sure

- ⊙ the cab area is isolated
- ⊙ the gear lever is in neutral
- ⊙ the storage lockers are open
- ⊙ a responsible person is on the coach

⊙ **the cab area is isolated**

⊙ **a responsible person is on the coach**

Your coach must never be left unattended if passengers still have access to it. In particular, they must not be able to get into the cab area of the vehicle. You or another responsible person must always be there to supervise the coach.

5.39 Mark **two** answers

You have parked and left your bus. The public will still have access to it. You should make sure that

- the door key is different to the ignition key
- the cab area is shut off
- a responsible person is on board
- all interior lights are on

the cab area is shut off

a responsible person is on board

Your bus must never be left unsupervised when passengers are still able to get back on board. The cab area must be protected, and either you or another responsible person must remain on board to ensure everyone's safety.

5.40 Mark **three** answers

When driving a double-deck bus on a steep camber you should be especially aware of

- lamp posts
- parking meters
- parked cars
- shop awnings
- litter bins
- traffic signs

lamp posts

shop awnings

traffic signs

When driving high-sided vehicles, such as double-deck buses, you must be aware of how road camber changes can affect your vehicle. As the bus leans towards the kerb, shop awnings, trees and street furniture, such as lamp posts, can get frighteningly close to passengers sitting on the top deck.

5.41 Mark **one** answer

What is the likely weight difference between an empty bus and a bus with 75 passengers on board?

- 5 tonnes
- 10 tonnes
- 15 tonnes
- 20 tonnes

5 tonnes

The way that your vehicle handles will be very different when it's full compared with when it's empty. Having 75 passengers on board could increase the weight of the bus by up to about 5 tonnes and the passengers may also have luggage.

All extra weight will have an effect on inertia and momentum: it will take longer to build up speed and the vehicle will maintain forward momentum. Advanced planning and controlled braking will be required to allow for this extra weight.

5.42 Mark **one** answer

It is important to be able to work out the weight difference between a full bus and an empty one. About how many passengers will equal 1 tonne in weight?

- 8
- 15
- 25
- 30

15

You should also make allowances for any luggage your passengers may bring on board. An average of two cases per passenger on a 50-seat coach will add about 1.5 tonnes to the overall weight of your bus or coach.

5.43 Mark **one** answer

It is only legal to drive an empty, half-cab bus when the passenger access has

- a vertical pole
- no high steps
- no obstructions
- a chain or strap

a chain or strap

You should never drive a half-cab bus in which you have no contact with the passengers unless a responsible person is in charge of the passenger saloon. If you do not have a responsible person in charge of the passenger saloon, the entrance should be secured with a chain or strap.

Always keep an eye on your nearside mirror when you are travelling slowly or are stationary in areas where pedestrians may attempt to jump aboard.

5.44 Mark **one** answer

You are driving a double-deck half-cab bus. Passengers can only be carried if

- no one uses the upper deck
- you can see them in your mirror
- a responsible person is in charge of them
- they are all travelling to the same destination

a responsible person is in charge of them

Under no circumstances should you drive a half-cab bus with passengers on board unless there is a responsible person in charge of them.

5.45 Mark **one** answer

While driving your half-cab bus you hear the three-bell signal from the conductor. This means

- stop when safe
- bus empty
- bus full
- move off when safe

bus full

One bell means 'stop', two bells mean 'move off when safe', and three bells are used to announce when the bus is full.

5.46  *Mark **one** answer*

It is legal to drive an empty, half-cab double-deck bus, but the passenger access must have

- a hand rail
- a vertical pole
- a chain or strap
- a warning notice

a chain or strap

The chain or strap will prevent any passengers jumping on board while you're stationary or waiting in traffic queues. You must not carry any passengers unless there's a responsible person on board to supervise.

5.47 *Mark **one** answer*

Buses and coaches used for school contract work MUST have

- yellow reflective signs
- only one door
- a conductor
- a 'no overtaking' sign

yellow reflective signs

Vehicles carrying school children display this sign to alert other drivers to the possible danger of young children crossing the road. As the bus driver, you must make every effort to ensure their safety when boarding or getting off your bus, as well as during their journey with you.

5.48 *Mark **one** answer*

You are driving a half-cab bus. The correct signal to move off when safe is

- one bell
- two bells
- three bells
- four bells

two bells

This is the correct signal to move off when safe.

5.49 *Mark **one** answer*

A passenger comments on exhaust smoke in the vehicle. You should

- report it as soon as you return to the depot
- stop and have the fault put right
- avoid heavy revving of the engine when stationary
- have the emissions checked at the next vehicle inspection test

- **stop and have the fault put right**

If exhaust fumes are getting into the vehicle this could cause a danger to your passengers. Stop and have the fault put right before continuing.

5.50 *Mark **one** answer*

What would you have to be especially aware of when driving a double-deck bus on a road with a steep camber?

- 'Keep Left' islands
- A smooth road surface
- Pedestrian crossings
- Overhanging trees

- **Overhanging trees**

A road which has a steep camber will slope sharply towards the kerb. You must be aware of the dangers this can present. The nearside wheels will be lower than the offside causing your bus to lean towards the pavement or verge. This brings a risk of collision with objects such as overhanging trees, lamp posts and bus stop roofs.

5.51 *Mark **two** answers*

You are driving a double-deck bus. Passenger care is important. You should

- assist passengers with special needs
- provide a commentary of the route
- listen to passengers while driving
- help passengers unfamiliar with the service
- carry passenger's luggage upstairs

- **assist passengers with special needs**
- **help passengers unfamiliar with the service**

Always show consideration to passengers whether they have special needs or not. Try to imagine what assistance you would like if you were in their position.

5.52  *Mark **one** answer*

Your bus is fitted with lifts or ramps for the less able-bodied. The equipment should only be operated by

- wheelchair attendants
- fully-trained people
- bus company employees
- accompanying nurses

fully-trained people

Make sure that you are fully trained in the safe use of lifts, ramps and securing devices. If you drive a vehicle fitted with this equipment, never let untrained people operate it. Look out for the safety of others at all times.

5.53 *Mark **one** answer*

Your conductor rings the bell twice. This means

- carry on past the next bus stop
- immediately carry out an emergency stop
- pull in at the next bus stop
- move off when it is safe to do so

move off when it is safe to do so

Make sure that you are both familiar with the correct signals. The conductor should ensure that all passengers are settled before signalling.

5.54 *Mark **one** answer*

You are driving a bus. The bell rings three times. This means

- pull in at the next stop
- move away when it is safe to do so
- an emergency on board
- your vehicle is full

your vehicle is full

The bell system is used to inform you using a predetermined set of codes. Never allow anyone to use the bells other than in the accepted way.

5.55 Mark **one** answer

What is a 'kneeling bus' designed to improve?

- Access for the disabled
- Stability when cornering
- Passenger comfort at higher speeds
- Access for the driver

Access for the disabled

Kneeling buses are equipped with air or hydraulic systems that allow the step level to be lowered. This improves access for disabled and elderly passengers; remember to raise the step before moving off.

5.56 Mark **one** answer

Your double-deck bus breaks down on a busy road. You should ask your passengers to move to the

- rear of the bus
- top deck
- lower deck
- front of the bus

front of the bus

The greatest risk to a stationary bus is being hit from behind. Moving your passengers forward could reduce the risk of injury.

5.57 Mark **one** answer

When you pull away from a bus stop watch out in particular for passengers who attempt to

- avoid paying the correct fare
- smoke in the lower saloon
- alight from the bus
- use an expired travel pass

alight from the bus

Even though you have started to move off, passengers may still try to get off the bus. You should also check your nearside mirror for any passengers trying to get on.

5.58  *Mark **three** answers*

A bus driver MUST not drive while

- ⊙ issuing tickets
- ⊙ the doors are open
- ⊙ wearing sunglasses
- ⊙ giving change
- ⊙ passengers are standing
- ⊙ luggage is being carried

⊙ **issuing tickets**

⊙ **the doors are open**

⊙ **giving change**

On regular services, traffic congestion can soon put you behind schedule. Nevertheless, you have a responsibility to your passengers at all times not to take shortcuts or jeopardise their safety. They are paying you for a service which must always deliver them safely to their destination.

5.59  *Mark **two** answers*

Your bus breaks down on the motorway. You have several passengers on board. You should

- ⊙ move the passengers to the rear
- ⊙ place a warning triangle in front of the bus
- ⊙ stop on the hard shoulder
- ⊙ move the passengers to the front

⊙ **stop on the hard shoulder**

⊙ **move the passengers to the front**

Stop as far to the left as possible on the hard shoulder. Make sure all your passengers have moved as far as possible to the front of the vehicle. Send a responsible person to the nearest telephone; you will be directed to this by small arrows on marker posts.

5.60  *Mark **one** answer*

As a bus driver your main aim should be

- ⊙ to keep strictly to the timetable
- ⊙ the safety of your passengers
- ⊙ service to your colleagues
- ⊙ to keep accurate details of ticket sales

⊙ **the safety of your passengers**

You should remember that, as a driver, you are there to provide a service. Your passengers rely on you to make sure that the journey is a safe and comfortable one.

5.61 *Mark **one** answer*

As the driver of a bus your FIRST priority is

- the safety and comfort of your passengers
- making sure that you are always on time
- making sure that your log book and tachograph are correctly completed
- making sure that your destination is clearly marked

the safety and comfort of your passengers

As the driver of a PCV you have responsibilities beyond those of other drivers. Your passengers have paid for a service, and should arrive at their chosen destination safely. Customers are more likely to travel with you again if they receive a safe, courteous and comfortable service.

5.62 *Mark **one** answer*

You are driving a one-person-operated bus. You are at a bus stop issuing tickets. You should

- be in gear without any signal
- be in gear and signalling
- signal only when ready to move away
- be in neutral but signalling to move off

signal only when ready to move away

Giving wrong signals causes uncertainty and confusion to other road users. Only give appropriate signals which are relevant to your intended actions.

5.63 *Mark **one** answer*

As the driver of a one-person-operated double-deck bus you should be constantly aware of passengers on the top deck. How should you do this?

- By counting passengers up and down the staircase
- By frequent checks upstairs while stopped at bus stops
- By listening to passengers in the upstairs gangway when approaching bus stops
- By making full use of the internal mirror system

By making full use of the internal mirror system

If you're driving a one-person-operated double-deck bus you must ensure that you can see passengers who are about to descend the stairs. Make sure that you can see them in the internal mirrors. Always consider their safety and avoid harsh braking and steering.

5.64  *Mark **one** answer*

When driving a double-deck bus, the internal mirror system is used to

- ⊙ watch for traffic on your right-hand side
- ⊙ keep a look out for any overtaking vehicles
- ⊙ keep a look out for passengers using the stairs
- ⊙ watch for cyclists on your left-hand side

⊙ **keep a look out for passengers using the stairs**

You must always be aware of anyone using the stairs. Be particularly careful to avoid any sudden movement, such as when braking or cornering, as this could cause them to stumble.

5.65 *Mark **one** answer*

You are stopping to collect passengers from a bus stop. Where should you pull up?

- ⊙ Close to the kerb
- ⊙ Away from the kerb
- ⊙ After the bus stop
- ⊙ Before the bus stop

⊙ **Close to the kerb**

A bus that has pulled half-way into a bus stop lay-by with the rear sticking well out into the road is a danger to other vehicles. If passengers are not waiting at the bus stop it can be tempting to pull up where they are. This may not be a safe place for your vehicle or for other road users. Be professional and be safe; pull up in the correct position.

5.66 *Mark **one** answer*

You should stop your bus to allow passengers to get on or off near

- ⊙ soft grass
- ⊙ guard rails
- ⊙ parked cars
- ⊙ the kerb

⊙ **the kerb**

You should stop as close to the kerb as you can, so that passengers can reach the safety of the pavement without any difficulty.

5.67 *Mark **one** answer*

A bus stop is blocked and you cannot pull into it. Before opening the exit door what is the most important action to take?

- Try to get the bus stop cleared
- Carry on to the next bus stop
- Check for traffic on the left
- Check for traffic on the right

Check for traffic on the left

You must take care of your passengers at all times. Ensure that you allow your passengers to get on or off the vehicle safely. If you're unable to stop close to the kerb, don't open the doors until you're sure it's safe. Always check the nearside mirror first.

5.68 *Mark **one** answer*

Several cars have parked blocking your bus stop. Before allowing passengers to get off you should

- move on to the next bus stop
- check it is clear of traffic on the left
- try and find the car owners
- check it is clear of traffic on the right

check it is clear of traffic on the left

Always check your nearside mirror before opening the door to allow passengers to alight. When you have stopped away from the kerb, it is important to warn the passengers to look out for cyclists and to expect a long step down onto the road. Be ready to offer assistance if required.

5.69 *Mark **one** answer*

What should you do before allowing passengers off your bus?

- Collect their used tickets
- Activate an audible warning system
- Check mirrors before opening doors
- Ask if they have luggage to collect

Check mirrors before opening doors

The safety of passengers is your main responsibility. Before you allow them to step down from the bus you should always check your mirrors to make sure that there's nothing approaching that could endanger them.

5.70 Mark **one** answer

Passengers may be in a hurry to get off the bus as you approach a bus stop. What should you do to reduce any dangers?

- Insist that passengers stay seated until the bus stops
- Pull up just before the stop and let passengers get off
- Let passengers on the bus before letting passengers off
- Not open the passenger doors until the bus stops

Not open the passenger doors until the bus stops

Passengers may be in a hurry to get off at their stop. Don't brake harshly or open the doors until the vehicle has stopped. Passengers may have left their seats early and be standing up waiting to get off. Due to the necessary fittings on board, such as handrails, poles and luggage racks, there's a substantial risk of injury. Put your passengers' safety first.

5.71 Mark **one** answer

You are driving a half-cab bus and carrying passengers. You must have

- a chain or strap across the doorway
- electrically operated doors
- school children only on board
- a responsible person in charge of them

a responsible person in charge of them

When you have no direct contact with your passengers, you must have a designated person in charge of the passenger saloon.

5.72 Mark **one** answer

You can drive a bus at night without having the interior lights on if

- the passengers want to sleep
- most passengers request it
- there are no standing passengers
- there are no passengers

there are no passengers

Whenever passengers are aboard, the interior lighting must be left on, but it may be turned off when the bus is empty.

5.73 *Mark **one** answer*

You are driving a bus in hot weather. May the passenger door be left open to let fresh air in?

- Yes, this is normal practice
- No, unless all passengers are seated
- Yes, unless carrying school children
- No, this is not allowed

No, this is not allowed

Under no circumstances should you drive with your passenger door open. Many vehicles have air-operated doors which close automatically when the clutch is released. Do not override this set-up. An open door invites people to make rash decisions to enter or leave the vehicle as you are about to move away, which can be extremely dangerous.

5.74 *Mark **two** answers*

Air suspension systems give

- increased fuel consumption
- uneven tyre wear
- increased speed
- even height
- a comfortable ride to passengers

even height

a comfortable ride to passengers

Air suspension can also help reduce wear on road surfaces, which is why it is also known as 'road-friendly suspension'.

5.75 *Mark **one** answer*

A disabled person is getting on your bus. They are having problems but say they can manage. What should you do?

- Be prepared to move off
- Smile and offer to help them
- Ask them politely to hurry up
- Do nothing, you can't leave your seat

Smile and offer to help them

Disabled people like to keep their independence. However, if they are having problems be prepared to offer help.

5.76  *Mark **one** answer*

TV and video equipment fitted to a coach must ONLY be used when

- ⊙ the coach is moving slowly
- ⊙ it cannot be seen by the driver
- ⊙ on long motorway journeys
- ⊙ the coach is on tour

⊙ **it cannot be seen by the driver**

Make sure that you are not distracted by any TV or video equipment fitted to your vehicle. Your main responsibility at all times is the safety and comfort of your passengers.

5.77  *Mark **one** answer*

What MUST new buses be fitted with, to benefit people with disabilities?

- ⊙ Internal mirror
- ⊙ Radio telephone
- ⊙ Automatic transmission
- ⊙ Priority seating

⊙ **Priority seating**

All new buses and coaches must be easily accessible for disabled people and others. They must have ramps, priority seating and colour contrast fittings.

5.78 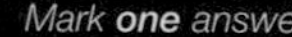 *Mark **one** answer*

Priority seating on a bus is designed for passengers

- ⊙ to store heavy luggage
- ⊙ with a weekly pass
- ⊙ who got on first
- ⊙ with disabilities

⊙ **with disabilities**

Since 2000, all new buses and coaches must be accessible to people with disabilities. These vehicles must have ramps, colour contrast and priority seating.

5.79 Mark **one** answer

A passenger using a wheelchair wants to get on your bus. When may you need to deny them access?

- When the wheelchair will not fit in the luggage rack
- When the boarding device has failed to work
- When the passenger must remain in a wheelchair
- When the heater on the vehicle is not working

When the boarding device has failed to work

It is unfortunate but machinery will break down despite best efforts to service it. Don't risk the health and safety of a person with a disability, or other passengers, by struggling to get them on without the proper equipment.

5.80 Mark **one** answer

Your bus is accessible to wheelchair users. You must always allow them access unless

- the designated space is occupied
- you are running behind schedule
- the traffic behind you will be held up
- you are shortly due to take a break

the designated space is occupied

It is illegal for bus and coach operators to discriminate against people with disabilities. You must always make reasonable adjustments to the way that any service is provided.

5.81 Mark **one** answer

You are driving a school bus. You MUST avoid all physical contact with school children other than

- in a medical emergency
- to prevent fare dodging
- when carrying luggage
- when fastening seat belts

in a medical emergency

All physical contact with school children should be avoided except in specific cases. Such as for genuine self defence, a medical emergency or to prevent a serious offence or threat to safety.

5.82 Mark **one** answer

Which should you wear when making a walk-round check of your coach?

- Ear protectors
- Protective goggles
- High-visibility vest
- Face mask

High-visibility vest

You should make yourself clearly visible when you are working outside your vehicle and near to moving traffic.

5.83 Mark **one** answer

You are about to drive on a route where you will be picking up wheelchair users. To accommodate them what MUST be checked before leaving the depot?

- Boarding device
- Radio
- Door seals
- Heater

Boarding device

To provide for people with disabilities you should make reasonable adjustments to your service. This is a legal requirement. You should make sure that any ramp or lift is in place and in good working order before leaving the depot.

5.84 Mark **one** answer

When should you NOT allow a wheelchair user onto your bus?

- When the lift has stopped working
- When the wheelchair will not fold up
- When the heater has stopped working
- When the wheelchair is too heavy to lift manually

When the lift has stopped working

You will not have failed in your statutory duties if the boarding device breaks down and there is no other means of assisting the passenger.

5.85 *Mark **one** answer*

You are unable to allow a person in a wheelchair to enter your bus. What would be the reason for this?

- Passengers are standing in a wheelchair space and cannot move elsewhere
- You will take time to load the wheelchair and fall behind schedule
- The wheelchair passenger will have to stand up
- You cannot fold down the wheelchair

Passengers are standing in a wheelchair space and cannot move elsewhere

If a wheelchair space is occupied by standing passengers and luggage you may not be able to allow them on the bus. This may occur on a bus that is almost full to capacity. You will not have failed in your statutory duties towards the wheelchair user.

5.86 *Mark **one** answer*

A bus driver should never allow passengers to

- sit in rear facing seats
- stand in the aisle
- stow their own luggage
- ride on an open platform

ride on an open platform

A bus driver is responsible for the safety of passengers on board. Anyone standing on an open platform is at risk should the driver have to brake suddenly or take a corner at speed.

section **six**

THE ROAD

This section covers

- Anticipation
- Hazard awareness
- Attention
- Speed and distance
- Reaction time
- Risk factors

6.1 Mark **one** answer

You will be driving a high-floor coach. You will be going over several high bridges. Why should you check the weather forecast?

- Rain can make crossing bridges very difficult for buses and coaches
- In hot weather the bridges might be closed to heavy traffic
- You won't be able to climb the bridges if it's frosty
- Some roads may be closed to certain vehicles in high winds

Some roads may be closed to certain vehicles in high winds

Some exposed places are frequently subject to high winds. These can include high-level bridges and roads, viaducts and some motorways. Check the weather forecast and plan an alternative route. Remember, you are responsible for your passengers' safety. DON'T ignore warnings of severe winds.

6.2 Mark **one** answer

As a bus driver, what should you do when overtaking a motorcyclist in strong winds?

- Sound the horn
- Pass close
- Use the nearside mirror
- Move back in early

Use the nearside mirror

Motorcyclists can be blown into your path in strong winds. Check your nearside mirror and allow them PLENTY of room as you overtake.

6.3 Mark **one** answer

You are driving a bus in strong winds. What should you do when overtaking a motorcyclist?

- Pass close
- Move back early
- Give a thank you wave
- Pass wide

Pass wide

In strong winds motorcyclists and cyclists are particularly vulnerable. When overtaking give them PLENTY of room and also check your nearside mirror as you pass.

6.4  *Mark **one** answer*

When overtaking a cyclist in heavy rain extra care has to be taken because of

- spray from your vehicle
- exhaust fumes from your vehicle
- noise from your vehicle
- the height of your vehicle

spray from your vehicle

When passing other road users, especially motorcyclists and cyclists, the spray from your vehicle could affect their control. Pass them leaving plenty of room, and check in your left-hand mirror as you pass to see whether they're still in control.

6.5 *Mark **two** answers*

What TWO effects will a strong side wind have on a bus?

- Steering will be easier
- The bus will tend to go off course
- Braking will be affected
- Stopping distance will be increased
- Steering will be more difficult
- Stopping distance will be decreased

The bus will tend to go off course

Steering will be more difficult

Be alert for places where the road is shielded from the wind. When you are steering into the wind you may suddenly find yourself making an unintentional change of direction.

6.6 *Mark **one** answer*

Double-deck buses are more likely than single-deck buses to be affected by

- strong winds
- heavy rain
- thick fog
- dense spray

strong winds

If you're driving a double-deck bus you'll feel the effect of the wind to a greater degree, due to the vehicle's extra height.

6.7 Mark **one** answer

As a bus driver what should you do when overtaking a motorcycle in strong winds?

- Pass close
- Move back early
- Pass wide
- Signal left

Pass wide

Motorcycles can be blown into your path in strong winds. Allow them plenty of room when you are overtaking.

6.8 Mark **one** answer

Spray suppression equipment fitted to buses is particularly useful when it is

- raining
- icy
- foggy
- windy

raining

If there's heavy rain the spray suppression equipment fitted on your vehicle will protect other road users from loss of vision when following or passing your vehicle. Check the wheel arches to ensure that the fitments haven't worked loose and that no parts have broken off. Well-maintained equipment will force the spray back down onto the road instead of to the rear and the sides of the vehicle.

6.9 Mark **one** answer

With a long bus, under normal driving conditions, when is it acceptable to straddle lanes?

- Only when joining a bus lane
- On all bends and corners
- On the approach to all roundabouts
- To avoid mounting the kerb

To avoid mounting the kerb

There are times when you might have to take up part of another lane in order to make a turn or manoeuvre. Be on your guard for other road users by using your mirrors to check all around your vehicle. Other traffic might try to move up alongside in the gap you've left to make your turn. Good planning and anticipation will allow you to signal your intentions to other road users and take up your position in good time.

6.10  *Mark **one** answer*

When parked on the road at night, buses and coaches must

- ⊙ be under street lights
- ⊙ be within 25 metres (82 feet) of a street light
- ⊙ have all of the interior lights switched on
- ⊙ have their sidelights on

⊙ **have their sidelights on**

Make sure that all your lights are working, and that they are clean. Your vehicle may cause other road users to slow down or stop, so they must be able to see you in good time.

6.11 *Mark **one** answer*

Unless there is street lighting, why could it be dangerous to overtake at night when driving a bus?

- ⊙ There may be unseen dips or bends in the road
- ⊙ You may dazzle other drivers
- ⊙ It is harder to concentrate
- ⊙ It is harder to keep control in the dark

⊙ **There may be unseen dips or bends in the road**

On unlit roads it is more difficult to see where the road bends or if there are junctions or dips. This could also prevent you from seeing oncoming traffic. Don't endanger your passengers. Unless the road is well lit or you are on a dual carriageway, ask yourself if overtaking is absolutely necessary.

6.12 *Mark **one** answer*

Why do some buses have marker lights along their sides?

- ⊙ To make them easier to overtake
- ⊙ To help the driver when reversing
- ⊙ To help any passengers getting on or off
- ⊙ To make them easier to see at junctions

⊙ **To make them easier to see at junctions**

Newer buses and coaches have marker lights along the side; these ensure that they are visible as they emerge from junctions and roundabouts, and in other situations.

6.13 Mark **one** answer

You are driving a bus. Where should you be most aware of the risk of grounding?

- On a hump bridge
- On a crawler lane
- On a left-hand bend
- On a narrow road

On a hump bridge

You must be aware of the risk of grounding, for example on a hump bridge. Look ahead for potential hazards and advance warning signs.

6.14 Mark **one** answer

Braking continuously can make brakes overheat. This will make

- the brakes work better
- braking less effective
- the brake pedal hard
- the air pressure build up

braking less effective

Whenever you brake, the moving energy of your vehicle is converted into heat. Continuous use of the brakes, particularly from high speed or on long steep descents, can cause the shoes and drums to overheat. This will make them less effective and in some cases they may not work at all.

6.15 Mark **one** answer

You are driving in a high wind. What do you need to be careful of?

- Fallen trees
- Poor visibility
- A risk of grounding
- Steep gradients

Fallen trees

In severe weather conditions you should be aware of the dangers of fallen trees or damaged branches that may fall on your vehicle. Be aware of the dangers and look out for fallen trees that may be lying across the road just around bends.

6.16 Mark **one** answer

You are driving a high-sided vehicle. You are about to drive over a high suspension bridge. What in particular do you need to be aware of?

- The swaying of the bridge
- The width of the lanes
- The effect of strong crosswinds
- The overhanging bridge cables

The effect of strong crosswinds

In exposed places the wind can be particularly strong. Make allowances for this especially when passing or being passed by other vehicles.

6.17 Mark **one** answer

You are driving through the night. You notice that your steering feels lighter than normal. What could this mean?

- That your tyres are losing pressure
- There is a leak in the power steering pump
- That there is ice or frost on the road
- There is not enough tread on your tyres

That there is ice or frost on the road

When you're in a warm cab you may not notice the drop in outside temperature. One of the first signs of an icy road is a lack of 'feel' in the steering.

6.18 Mark **one** answer

You are in the centre lane of a motorway and overtaking another vehicle. What should you do before returning to the left-hand lane?

- Signal left then check your mirror
- Wait for the other driver to flash their headlights
- Check ahead and then your nearside mirror
- Check behind for fast traffic in the right-hand lane

Check ahead and then your nearside mirror

Never return to the left-hand lane until you are sure that you are well clear of the vehicle you have just overtaken. Don't cut in too soon and don't rely on the other driver flashing you in. Make your own judgement!

6.19 Mark **one** answer

When approaching a zebra crossing you should

- stop before the zigzag lines
- wave pedestrians across the road
- sound the horn and flash headlights
- be prepared to stop in good time

be prepared to stop in good time

Always keep your speed down on the approach to zebra crossings. This will allow you to stop safely if necessary. On the approach look well ahead for anyone about to cross.

6.20 Mark **one** answer

You are driving a high-sided vehicle on a motorway. You should be ESPECIALLY aware of the effects of crosswinds

- on high bridges
- in cuttings
- in tunnels
- when passing signs

on high bridges

High-sided vehicles are very vulnerable to strong winds. In bad weather listen to or watch out for weather forecasts. You might need to alter your route or even cancel your journey altogether.

6.21 Mark **one** answer

You are on a motorway in a high-sided vehicle. You should be ESPECIALLY aware of the effects of crosswinds

- when passing signs
- on exposed sections
- in contraflow systems
- in service areas

on exposed sections

When the weather is bad, listen to and watch out for weather forecasts. Motorways in particular have exposed sections of road, placing high-sided vehicles at risk.

6.22 Mark **one** answer

You are driving a high-sided vehicle in very windy conditions. Which of the following should you avoid if possible?

- Suspension bridges
- Steep hills
- Country lanes
- Road tunnels

Suspension bridges

In windy weather try to avoid routes where you would have to drive across suspension bridges and other exposed stretches of road. Think about other factors, such as ferry cancellations, that might lead to changes in your route or rest periods.

6.23 Mark **one** answer

The conditions are very windy. You are driving a high-sided vehicle. Which of the following should you avoid if possible?

- Road tunnels
- Steep hills
- Country lanes
- Viaducts

Viaducts

Try to avoid routes where you would have to negotiate viaducts and other high and exposed places when it is very windy. You may need to alter your route or rest stops and consider other factors such as ferry cancellations.

6.24 Mark **one** answer

You are driving in heavy rain. Your steering suddenly feels very light. What should you do?

- Brake very sharply
- Steer towards the centre line
- Ease off the accelerator
- Increase your speed

Ease off the accelerator

In wet conditions water can build up between your tyres and the road surface. This is known as aquaplaning and will cause your vehicle to slide. Tyres will not grip in this situation. Try to regain control by easing off the accelerator to gradually lose speed. Do not brake or steer until tyre grip is restored.

6.25 Mark **one** answer

Why should you be especially aware of parked cars when driving at night?

- There are more of them
- They are more likely to move off
- The drivers may be drunk
- They can park without lights

They can park without lights

Vehicles below 1525 kg are permitted to park without lights on roads with a speed limit no greater than 30 mph. In dark streets you may not be able to see them clearly.

6.26 Mark **one** answer

You are waiting at a T-junction. A vehicle is coming from the right with the left signal flashing. What should you do?

- Move out and accelerate hard
- Wait until the vehicle starts to turn in
- Pull out before the vehicle reaches the junction
- Move out slowly

Wait until the vehicle starts to turn in

Try to anticipate the actions of other road users. Their signals might be misleading. When you're waiting at a junction, don't emerge until you're sure of their intentions.

6.27 Mark **one** answer

On a motorway what do signs showing a crawler lane suggest?

- Advance warning for a steep downhill section
- Only lorries and buses are allowed to use that lane
- Vehicles fitted with speed limiters must use that lane
- There will be a long, gradual uphill gradient ahead

There will be a long, gradual uphill gradient ahead

Due to its size and weight overtaking in a large heavy vehicle will take much longer than in a car. First ask yourself if overtaking is really necessary. The combination of a heavy load, a speed limiter and a gradient may leave you without the power to overtake safely.

6.28   *Mark two answers*

You are about to pass this car. What are the TWO main hazards you should be aware of?

- Bright sunshine reflecting off the car windscreen
- The driver's side door may suddenly open
- The parked car may move off with no warning
- The narrow pavement on the right

- **The driver's side door may suddenly open**
- **The parked car may move off with no warning**

You do not know what the driver of this car will do. Be prepared for any hazard. The driver may not have seen you. Planning ahead will allow you to be in the correct gear and at the correct speed to be able to deal safely with this hazard.

6.29  *Mark one answer*

You have parked your vehicle on a two-way road at night. You should

- leave the lights on
- switch off all lights
- leave your lights on if you have parked on the right-hand side
- switch off your lights if you have parked underneath a street lamp

- **leave the lights on**

Large vehicles are required by law to leave lights on when parked at night, unless in a designated off-road parking area. Also, unless you're in a one-way street, you must only park on the left-hand side. It's generally much better to park off-road if you can, particularly if you're going to be stationary for a long period of time.

6.30 Mark **two** answers

When driving, on which TWO occasions would you be most likely to experience weight transfer?

- Reversing
- Braking
- Overtaking
- Unloading
- Cornering
- Loading

- **Braking**
- **Cornering**

You must take extra care when your vehicle is carrying a load. When braking or cornering, the vehicle's weight will transfer. When cornering, weight will be transferred away from the direction in which you're turning. If you are also braking, weight can be transferred in several different directions.

6.31 Mark **three** answers

When driving a laden vehicle downhill, the effect of gravity will tend to

- make the vehicle use more fuel
- make the vehicle's speed increase
- require more braking effort
- require less braking effort
- increase stopping distances
- reduce stopping distances

- **make the vehicle's speed increase**
- **require more braking effort**
- **increase stopping distances**

Always plan ahead; take note of warning signs informing you of the gradient of the hill. Make sure you reduce your speed and select an appropriate lower gear in good time.

6.32 Mark **one** answer

Long vehicles need to straddle lanes

- to avoid mounting the kerb
- to avoid braking sharply
- when driving on motorways
- when coming to contraflow systems

- **to avoid mounting the kerb**

When driving a long vehicle around corners it's sometimes necessary to adopt a different road position to avoid mounting the kerb or colliding with street furniture such as lamp posts, traffic signs, etc. Other road users may not understand what you intend to do next. Watch them carefully and always signal in good time.

6.33 Mark **one** answer

When driving in windy weather, you should

- drive in a normal manner in exposed areas
- anticipate how conditions may affect other road users
- never alter your intended route if this would lengthen a journey
- always overtake smaller or vulnerable vehicles quickly

anticipate how conditions may affect other road users

Cyclists and motorcyclists are very vulnerable in high winds. They can be blown into your path. Plan ahead and give them a wide berth.

6.34 Mark **one** answer

You are driving a high-sided vehicle on a motorway. You should be especially aware of the effects of crosswinds on your vehicle

- when travelling in cuttings
- after passing motorway bridges
- after passing motorway signs
- when travelling in tunnels

after passing motorway bridges

Bridges provide shelter from the wind. The force of the wind after passing a bridge can be stronger than expected. Be prepared for this and be ready to react.

6.35 Mark **two** answers

High-sided vehicles can be affected by side winds. In which TWO situations is this most likely?

- Narrow country roads
- Open roads
- Motorway flyovers
- Motorway underpasses
- Built-up areas
- Roads with speed humps

Open roads

Motorway flyovers

As a driver of a large vehicle you should listen to weather forecasts, and plan your route accordingly. You're most likely to be subjected to high winds where there are, high-level bridges, high-level roads, exposed viaducts, exposed stretches of motorway.

6.36 Mark **two** answers

You are driving a high-sided vehicle. Which of these places may cause you problems on a windy day?

- Road tunnels
- High-level roads
- Dead ground
- Ring roads
- Exposed viaducts
- Residential roads

High-level roads

Exposed viaducts

Listen to the weather forecasts and plan your route to avoid exposed roads. If you can delay your journey or take an alternative route you could save yourself, your employer and the emergency services a lot of unnecessary work and expense.

6.37 Mark **one** answer

Which of the following vehicles is least likely to be affected by high winds?

The car is the most stable of the vehicles shown. All vehicles are affected by crosswinds and buffeting from larger vehicles. Be aware that your speed and road position could cause unnecessary turbulence when passing smaller vehicles.

6.38 Mark **one** answer

What is a 'buffer' lane?

- A lane for large vehicles blown off course
- A lane for overtaking
- A lane to park in until the wind drops
- The only lane to be used in high winds

A lane for large vehicles blown off course

During high winds one of the lanes on high bridges might be closed to traffic to create a 'buffer' lane. This lane is kept free to prevent vehicles being blown into the path of other road users in the next lane. The closure of this lane may cause traffic congestion and delay.

6.39 Mark **one** answer

In high winds where would you expect to find 'buffer' lanes?

- In built-up areas
- On high bridges
- On country roads
- In roadworks

On high bridges

If your route takes in any locations that are frequently subjected to high winds, such as, high-level bridges, high-level roads, exposed viaducts or exposed stretches of motorway, listen to the weather forecasts, which will inform you of any need to replan your route.

6.40 Mark **one** answer

When is a 'buffer' lane most likely to be in use?

- When windy
- When raining
- When foggy
- When icy

When windy

A buffer lane is established when the wind begins to cause a risk to high-sided vehicles. At other times it will be a normal lane. Don't use the buffer lane unless your vehicle has been blown off course into it, or you need to use it to avoid an incident or collision. Leave it free, however heavy the traffic.

6.41 Mark **one** answer

How can you best control your vehicle when driving on snow in windy conditions?

- By keeping the engine revs high and spinning the wheels
- By driving in your very lowest crawler gear
- By keeping the engine revs high and slipping the clutch
- By driving slowly in as high a gear as possible

By driving slowly in as high a gear as possible

Driving slowly will give you better control of your vehicle. By using a high gear you reduce the chance of your wheels spinning and skidding on the snow.

6.42 *Mark **one** answer*

You are driving a large vehicle in gusty conditions. Which of the following is most likely to be affected when you overtake it?

- A motorcycle
- A flat-bed lorry
- A car
- A loaded tanker

A motorcycle

Give motorcyclists extra room in windy conditions. A combination of gusty conditions and buffeting caused by your vehicle can easily upset the motorcyclist's control and balance.

6.43 *Mark **one** answer*

You are driving on a motorway in high winds. You are overtaking a motorcyclist. You should be especially aware of the effects caused by

- exhaust smoke
- engine noise
- buffeting
- tyre noise

buffeting

Always watch motorcyclists carefully in your nearside mirror when you overtake them. Give them plenty of room as the rider might wobble or be blown off course.

6.44 *Mark **one** answer*

In gusty winds on a motorway you must be aware of motorcyclists as they may

- be blown into your path
- leave at the next exit
- suddenly stop on the hard shoulder
- position to turn right

be blown into your path

On motorways there are often exposed stretches of road where there are strong crosswinds. A gust of wind can force a motorcyclist to swerve across the lanes. GIVE THEM PLENTY OF ROOM!

6.45 *Mark **three** answers*

Which road users are in the most danger from the buffeting effects of large vehicles?

- ⊙ Lorry drivers
- ⊙ Coach drivers
- ⊙ Tractor drivers
- ⊙ Pedestrians
- ⊙ Horse riders
- ⊙ Cyclists

⊙ **Pedestrians**

⊙ **Horse riders**

⊙ **Cyclists**

Remember that buffeting can affect other road users including

- cars towing caravans
- motorcyclists.

6.46 *Mark **four** answers*

Which road users would be most affected by turbulence caused by your vehicle?

- ⊙ Pedestrians
- ⊙ Car drivers towing caravans
- ⊙ Drivers of skip lorries
- ⊙ Cyclists
- ⊙ Coach drivers
- ⊙ Horse riders

⊙ **Pedestrians**

⊙ **Car drivers towing caravans**

⊙ **Cyclists**

⊙ **Horse riders**

Be considerate when passing more vulnerable road users. Give them plenty of room, don't use the size of your vehicle to intimidate other road users.

6.47 *Mark **four** answers*

Turbulence is created by large vehicles travelling at speed. This is most likely to be a danger to

- ⊙ low-loaders
- ⊙ cyclists
- ⊙ pedestrians
- ⊙ motorcyclists
- ⊙ tankers
- ⊙ caravans

⊙ **cyclists**

⊙ **pedestrians**

⊙ **motorcyclists**

⊙ **caravans**

Passing too close to any of the above will create turbulence which could affect their balance or control. Don't be guilty of putting others in danger through thoughtless or inconsiderate driving.

6.48 Mark **one** answer

You are overtaking a motorcycle in windy conditions. Why should you always check your nearside mirror?

- To check your road position
- To see if the rider is still in control of the motorcycle
- To see if other vehicles have been affected
- To check if it is properly adjusted

- **To see if the rider is still in control of the motorcycle**

You must check the nearside mirror during and after overtaking a motorcyclist. Make sure that the rider is still in control and that your vehicle hasn't caused buffeting.

6.49 Mark **three** answers

Which THREE of the following are most likely to be affected by high winds?

- Slow-moving vehicles
- Cyclists
- Vehicles towing caravans
- Curtain-sided vehicles
- Track-laying vehicles
- Front-wheel drive vehicles

- **Cyclists**
- **Vehicles towing caravans**
- **Curtain-sided vehicles**

Very windy conditions can cause certain types of vehicles to be blown off course. Be aware of these and allow extra room when overtaking.

6.50 Mark **one** answer

You are driving a high sided vehicle on a motorway. You should be especially aware of the effects of crosswinds on your vehicle when

- travelling in cuttings
- travelling through tunnels
- driving across viaducts
- passing motorway signs

- **driving across viaducts**

On motorways you should be especially careful when driving over bridges and viaducts which are frequently subjected to high winds. Be prepared to reduce your speed.

6.51 Mark **one** answer

On a motorway the surface is still wet after rain. You should take extra care when overtaking because

- wet roads may create more buffeting
- other vehicles will have their lights on
- vehicles may be parked on the hard shoulder
- the road may still be slippery

the road may still be slippery

Rain reacts with oil, dirt and debris on the surface, reducing grip between the tyres and the road.

6.52 Mark **one** answer

The road is wet. Why might a motorcyclist steer around drain covers on a bend?

- To prevent the motorcycle skidding
- To avoid puncturing the tyres
- To help steer around the bend
- To avoid splashing pedestrians

To prevent the motorcycle skidding

Drain covers usually have a metal surface. When wet they can cause the motorcycle to skid.

6.53 Mark **one** answer

In heavy rain what is the least amount of space you should allow for braking?

- The normal distance
- Twice the normal distance
- Three times the normal distance
- Five times the normal distance

Twice the normal distance

Your tyres could lose their grip in wet conditions. If you're travelling in heavy rain you should be aware that it could take twice as long for you to stop as in dry weather. Therefore increase your distance from the vehicle in front.

6.54 Mark **three** answers

You are driving on a motorway. Your view ahead is poor due to heavy spray. Which THREE of the following should you do?

- Move into the lane on the right
- Use the four-second rule
- Switch on your dipped headlights
- Switch on your full-beam headlights
- Reduce your speed

- **Use the four-second rule**
- **Switch on your dipped headlights**
- **Reduce your speed**

If you're travelling on a motorway and your view ahead is poor then you should reduce your speed. Leave about four seconds between you and the vehicle in front, and make sure that others can see you by using your dipped headlights.

6.55 Mark **one** answer

When overtaking on motorways in very wet weather, what is the main danger that can affect your vehicle?

- Your engine may get flooded
- Your braking distance may be reduced
- Your steering may become heavy
- Your tyres may lose grip

- **Your tyres may lose grip**

Water can form a layer between the road and the tyre resulting in a loss of contact with the road. This is known as aquaplaning.

6.56 Mark **one** answer

Overtaking on a motorway in heavy rain needs extra care because of

- slippery manhole covers
- spray from traffic
- reduced braking distances
- bright reflections

- **spray from traffic**

Other drivers can be affected by the spray created by your vehicle, causing them to be temporarily blinded. Always take care when you need to change lanes, give a signal in good time and watch your mirrors carefully before pulling out in these conditions.

6.57 Mark **one** answer

Visibility can be worse when driving at higher speeds in wet weather because

- drivers always bunch together
- headlights will dazzle you more easily
- of people driving at different speeds
- more spray is thrown up

more spray is thrown up

The faster a wheel turns, the more spray is thrown up from the road to the side and rear of the vehicle. Always use dipped headlights in poor visibility caused by rain and spray.

6.58 Mark **one** answer

You intend to overtake a large vehicle that is throwing up spray. You should

- get much closer before moving out
- wait until the other driver gives a left signal
- move out earlier than normal
- wait for the other vehicle to slow down on a hill

move out earlier than normal

If you wish to overtake a vehicle that's throwing up spray, move out to overtake earlier than normal. This will prevent you being affected by the rear spray as well as the side spray as you pass.

6.59 Mark **one** answer

Your vehicle is fitted with spray suppression equipment. What effect will this have on other drivers if it is NOT in good working order?

- Their vision will be increased
- Their vision will be reduced
- They will be able to overtake quickly
- They will be able to follow closely

Their vision will be reduced

Spray suppression equipment reduces the amount of spray thrown up to other road users. Check the equipment regularly to make sure it is secure.

6.60 *Mark* ***one*** *answer*

The purpose of the brushes fitted to this vehicle is to

- clear mud from the tyres on building sites
- remove objects from the tyre tread
- stop snow building up behind the wheel
- reduce spray and increase visibility

reduce spray and increase visibility

The brushes are part of a spray suppression system which stops water from being thrown up at the sides and to the rear of the vehicle. Check them regularly for security, and if they become worn make sure they are replaced.

6.61 *Mark* ***one*** *answer*

You should check your vehicle's spray suppression equipment

- only when you will be using a motorway
- before setting out on a journey
- only at the start of winter as a pre-winter check
- yearly before the MOT test

before setting out on a journey

You should check all your spray suppression equipment before setting out. Bear in mind that the weather may change during the course of the journey.

6.62 *Mark* ***one*** *answer*

In wet weather, following drivers will be able to see better if your vehicle is fitted with

- spray reducers
- side-panel skirts
- wind deflectors
- a catalytic converter

spray reducers

Spray reducers or spray suppression equipment are attachments fitted around the wheel arch area of large vehicles. They effectively trap the water thrown up from the wheels when driving on wet roads. This improves visibility for you and other drivers who wish to overtake.

6.63  Mark **one** answer

This vehicle is fitted with spray suppression equipment. This will be most useful when it is

- raining
- snowing
- windy
- foggy

- **raining**

The spray suppression equipment helps prevent water being thrown up and causing reduced visibility. Driving at a reduced speed in wet weather conditions will also help to reduce the amount of water thrown up by your vehicle.

6.64 Mark **one** answer

When driving through deep water you should drive

- slowly in a low gear with engine speed high
- slowly in a high gear with engine speed low
- as quickly as possible to cause less delay
- at normal speed if you have spray reducers fitted

- **slowly in a low gear with engine speed high**

It is important to keep the engine speed high to prevent water entering the engine through the exhaust system. It may be necessary to slip the clutch in these circumstances to keep the road speed as low as possible.

6.65 Mark **one** answer

You are approaching a working snow plough on a motorway. You should not overtake because

- it is illegal to overtake snow ploughs
- snow ploughs are left-hand drive only
- your speed could cause snow to drift behind
- there may be deep snow ahead

- **there may be deep snow ahead**

There is no way of knowing how deep the snow could be ahead. If you overtake and then become stuck in the snow you may cause problems for the snow plough, particularly if you block the road.

6.66 Mark **three** answers

You are driving in heavy rain. Why is there a need to increase your distance from the vehicle in front?

- To prevent rain entering the vehicle's braking system
- The tyres will have less grip on the road surface
- Spray from traffic will make it difficult to see ahead
- To reduce the risk of water spraying into filters
- Normal stopping distances could be doubled

- **The tyres will have less grip on the road surface**
- **Spray from traffic will make it difficult to see ahead**
- **Normal stopping distances could be doubled**

Extra care is needed when driving in adverse weather conditions. Reduce your speed and switch on dipped headlights. Tyres will have less grip on a wet road so it will take longer to stop. Spray from large vehicles will be an added hazard, especially on motorways.

6.67 Mark **one** answer

You are driving a large vehicle on a motorway. Why should you slow down when the roads are very wet?

- To force other drivers to act properly and slow down
- To reduce the amount of spray thrown up
- To prevent water entering the braking system
- To stop the electrics getting wet

- **To reduce the amount of spray thrown up**

Driving at high speed on a wet motorway can seriously reduce vision. Spray thrown up by large, fast-moving vehicles can make it very difficult for other drivers to see ahead.

6.68 Mark **one** answer

You are driving on a motorway in heavy rain. When would you be allowed to use high-intensity rear fog lights?

- When visibility is more than 100 metres (328 feet)
- Only when the national speed limit applies
- Only when you are being followed closely by other traffic
- When visibility is reduced to 100 metres (328 feet) or less

- **When visibility is reduced to 100 metres (328 feet) or less**

Heavy rain and the resulting spray from higher speeds and large vehicles can seriously affect visibility on the motorway. Reduce your speed and use your headlights. Do not use high-intensity rear lights UNLESS visibility is reduced to 100 metres (328 feet) or less.

6.69 Mark **one** answer

You are driving on a motorway in heavy rain. What could cause your steering to be less responsive?

- Water reducing the tyre grip on the road
- Tyres becoming hotter in the bad weather
- Braking gently and in good time
- Water entering the braking system

- **Water reducing the tyre grip on the road**

Be careful when driving in bad weather. Steering can be less responsive when the roads are wet because water prevents the tyres from gripping the road. If this happens, ease off the accelerator and slow down gradually.

6.70 Mark **one** answer

What causes extra danger when overtaking in rain?

- Other vehicles driving slowly
- Vehicles wandering across lanes
- Increase in vehicle noise
- Spray from large vehicles

- **Spray from large vehicles**

Other vehicles might create heavy spray, so you must be cautious when you're overtaking. Severe spray can result in a complete loss of vision as you overtake. Be aware of this and anticipate it happening. Spray from your vehicle could cause the driver of an overtaking vehicle to lose visibility. You should be aware of this as smaller vehicles overtake you.

6.71 Mark **three** answers

A vehicle travelling downhill will

- need more engine power
- need more braking effort
- take longer to stop
- need a shorter stopping distance
- require less braking effort
- increase speed quickly

- **need more braking effort**
- **take longer to stop**
- **increase speed quickly**

When a vehicle is stationary on level ground the only force acting on it is the downward pull of gravity. When travelling on a downhill gradient the effect of gravity will tend to make the vehicle's speed increase, require more braking effort and increased stopping distances.

6.72 Mark **one** answer

The road is wet. Why should you slow down as you approach this pedestrian?

- Because there are no road markings
- To avoid splashing them
- Because they have priority
- To encourage them to cross

- **To avoid splashing them**

Drive with consideration along wet roads, especially if pedestrians are walking or standing near the kerb.

6.73 Mark two answers

Tailgating another vehicle is dangerous because

- your job could be at risk
- your braking time is increased
- your view to the rear is reduced
- your view ahead is reduced
- your room for braking is reduced

your view ahead is reduced

your room for braking is reduced

Tailgating is very dangerous because there is no safety distance in which to stop between yourself and the driver in front. It also intimidates the driver you are following.

6.74 Mark one answer

Hazard warning lights may be used while moving when

- you have just overtaken another vehicle
- you need to reverse for some distance
- traffic ahead is slowing quickly on a motorway
- one of your lights has failed

traffic ahead is slowing quickly on a motorway

While moving, hazard warning lights may only be used on a motorway or unrestricted dual carriageway to warn drivers behind of a need to slow down, due to a temporary obstruction ahead.

6.75 Mark one answer

You are driving in town and see these lights flashing. What would you expect to see ahead?

- Contraflow system
- Uneven road surface
- Children crossing the road
- Roadworks ahead

Children crossing the road

These lights warn of children likely to be crossing the road on their way to and from school. Slow down and watch out for them.

6.76 *Mark **one** answer*

Where are these lights found?

- On approach to a level crossing
- Near a fire station
- On approach to a motorway
- Near a school

Near a school

Flashing amber lights are found near schools. They warn you that children are likely to be crossing the road to and from school. Drive slowly until you are clear of the area.

6.77 *Mark **one** answer*

You are allowed to use hazard warning lights while moving when

- towing another vehicle
- an overtaking lorry has cleared the front of your vehicle
- being towed by another vehicle
- traffic ahead on a motorway is slowing down quickly

traffic ahead on a motorway is slowing down quickly

Hazard warning lights may only be used while moving when driving on motorways, or unrestricted dual carriageways. You can only use them to warn drivers behind you of a hazard or obstruction ahead.

6.78 *Mark **three** answers*

What extra problems may you have when driving at night?

- Increased overtaking distances
- An increase in traffic
- Reduced visibility
- Reduced braking distances
- Dazzle from other vehicles
- Becoming tired

Reduced visibility

Dazzle from other vehicles

Becoming tired

Make sure that you drive within the speed limit, even if the roads appear to be empty. You must be able to stop safely in the distance that you can see clear ahead, which will be the distance illuminated by your headlights or by street lights.

6.79 Mark **one** answer

You should take extra care when overtaking at night because

- every driver will normally be tired
- large vehicles are subject to a 10% speed reduction
- speed and distance are harder to judge
- most towns are not adequately lit

speed and distance are harder to judge

In the darkness it will be difficult to assess the road ahead, especially if there are bends or hills which may prevent you from seeing an oncoming vehicle.

6.80 Mark **one** answer

You are driving along a motorway in thick fog at night. The reflective studs are red on your left and white on your right. You are driving

- in the right-hand lane
- on the hard shoulder
- in the left-hand lane
- in the middle lane

in the left-hand lane

The red studs indicate the hard shoulder. Always use more than one reference point at all times. This will help you to be more certain of your position.

6.81 Mark **one** answer

You are driving on a three-lane motorway. You are about to move into the middle lane to overtake a slower vehicle. You should check

- for traffic in the right-hand lane returning to the middle lane
- for traffic which is intending to leave at the next exit
- the nearside mirror before pulling out
- for any traffic behind that is trying to pass you on the left

for traffic in the right-hand lane returning to the middle lane

Traffic returning from the right-hand lane can be a hazard to be aware of when overtaking. Always check your blind spot before changing lanes.

6.82 Mark **one** answer

Before overtaking or changing lanes on a motorway you should always

- check your mirrors carefully
- change to a lower gear
- look over your left shoulder
- increase your speed gently

check your mirrors carefully

Check your mirrors to ensure that it is safe to overtake. Remember that traffic coming up behind you will be travelling at a faster speed.

6.83 Mark **one** answer

You are driving at the maximum speed limit for your vehicle on a clear motorway. You should keep to

- any one of the lanes
- the middle lane
- the right-hand lane
- the left-hand lane

the left-hand lane

You should remain in the left-hand lane unless you are overtaking other vehicles. Don't be inconsiderate and hog the centre or right-hand lane of a two-lane motorway.

6.84 Mark **one** answer

You are driving in the left-hand lane of a motorway. You see another large vehicle merging from a slip road. It is travelling at the same speed as you. You should

- try to race and get ahead of it
- leave the other vehicle to adjust its speed
- stay at the maximum speed allowed for your vehicle
- be ready to adjust your speed

be ready to adjust your speed

Be alert for this type of situation developing; it is not always possible to change lanes safely. The merging driver has a responsibility to give way if necessary. Don't change lanes if it will inconvenience or endanger other road users on the main carriageway.

6.85 Mark **two** answers

When driving in the left-hand lane of a motorway you see merging vehicles travelling at the same speed as you. You should

- try and accelerate past them
- move to the next lane if safe
- allow the traffic to merge by adjusting your speed
- expect the traffic to let you pass

- **move to the next lane if safe**
- **allow the traffic to merge by adjusting your speed**

Only change lanes if doing so will not inconvenience other road users on the main carriageway. Merging drivers have a responsibility to give way, if necessary, and not force their way into the main carriageway. Planning ahead will ensure you are well prepared to deal with these situations.

6.86 Mark **three** answers

You should take extra care before moving into the centre lane of a three-lane motorway because

- the centre lane is narrower
- another vehicle might be planning to use the same lane
- other drivers need time to react
- car drivers might not know they must give way to large vehicles
- the bridge height clearance will be less in that lane
- traffic from behind may be travelling much faster than you

- **another vehicle might be planning to use the same lane**
- **other drivers need time to react**
- **traffic from behind may be travelling much faster than you**

You should plan ahead to assess the actions of other vehicles using the road. Always indicate your intentions in good time, this will allow others to revise their course of action if necessary. Always check your blind spots before changing lanes.

6.87 Mark **one** answer

Normally, vehicles over 7.5 tonnes maximum authorised mass may use the right-hand lane of a motorway only when

- it is a three-lane motorway
- there are vehicles on the hard shoulder
- it is a two-lane motorway
- other vehicles are turning right

- **it is a two-lane motorway**

Goods and passenger vehicles with, a MAM of more than 7.5 tonnes, those required to be fitted with a speed limiter, and vehicles towing trailers, must not use the right-hand lane on motorways with more than two lanes, unless there are exceptional circumstances.

6.88 Mark **one** answer

You have just overtaken another vehicle on a motorway. When moving back to the left you should avoid

- cutting in
- increasing your speed
- changing gear
- signalling

- **cutting in**

Always check your nearside mirror carefully before moving back to the left after overtaking. Don't rely on the other driver flashing their headlights. Remember, The Highway Code explains that the correct interpretation of this is simply 'I am here'.

6.89 Mark **one** answer

What is a crawler lane for?

- To enable other traffic to overtake on the nearside
- To enable large vehicles to pull over and park out of the way
- To enable slow-moving traffic to move further over to the left on uphill gradients
- To enable emergency vehicles to get to the scene of an accident quicker

- **To enable slow-moving traffic to move further over to the left on uphill gradients**

On a motorway where there's long uphill gradients there may be a crawler lane. This type of lane helps the traffic to flow by diverting the slower, heavy vehicles into an extra lane on the left.

6.90 *Mark **one** answer*

You see this sign on a motorway. It means you are coming to a

- long downhill slope
- long uphill slope
- 'lorries only' lane
- service area

long uphill slope

The term 'crawler lane' doesn't mean the lane is only for extremely slow vehicles. It is advising you of an extra lane on the left. Crawler lanes are usually built on sections of road where the length of the gradient is such that some large vehicles will be slowed to the point where they become a hazard for other road users.

6.91 *Mark **one** answer*

You should use a crawler lane

- to let faster traffic overtake you
- when turning right from major roads
- for parking when having a break
- when slowing down for a motorway exit

to let faster traffic overtake you

Many vehicles are very powerful and can maintain speed even when climbing a gradient. Even if your vehicle is capable of maintaining speed, you can still use the crawler lane to allow other road users to overtake safely.

6.92 *Mark **one** answer*

Before overtaking you should

- flash your headlights to oncoming traffic
- look ahead for right-turn lane markings
- drive very close to the vehicle in front
- make a final check in your left mirror

look ahead for right-turn lane markings

Before overtaking look well ahead for road markings and traffic signs which indicate a right turn ahead. If a vehicle is turning right you could risk a collision.

6.93 *Mark* ***three*** *answers*

You should not overtake when

- there are signs and road markings that allow you to
- you are unable to see clearly ahead
- you would have to break the speed limit
- your view of the road ahead is clear
- approaching motorway exits or slip roads
- other road users would have to slow down

- **you are unable to see clearly ahead**
- **you would have to break the speed limit**
- **other road users would have to slow down**

Never commit yourself to an overtaking manoeuvre with a large vehicle unless you are absolutely certain you have the time and space to see it through safely. Don't take unnecessary risks which endanger other road users.

6.94 *Mark* ***one*** *answer*

After overtaking another large vehicle how would you know when it was safe to move back to the nearside lane?

- By waiting for the driver you have just overtaken to flash the headlights
- By checking your nearside mirror
- By using your hazard warning lights as a signal
- By moving over to the nearside in the hope that the other vehicle will slow down

- **By checking your nearside mirror**

While overtaking you'll need to judge carefully when to pull back into the nearside lane. Don't cut in too soon on the vehicle you've overtaken – leave a safety margin. Check your left-hand (nearside) mirror to make sure the rear of your vehicle is well clear. You should allow for the length of both vehicles and take into account the speed difference. Don't rely on signals from other drivers. They may be signalling to someone else.

6.95 *Mark* ***one*** *answer*

You are driving on a dual carriageway and intend to overtake the vehicle ahead. Behind there is a car approaching quickly in the right-hand lane. You should

- keep behind the slower vehicle
- signal and move out
- move up closer to the slower vehicle
- stay on the left, large vehicles cannot use the right-hand lane

- **keep behind the slower vehicle**

This will allow the faster-moving vehicle to overtake safely. If you pull out to overtake at this time, you will cause the car behind to brake sharply. Don't use the size of your vehicle to intimidate. Be professional and show consideration to other road users.

6.96 Mark **one** answer

What should you do after overtaking on a dual carriageway?

- Move back to the left as soon as possible
- Indicate left then right
- Wait until the other driver flashes their headlights
- Switch your rear lights on and off

Move back to the left as soon as possible

When you are sure it is safe, signal if necessary and move back to the left. Don't drive for long distances in the centre or right-hand lane unnecessarily.

6.97 Mark **one** answer

You are turning right at a roundabout driving a long vehicle. You need to occupy the left-hand lane. You should check mirrors and

- signal left on approach
- signal right on approach
- avoid giving a signal on approach
- signal right after entering the roundabout

signal right on approach

There are times when, due to the size of your vehicle, you'll have to take up part of another lane. If you need to do this, make sure that you use effective observation all around. Be aware that other road users might not understand the reasons for your position on the road. You should signal your intentions and take up your position in good time.

6.98 Mark **one** answer

Long vehicles need to straddle lanes

- to avoid braking sharply
- when driving on motorways
- to avoid mounting the kerb
- when coming to contraflow systems

to avoid mounting the kerb

When you have to straddle the lanes at small roundabouts or junctions, always signal in good time. Be alert for inexperienced road users who may, without realising, put themselves into a dangerous position.

6.99 Mark **two** answers

When approaching these roadworks, you should NOT

- start to overtake
- increase speed
- flash your headlights
- give any signals

- **start to overtake**
- **increase speed**

Slow down and look out for warning signs. Always obey speed limits at roadworks. Look for workers stepping into the road.

Don't use the size of your vehicle to force your way through. If the obstruction is on your side of the road, give way to oncoming traffic. Look for and act according to signals given by the person in charge of a 'Stop-Go' board or temporary traffic lights.

6.100 Mark **one** answer

It is very windy. You are about to overtake a motorcyclist. You should

- allow extra room
- overtake slowly
- sound your horn as you pass
- keep close as you pass

- **allow extra room**

Cyclists and motorcyclists may become unbalanced by your vehicle passing too close. Plan ahead and give them plenty of room. Remember that your large vehicle can cause a vacuum which will suck the rider towards it. The noise and close proximity of your vehicle can also startle them, which could cause them to swerve suddenly.

6.101 Mark **one** answer

You are driving behind two cyclists. They are approaching a roundabout in the left-hand lane. What should you expect them to do?

- Go in any direction
- Turn left
- Turn right
- Go straight ahead

- **Go in any direction**

When following cyclists into a roundabout be aware that they might not take the exit you expect them to. Cyclists approaching in the left-hand lane may be turning right. They may not have been able to get into the correct lane due to busy traffic. Be courteous and give them room.

6.102 Mark **one** answer

You should never attempt to overtake a cyclist

- on a roundabout
- before you turn left
- before you turn right
- on a one-way street

before you turn left

When you are driving a large vehicle always make good use of your nearside mirror before you turn left. Cyclists don't always understand the reasons why a large vehicle will adopt a position away from the kerb before turning left. Wait for them to pass the junction before you turn left.

6.103 Mark **one** answer

You are about to overtake a lorry. You should

- look well ahead for uphill gradients
- check your position in the left mirror
- quickly change to a higher gear
- close right up before pulling out

look well ahead for uphill gradients

Plan your overtaking carefully. The weight of your vehicle combined with the restrictions imposed by a speed limiter are factors you should take into consideration.

6.104 Mark **one** answer

You are in the left-hand lane on a three-lane motorway. Before you overtake you should check for any vehicles in the right-hand lane that might be about to

- move to the right
- move back to the left
- cut in sharply behind you
- accelerate briskly in front of you

move back to the left

Vehicles overtaking in the right-hand lane may return to the centre lane when they have finished their manoeuvre. You should look for this before starting to pull out. Don't rely on the size of your vehicle to claim right of way.

6.105 *Mark* ***three*** *answers*

Normally white lights on a vehicle at night show you that the vehicle is

- moving away from you
- moving towards you
- ahead of you and braking
- stationary facing you
- stationary and facing away from you
- reversing towards you

- **moving towards you**
- **stationary facing you**
- **reversing towards you**

Other road users must be able to recognise the size of your vehicle and which way you are going.

6.106 *Mark* ***three*** *answers*

When driving at night you should make sure all your lights are clean and working correctly. Why is this?

- To enable you to see ahead properly
- To prevent the battery from overcharging
- So that other road users can see the size of your vehicle
- So that the intensity of street lighting can be reduced
- To allow following drivers to use dipped headlights
- So that other road users are aware of your direction of travel

- **To enable you to see ahead properly**
- **So that other road users can see the size of your vehicle**
- **So that other road users are aware of your direction of travel**

See and be seen. Driving at night when your vehicle is poorly lit is dangerous for you and other road users and pedestrians.

6.107 *Mark* ***one*** *answer*

High-intensity rear fog lights should be used when visibility is less than

- 100 metres (328 feet)
- 200 metres (656 feet)
- 300 metres (984 feet)
- 400 metres (1312 feet)

- **100 metres (328 feet)**

Large vehicles are no more visible than other vehicles in dense fog. If visibility is seriously reduced, use your fog lights to help other drivers see you.

6.108 Mark **one** answer

You should switch off fog lights when visibility is more than

- ⊙ 10 metres (32 feet)
- ⊙ your stopping distance
- ⊙ your separation distance
- ⊙ 100 metres (328 feet)

⊙ **100 metres (328 feet)**

Do not drive with front or rear fog lights switched on unnecessarily. The glare from them can dazzle other drivers.

6.109 Mark **one** answer

You should switch off rear fog lights when visibility is more than

- ⊙ 10 metres (32 feet)
- ⊙ 50 metres (164 feet)
- ⊙ 75 metres (246 feet)
- ⊙ 100 metres (328 feet)

⊙ **100 metres (328 feet)**

Be professional; switch off your fog lights when visibility improves. Don't cause unnecessary glare or distraction to other drivers.

6.110 Mark **one** answer

In fast traffic a two-second gap from the vehicle in front may be enough only when conditions are

- ⊙ dry
- ⊙ wet
- ⊙ damp
- ⊙ foggy

⊙ **dry**

You must be aware that when the weather is bad, you will have to keep a greater distance from the vehicle in front because it will take you further to stop. In wet weather it will take twice as far; in icy weather this could increase to ten times the distance.

6.111 Mark one answer

When driving in traffic on a motorway you see a lorry too close behind. You should

- increase your distance from the vehicle in front
- touch the brake pedal sharply to show your brake lights
- briskly accelerate away from the vehicle behind
- switch your rear fog lamps on and off

increase your distance from the vehicle in front

The faster the traffic is moving, the greater the distance which needs to be kept between vehicles to maintain safety margins. If you find another vehicle driving too close behind you, gradually reduce your speed to increase your distance from the vehicle in front. You'll then be able to brake more gently when you need to, reducing the likelihood of the vehicle behind running into the back of your vehicle

6.112 Mark one answer

Another vehicle has overtaken you and has pulled in too close in front. You should

- slow down
- drive on close behind
- overtake the vehicle
- flash your headlights

slow down

Always maintain a safe following distance from the vehicle in front. If another vehicle pulls into the gap you have left slow down to re-establish a safe following distance.

Following too close is dangerous and places you and other road users in unnecessary danger; your view of the road ahead will be seriously reduced, and you won't be able to see or plan effectively.

6.113 Mark one answer

At 50 mph (80 kph) what gap should you leave behind the vehicle in front on a dry, level road?

- One vehicle length
- Two vehicle lengths
- A minimum one-second gap
- A minimum two-second gap

A minimum two-second gap

'Tailgating' – travelling too close to the vehicle in front – is a very dangerous practice. Don't do it.

It's essential that you understand the distance it will take for you to stop in an emergency. Leave at least a two-second gap in good conditions and increase this to four seconds in wet weather.

6.114 *Mark **one** answer*

You are behind a large vehicle. How can you improve your view ahead?

- Stay further back
- Move over to the right
- Move over to the left
- Overtake as soon as you can

Stay further back

Leaving a safety margin and staying well back from the vehicle in front will improve your view of the road ahead. This will give you more time and room to react to hazards. Use the two-second rule to ensure you're not too close. Do not move out to the right as this could put you into the path of an oncoming vehicle, and may cause a head-on collision.

6.115 *Mark **two** answers*

You should overtake at night only when

- you can see well ahead
- you can do so without cutting in
- there is an overtaking lane
- you are outside built-up areas
- the road is well lit

you can see well ahead

you can do so without cutting in

It is more difficult to judge speed and distance accurately in the dark. Darkness can also hide bends and dips in the road. Plan ahead, and be sure that you have time and space to complete your overtaking safely.

6.116 *Mark **one** answer*

When driving in snow, stopping distances may be increased by up to how many times, compared with a dry road?

- Two
- Four
- Five
- Ten

Ten

In icy or snowy weather your stopping distance can increase by up to ten times. Because snowy weather increases the distance needed to stop, you must look well ahead and leave a good safety margin. It's easy to underestimate the different stopping distances needed in bad weather.

6.117 Mark **one** answer

When required to slow down or stop on an icy road you should make sure that

- braking is gentle and in good time
- retarders are always used
- downward gear changes are made
- the parking brake is used in a rapid on-and-off movement

- **braking is gentle and in good time**

When you have to slow down or stop you should avoid harsh, late braking. If you're planning ahead with good anticipation you can reduce the need to brake harshly. Brake gently and in good time to ensure control of your vehicle. This is particularly important on icy or slippery roads.

6.118 Mark **two** answers

You are driving a vehicle in icy weather. All braking must be done

- suddenly
- by 'pumping' the brakes
- gently
- by using the gears first
- over longer distances

- **gently**
- **over longer distances**

All braking should be controlled, in good time and when travelling in a straight line. Avoid braking and turning at the same time. Look well ahead to assess and plan your actions.

6.119 Mark **one** answer

You should use the 'two-second rule'

- before restarting the engine after it has stalled
- to keep a safe distance from the vehicle in front
- before using the 'Mirror - Signal - Manoeuvre' routine
- when emerging on wet roads

- **to keep a safe distance from the vehicle in front**

To measure this, choose a fixed reference point, such as a bridge, sign or tree. When the vehicle ahead passes the object, say to yourself 'Only a fool breaks the two-second rule.' If you reach the object before you finish saying this you're TOO CLOSE.

6.120 Mark **one** answer

Following a large goods vehicle too closely is dangerous because

- your field of vision is seriously reduced
- slipstreaming will reduce wind effect
- your engine will overheat
- your brakes need a constant cooling effect

your field of vision is seriously reduced

Staying back will increase your view of the road ahead. This will help you to see any hazards that might occur and allow you more time to react.

6.121 Mark **one** answer

You are following a vehicle on a wet road. You should leave a time gap of at least

- one second
- two seconds
- three seconds
- four seconds

four seconds

Wet roads will increase the time it will take you to stop. Four seconds is the MINIMUM gap you should leave on wet roads, this is double the gap you should normally keep from the vehicle in front on good, dry roads.

6.122 Mark **one** answer

The entrances to roundabouts are often slippery when wet. You should always

- keep in the left-hand lane
- brake in good time
- use the handbrake
- stop before emerging

brake in good time

The entrances to roundabouts are often worn which can make the surface slippery, especially when wet. You should always plan your approach and brake in good time.

6.123 Mark **one** answer

You become stuck in snow. What might help you to move off?

- Trolley jack
- Can of de-icer
- Wheel brace
- Shovel

Shovel

A shovel can be used to clear away deep snow, and to make a clear path for the vehicle to pull away in. Cloth sacks can be placed under the wheels in order for them to have something to grip on while the vehicle pulls clear.

6.124 Mark **one** answer

What might help you to move off when you are stuck in snow?

- Trolley jack
- Cloth sacks
- Wheel brace
- Can of de-icer

Cloth sacks

Cloth sacks placed under the wheels will provide extra grip. It will also be useful to carry a shovel in your vehicle.

6.125 Mark **one** answer

Before braking in wet conditions you should make sure, as far as possible, that

- the gear lever is in neutral
- all spray suppression equipment is working
- there is no mist on your rear-view mirrors
- your vehicle is travelling in a straight line

your vehicle is travelling in a straight line

If you need to brake when the road surface is wet, do so while your vehicle is travelling in a straight line. This will lessen the risk of skidding. As a professional driver you should be in the routine of braking in good time, so that you aren't braking and changing direction at the same time.

6.126 Mark **one** answer

You are driving a fully-laden vehicle. You are approaching an uphill gradient as you are overtaking another vehicle. Which of the following is NOT correct?

- You will be able to get past quicker
- The extra weight will make you slower
- It will take you longer to get past
- You will need more power from the engine

You will be able to get past quicker

Always plan well ahead before overtaking. Take into consideration the size of your vehicle. The load on your vehicle will influence its handling and speed characteristics.

6.127 Mark **one** answer

You are driving at night in a built-up area. To ensure that you can be seen you should use

- ⊙ dipped beam headlights
- ⊙ main beam headlights
- ⊙ side lights only
- ⊙ front fog lights only

⊙ **dipped beam headlights**

Using dipped headlights will help others see you and also aids your visibility if the street lighting changes or isn't working.

6.128 Mark **one** answer

You are on a motorway and there is a strong crosswind. Which of these vehicles is particularly at risk?

- ⊙ A motorcycle
- ⊙ A taxi
- ⊙ A sports car
- ⊙ A road tanker

⊙ **A motorcycle**

Motorcycles can be very vulnerable to strong crosswinds. Allow extra room when overtaking them in windy weather. Check your nearside mirror while alongside and before moving back to the left.

6.129 Mark **one** answer

You are driving at a speed of 50 mph (80 kph) in good, dry conditions. What distance should you stay behind the vehicle in front?

- ⊙ At least 20 metres (66 feet)
- ⊙ At least 30 metres (98 feet)
- ⊙ At least 40 metres (131 feet)
- ⊙ At least 50 metres (164 feet)

⊙ **At least 50 metres (164 feet)**

You should always leave a safety margin between you and the vehicle in front. This gap will give you a better view of the road ahead. It will also allow you more time to react if the traffic in front changes speed or direction.

6.130 *Mark **one** answer*

You are on a motorway just after heavy rain. Spray is being thrown up causing poor visibility. What should you do?

- Keep a two-second gap
- Use sidelights only
- Remove spray suppression equipment
- Leave a greater separation distance

Leave a greater separation distance

When visibility is poor and the road is wet leave a greater separation distance. You should leave at least a four-second time gap from the vehicle in front. You should also reduce speed and use dipped headlights.

6.131 *Mark **one** answer*

Spray is causing poor visibility on the motorway. What should you do?

- Use a two-second gap
- Use sidelights only
- Slow to a safe speed
- Remove spray suppression equipment

Slow to a safe speed

Spray from other vehicles, particularly lorries, will reduce visibility. Slow down and leave a greater separation distance from the vehicle in front. You should also use dipped headlights.

6.132 *Mark **one** answer*

You are driving in snow. Care should be taken when using the endurance brake (retarder) because it may cause

- additional brake wear
- an increase in speed
- the drive-wheels to lock
- compressed air to escape

the drive-wheels to lock

When operating independent retarders, care must be taken when descending snow covered gradients and other slippery surfaces. Harsh use could cause the drive-wheels to lock.

6.133 Mark **one** answer

You overtake a cyclist on a two-way road. What should you do?

- Pass closely staying about 1 metre (3 feet 3 inches) from the kerb
- Go past quickly and move back to the left sharply
- Leave plenty of room and check your nearside mirror before returning
- Use a right-turn signal after pulling out

- **Leave plenty of room and check your nearside mirror before returning**

Only overtake when it is safe to do so. Never force other vehicles to move for you. Be patient and stay well back from the cyclist until there is a safe overtaking gap.

6.134 Mark **one** answer

Your lorry has a curtain-side body. Your route will take you over several high-level bridges. Why is it particularly important to check the weather forecast?

- Rain can make crossing bridges very difficult for large vehicles
- In hot weather the bridges might be closed to heavy traffic
- You won't be able to climb the bridges if it's frosty
- Some routes may be closed to certain vehicles in high winds

- **Some routes may be closed to certain vehicles in high winds**

In exposed places such as high-level bridges and roads, viaducts or some motorways, the wind can be particularly strong. If you're driving a high-sided vehicle make sure that you check the weather forecast and plan an alternative route, just in case.

6.135 Mark **one** answer

You want to join a motorway. Traffic is flowing freely on the motorway. What should you do?

- Keep to a low speed until you see a gap on the motorway
- Build up your speed on the slip road before joining the motorway
- Stop at the start of the slip road and move off when there is a gap
- Use the hard shoulder if necessary, to build up speed

- **Build up your speed on the slip road before joining the motorway**

Normally you should avoid having to stop before joining a motorway. Use the slip road to build up your speed so that you can emerge safely. If it's extremely busy there may be rare occasions when you have to stop and then filter into the traffic. This is most likely to happen at roadworks and where there are contraflow systems.

6.136 *Mark **one** answer*

Before driving your lorry in high winds, you should always

- check your wind deflector
- check your spray suppression equipment
- plan your journey well in advance
- only half load your lorry

plan your journey well in advance

Plan your route with care. Take into account whether the road will be exposed and if there will be bridges or viaducts to cross. Be sensible and avoid these areas if possible in high winds.

6.137 *Mark **one** answer*

You are overtaking another lorry. Due to an uphill gradient you start to lose speed. You should

- continue at the same speed and position
- try to force the vehicle you were overtaking to drop back
- try to force the vehicle you were overtaking to speed up
- ease off and drop behind the vehicle you were trying to overtake

ease off and drop behind the vehicle you were trying to overtake

If you try to overtake another vehicle and you realise that you're unable to complete the manoeuvre, ease off the accelerator and drop back behind the vehicle. If the vehicle you're trying to overtake is large then it will take longer to pass. You should assess whether you have the time and the power to complete the manoeuvre BEFORE you try to overtake.

6.138 *Mark **one** answer*

When driving an empty curtain-sided vehicle, how could you reduce crosswind problems on exposed bridges?

- Tie just one curtain side back and lock open the rear doors
- Leave both curtain sides closed
- Tie both curtain sides at one end of the vehicle
- Tie the curtain sides halfway back

Tie both curtain sides at one end of the vehicle

If you're driving an empty curtain-sided vehicle, you can help to lower the resistance to side winds if you tie back the curtains. The air will be able to flow across the flat bed of the vehicle and lessen any loss of control, particularly when crossing exposed viaducts or bridges.

6.139  *Mark **one** answer*

A high-sided vehicle will be MOST affected by crosswinds when it is

- ⊙ stationary
- ⊙ travelling loaded
- ⊙ reversing
- ⊙ travelling empty

⊙ **travelling empty**

Take care if you are driving an empty high-sided vehicle when the wind is blowing across the road you are travelling on. Watch for places where the conditions could suddenly change, such as a gap in the trees or when passing under a bridge.

6.140 *Mark **one** answer*

You are driving an empty curtain-sided vehicle. Why might you consider tying the curtains open?

- ⊙ To use less fuel
- ⊙ It is a legal requirement
- ⊙ To prevent the curtains tearing
- ⊙ To reduce the effect of crosswinds

⊙ **To reduce the effect of crosswinds**

Closed curtains on large empty vehicles can hold the wind. Strong side winds can actually lift and blow the semi-trailer off course as the vehicle is travelling along the road.

6.141 *Mark **one** answer*

A box van will be MOST affected by crosswinds when it is

- ⊙ travelling empty
- ⊙ stationary
- ⊙ travelling loaded
- ⊙ reversing

⊙ **travelling empty**

High-sided vehicles such as box vans are affected by strong winds, particularly when unladen. Reduce your speed and stay alert for other road users who are also affected by weather conditions.

6.142 *Mark **three** answers*

In high winds, drivers of lorries approaching high bridges or viaducts should expect

- lower speed limits
- minimum speed limits
- no restrictions for loaded vehicles
- lane closures
- no restrictions for lorries
- diversions

lower speed limits

lane closures

diversions

You might be delayed by road closures or diversions. Consider this when you're planning your rest stops. Delays will add to your driving time.

6.143 *Mark **one** answer*

Which of these vehicles is MOST at risk from high crosswinds?

- A laden lorry with box body
- An unladen lorry with box body
- An unladen lorry with platform body
- A laden lorry with platform body

An unladen lorry with box body

The combination of an unladen vehicle with high sides will leave it vulnerable to the effects of strong winds. An evenly distributed load will keep the vehicle more stable and less likely to be blown off course. The higher your vehicle, the more it will be affected by strong winds. Be aware that it may become unstable or difficult to control.

6.144 *Mark **one** answer*

Which vehicle is most at risk when being driven in strong crosswinds?

- A box van carrying light goods
- An unladen lorry with platform body
- A container vehicle with a heavy load
- A low-loader carrying heavy machinery

A box van carrying light goods

High-sided vehicles catch the wind more than flat-bed vehicles. You should be aware of the places where you are likely to be at risk.

6.145 Mark **one** answer

In strong winds an overtaking lorry can affect other road users. Which vehicle is most at risk?

- A car
- A furniture van
- A motorcycle
- A coach

A motorcycle

Road users, such as motorcyclists, cyclists and vehicles towing caravans could be blown off course by high winds. You should be aware of this when you're following or planning to overtake them. When you overtake your vehicle could cause buffeting to these types of vehicle.

6.146 Mark **two** answers

Which TWO types of vehicle are most at risk in windy conditions?

- High-sided lorries
- Saloon cars
- Unladen vans
- Single-deck buses
- Tractor units

High-sided lorries

Unladen vans

The higher the sides of your vehicle, the more the vehicle will be buffeted by strong winds. The large area of bodywork will present a resistance to crosswinds, and this in turn will affect the control you have on the vehicle. The risk of loss of control will be increased if your vehicle isn't carrying a load. The vehicle will be lighter and so could be more easily pushed off course by the wind.

6.147 Mark **one** answer

When are air deflectors most effective?

- When there is a crosswind
- When there is a headwind
- When reversing
- When there is a strong tailwind

When there is a headwind

Cab mounted air deflectors and lower panels will streamline the vehicle and it will, therefore, offer less resistance to the air around it. This will decrease its fuel consumption. Conserving energy and resources should be a concern for all drivers on the road.

6.148 Mark **two** answers

You are driving your lorry on the motorway. Visibility is reduced by heavy rain and spray. You should

- maintain a constant speed
- use main beam headlights
- double your dry weather separation distance
- stay in the left-hand lane
- obey advisory speed limit signs

- **double your dry weather separation distance**
- **obey advisory speed limit signs**

Wet roads reduce tyre grip and can make the surface even more slippery. Give yourself plenty of time and room for slowing down and stopping. Keep well back from other vehicles. Advisory signs are set by the police and should be adhered to when they are shown.

6.149 Mark **one** answer

Before driving your lorry from a wet construction site at the side of a motorway, you should

- inform the local council
- hose down the road
- hose down the wheels
- inform the lorry operator

- **hose down the wheels**

It is important that you prevent any mud or debris from being deposited on the road. This can cause danger to other road users. If possible, hose the mud off your vehicle before driving on the public road.

6.150 Mark **one** answer

You are driving a lorry from a wet construction site onto a motorway. You must take extra precautions before driving because

- your lorry will be unladen and liable to 'bounce'
- it is an offence to emerge from a works site straight onto a motorway
- your lorry's spray suppression equipment will be inoperative
- it is an offence to deposit mud on a road

- **it is an offence to deposit mud on a road**

You should take all possible precautions to prevent any mud being deposited on the road as this is a hazard to other road users. It is also an offence for which you could be prosecuted.

6.151 Mark **one** answer

Before raising the body of a tipper lorry you should make sure the ground is

- soft and level
- soft and downhill
- solid and uphill
- solid and level

solid and level

When discharging a load from a tipper vehicle the centre of gravity is raised to a critical position. It's vitally important the vehicle is on a level, solid surface before engaging the hoist mechanism.

6.152 Mark **one** answer

You are driving a lorry weighing more than 7.5 tonnes maximum authorised mass. You may only use the right-hand lane to overtake on a motorway with

- two lanes
- three lanes
- a 50 mph speed limit
- a 40 mph speed limit

two lanes

You may use the right hand lane to overtake only on a two-lane motorway. Lorries weighing more than 7.5 tonnes maximum authorised mass, those required to be fitted with speed limiters, and those towing trailers are NOT allowed to use the far right-hand lane of a motorway with three or more lanes, except in special circumstances.

6.153 Mark **one** answer

You are driving on a motorway. You look in your mirrors and see smoke coming from your rear tyres. What should you do?

- Reduce speed for the rest of your journey
- Drive on the hard shoulder until the smoke stops
- Stop as soon as it's safe to do so
- Ignore it, this is normal when driving at speed

Stop as soon as it's safe to do so

Your tyre may burst or shred if it becomes overheated. This could result in serious loss of control. Stop on the hard shoulder as soon as it's safe to do so and call for help.

6.154 *Mark **one** answer*

You are on a wet level road. At 50 mph what gap should you leave from the vehicle in front?

- One second minimum
- Two seconds minimum
- Three seconds minimum
- Four seconds minimum

Four seconds minimum

Stopping distances can at least double on wet roads. Always drive in accordance with the road and weather conditions.

6.155 *Mark **one** answer*

You are driving an articulated lorry on a three-lane motorway. When can you drive in the right-hand lane?

- When overtaking a slow-moving car in the middle lane
- When the escort vehicle of an oversized load signals you to pass
- If no speed limiter is fitted to your lorry
- If your lorry is unladen

When the escort vehicle of an oversized load signals you to pass

Articulated lorries are prohibited from driving in the right-hand lane of motorways with three or more lanes except when an escort vehicle gives you a signal, when road signs indicate or when directed by a police officer.

6.156 *Mark **one** answer*

You are driving on a motorway after heavy rain. Visibility is low because of spray being thrown up by other lorries. You should

- use dipped headlights
- use sidelights only
- remove spray suppression equipment
- use the two-second rule

use dipped headlights

If visibility is reduced use dipped headlights to make yourself seen. During and after heavy rain you should also reduce speed and increase your distance from the vehicle in front.

section **seven**

ACCIDENT HANDLING

This section covers

- Reducing risk
- Injuries
- Casualties

7.1 *Mark* ***one*** *answer*

You are driving a coach carrying elderly people. You arrive at the scene of an accident. The emergency services have already arrived. You should

- ask your passengers to find out what is happening
- not tell passengers anything in case you upset them
- leave the passengers on the bus and see what is happening yourself
- tell the passengers what is happening without upsetting them

tell the passengers what is happening without upsetting them

You should reassure passengers when letting them know what has happened. Confirm to them that the emergency services are in attendance.

7.2  *Mark* ***one*** *answer*

Your bus and other vehicles have been involved in an accident. You should

- switch off their headlights
- switch off the fuel supply
- turn vehicles the right way up
- always pull casualties out of their vehicles

switch off the fuel supply

The risk of fire will be reduced if all fuel supplies are switched off.

7.3 *Mark* ***one*** *answer* NI EXEMPT

Your bus has hit a parked vehicle. The owner cannot be found. You must report the accident

- to the police within seven days
- to the owner as soon as possible
- to the owner within seven days
- to the police within 24 hours

to the police within 24 hours

If you damage a parked vehicle and the owner isn't around, you must report it to the police within 24 hours. This applies to any property you might have damaged. In Northern Ireland all accidents must be reported to the police immediately.

7.4  *Mark **one** answer*

You are treating a passenger who is in shock. You should

- ⊙ give them liquids
- ⊙ keep them moving
- ⊙ encourage them to sleep
- ⊙ keep them warm

⊙ **keep them warm**

Knowing what to do at a crash scene could save lives. Stay calm and in command of the situation. Call the emergency services. They're the experts and know how to deal with injured or shocked victims. First aid is very important, but the correct procedure is vital. Although not obviously injured, passengers may be suffering from shock. Reassure them and keep them warm. Don't give them anything to eat or drink.

7.5 *Mark **one** answer*

A passenger on your bus has stopped breathing. You help them by giving mouth to mouth resuscitation. When should you stop doing this?

- ⊙ When they can breathe on their own
- ⊙ When you think the passenger has died
- ⊙ When their skin colour has turned blue
- ⊙ When you think the ambulance is coming

⊙ **When they can breathe on their own**

You should only stop resuscitation when the passenger can breathe on their own or a professional medical person can take over.

7.6 *Mark **one** answer*

Your bus is involved in an accident. You have a passenger who is unconscious but still breathing. What should you do?

- ⊙ Get medical help
- ⊙ Check their pulse
- ⊙ Give them liquid
- ⊙ Lie them on their back

⊙ **Get medical help**

If one of your passengers is unconscious but breathing get medical help immediately. Only move the casualty if there's danger of further injury. Call the experts: dial 999.

7.7 *Mark **one** answer*

Your bus is stopped at the scene of an accident. Why should you consider moving your passengers to the front of the bus?

- To improve weight distribution
- To reduce the risk of injury from behind
- To be nearer emergency exits
- To be witnesses of the accident

To reduce the risk of injury from behind

You'll need to decide whether it's appropriate for passengers to move to a safer position if another vehicle could run into the back of the bus.

7.8 *Mark **one** answer* NI EXEMPT

Your bus hits a low railway bridge. Nobody is injured. You should report the accident

- immediately to your employer
- within 24 hours to the railway authority
- within seven days to the police
- immediately to the railway authority

immediately to the railway authority

If your bus hits a railway bridge you MUST inform the railway authorities immediately due to the possibility of structural damage to the bridge. You should find the telephone number on or near the bridge. It's very important to do this as soon as possible so that all rail traffic is stopped. You must also inform the police immediately or in any case within 24 hours.

7.9 *Mark **one** answer*

While going through a tunnel your coach catches fire. It cannot be driven any further. What should you do?

- Move the passengers to the rear of the coach
- Get the passengers off, keeping them together
- Make sure the passengers stay in their seats
- Move the passengers to the front of the coach

Get the passengers off, keeping them together

If your coach catches fire and it is unsafe to go any further, pull over to the side, switch the engine off and switch on your hazard warning lights.

Your immediate responsibility is to your passengers. Get them off the coach, keep them together and take them to the nearest emergency exit.

7.10 *Mark* ***two*** *answers*

You are driving a loaded school bus. Looking in your mirror you see smoke from the engine compartment at the rear. You must

- stop as quickly and safely as possible
- open the engine covers to investigate
- drive to the bus station for a replacement vehicle
- get everyone off the bus quickly
- move the passengers to the front away from danger

stop as quickly and safely as possible

get everyone off the bus quickly

Smoke from the engine compartment is very serious, as fire within a vehicle can spread very quickly. Your first priority is to make sure that all passengers get off the bus as quickly and safely as possible.

7.11 *Mark* ***one*** *answer*

You are driving in a tunnel. Your bus catches fire and you cannot drive out. After stopping, what should you do?

- Move the passengers to the nearest tunnel exit
- Use the extinguisher to put out the fire
- Keep the passengers together in front of the vehicle
- Stand behind your vehicle and warn other drivers

Move the passengers to the nearest tunnel exit

If you break down or there is an incident in a tunnel, your first priority is to your passengers. If your vehicle catches fire and you can drive it out of the tunnel, you should do so. If you can't do this,pull over to the side and switch off the engine. Move your passengers calmly but quickly to the nearest exit.

7.12  *Mark* ***one*** *answer*

In the UK the headroom under bridges, unless otherwise shown, is AT LEAST

- 4.8 metres (16 feet)
- 5 metres (16 feet 6 inches)
- 6 metres (19 feet 8 inches)
- 8 metres (26 feet 3 inches)

5 metres (16 feet 6 inches)

You must always be aware of the height of the vehicle you're driving. There are about 800 incidents a year where vehicles or their loads hit railway or other bridges. Every effort should be made to prevent this happening. If you hit a bridge you must report it to the police and if it's a railway bridge you must also report it to the relevant railway authority. Failure to report an incident involving a railway bridge is an offence.

7.13 *Mark **one** answer*

You are approaching a bridge that has NO height restriction on it. The height of the bridge will be at least

- 3.6 metres (11 feet 10 inches)
- 4.4 metres (14 feet 5 inches)
- 4.8 metres (16 feet)
- 5 metres (16 feet 6 inches)

5 metres (16 feet 6 inches)

The headroom under bridges in the UK is at least 5 metres (16 feet 6 inches), unless otherwise indicated. Where the overhead clearance is arched, this headroom is normally only between the limits marked.

7.14 *Mark **two** answers*

A laminated windscreen is one which

- will not shatter
- does not mist up
- has a plastic layer
- cuts down on glare

will not shatter

has a plastic layer

Windscreens are either laminated or toughened. The main difference is that toughened screens shatter, whereas a laminated screen will crack. A small crack may quickly become larger if the screen flexes as the vehicle is being driven.

7.15 *Mark **three** answers*

You are the first to arrive at the scene of an accident. Someone is unconscious. Which of the following should be given urgent priority to help them?

- Try to get them to drink water
- Look for any witnesses
- Clear the airway and keep it open
- Check that they are breathing
- Stop any bleeding
- Take the numbers of any vehicles involved

Clear the airway and keep it open

Check that they are breathing

Stop any bleeding

Gently tilt the head to clear the airway. Check for at least ten seconds that the casualty is breathing by looking for movement in the chest, listening for sounds and feeling for breath on your cheek. Apply pressure to any wound that is bleeding, using the cleanest material available; avoid pressing on anything caught in the wound.

7.16 Mark *one* answer

What must you do if you are involved in an accident?

- Drive on for help
- Inform the police within seven days
- Stop at the scene of the accident
- Drive to the nearest police station

Stop at the scene of the accident

If your vehicle is involved in a traffic incident you must stop. If there is injury or damage to any other person or vehicle, or animals not in your vehicle or to roadside property, you should stop at the scene and comply with certain legal obligations specified in The Highway Code.

7.17 Mark *one* answer NI EXEMPT

Your vehicle has been involved in an accident where someone is injured. You do not produce the required insurance certificate at the time of the accident. You must report the accident to the police as soon as possible, or in any case within

- 24 hours
- 48 hours
- 72 hours
- seven days

24 hours

If you don't give your name and address at the time of the accident, report the accident to the police as soon as reasonably practicable, or in any case within 24 hours. If any other person is injured and you don't produce your insurance certificate at the time of the accident to the police, or to any other person who has reasonable grounds to request it, you must also

- report the accident to the police as soon as possible, or in any case within 24 hours
- produce your insurance certificate to the police either when reporting the accident or within seven days (five days in Northern Ireland) at any police station you select.

7.18 *Mark **one** answer*

At the scene of an accident you see a plain orange rectangle displayed on one of the vehicles. This tells you that the vehicle

- is carrying dangerous goods
- is carrying a First Aid kit
- is carrying medical supplies
- is unladen

is carrying dangerous goods

Vehicles that carry dangerous goods have badges displayed on the side and rear. These are coloured orange and show the type of material that's being carried. Make a note of this and report it to the emergency services when you contact them.

7.19 *Mark **one** answer*

You arrive at an accident where someone is suffering from severe burns. Which of the following would help?

- Douse the burns with cold water
- Remove anything stuck to the burns
- Burst blisters that form on the burns
- Apply ointment to the burns

Douse the burns with cold water

Cold water will cool the burning tissue, help prevent further damage, reduce swelling, minimise shock and alleviate pain. Use water, or another liquid, that is clean and non-toxic.

7.20 *Mark **one** answer*

You arrive at the scene of an accident. A pedestrian is bleeding heavily from a leg wound. What should you do?

- Apply firm pressure to the wound
- Dab the wound to stop the bleeding
- Keep both legs flat on the ground
- Wrap an ice pack near the wound

Apply firm pressure to the wound

Control blood loss by applying pressure over the wound and raising the leg if possible.

7.21 Mark **one** answer

An accident has just happened. An injured person is lying in the busy road. What is the first thing you should do to help?

- Treat the person for shock
- Warn other traffic
- Place them in the recovery position
- Make sure the injured person is kept warm

- **Warn other traffic**

You could do this by displaying an advanced warning signal, if you have one, or switching on hazard warning or other lights. You could also use any other means that does not put you at risk.

7.22 Mark **three** answers

You are the first person to arrive at an accident where people are badly injured. Which THREE should you do?

- Switch on your own hazard warning lights
- Make sure that someone telephones for an ambulance
- Try and get people who are injured to drink something
- Move the people who are injured clear of their vehicles
- Get people who are not injured clear of the scene

- **Switch on your own hazard warning lights**
- **Make sure that someone telephones for an ambulance**
- **Get people who are not injured clear of the scene**

If you're the first to arrive at the scene, further collisions and fire are the first concerns. Switching off vehicle engines will reduce the risk of fire. Switch on hazard warning lights to warn other traffic. Don't assume someone else has called the emergency services, do it yourself. Don't move casualties trapped in vehicles unless they're in danger.

7.23 Mark *three* answers

You arrive at a serious motorcycle accident. The motorcyclist is unconscious and bleeding. Your main priorities should be to

- try to stop the bleeding
- make a list of witnesses
- check the casualty's breathing
- take the numbers of the vehicles involved
- sweep up any loose debris
- check the casualty's airways

- **try to stop the bleeding**
- **check the casualty's breathing**
- **check the casualty's airways**

At a traffic incident the danger of further collisions and fire need to be dealt with first. Injuries should be dealt with in the order, Airway, Breathing, Compressions and bleeding. Do not remove a motorcyclist's helmet unless it is essential to do so.

7.24 Mark *one* answer

You arrive at an accident. A motorcyclist is unconscious. Your first priority is the casualty's

- breathing
- bleeding
- broken bones
- bruising

- **breathing**

The first priority when dealing with an unconscious person is to make sure they can breathe. This may involve clearing their airway if they're having difficulty or some obstruction is obvious but don't attempt to remove a motorcyclist's safety helmet unless it's essential – serious injury could result. At the scene make sure there is no danger from further collisions or fire before dealing with any casualties.

7.25 Mark *three* answers

You arrive at the scene of an accident. It has just happened, and someone is unconscious. Which of the following should be given urgent priority to help them?

- Clear the airway and keep it open
- Try to get them to drink water
- Check that they are breathing
- Look for any witnesses
- Stop any heavy bleeding
- Take the numbers of vehicles involved

- **Clear the airway and keep it open**
- **Check that they are breathing**
- **Stop any heavy bleeding**

Stay with the casualty and make sure someone rings for an ambulance.

7.26 *Mark **three** answers*

You have stopped at the scene of an accident to give help. Which THREE things should you do?

- Keep injured people warm and comfortable
- Keep injured people calm by talking to them reassuringly
- Keep injured people on the move by walking them around
- Give injured people a warm drink
- Make sure that injured people are not left alone

- **Keep injured people warm and comfortable**
- **Keep injured people calm by talking to them reassuringly**
- **Make sure that injured people are not left alone**

If you stop to give help and there are casualties, don't move injured people unless there is further danger. Don't give them anything to drink.

7.27 *Mark **three** answers*

You arrive at the scene of an accident. It has just happened and someone is injured. Which of the following should be given urgent priority?

- Stop any severe bleeding
- Get them a warm drink
- Check that their breathing is OK
- Take numbers of vehicles involved
- Look for witnesses
- Clear their airway and keep it open

- **Stop any severe bleeding**
- **Check that their breathing is OK**
- **Clear their airway and keep it open**

Where possible call the emergency services first. If you are able to give first aid, remember DR ABC. Check for Danger. Check the casualties Response. Then check their Airway, Breathing, Circulation, giving Compressions if necessary, and bleeding. If you feel you are not capable of carrying out first aid, then consider doing some training. It could save a life.

7.28 *Mark **four** answers*

You are at the scene of an accident. Someone is suffering from shock. You should

- reassure them constantly
- offer them a cigarette
- keep them warm
- avoid moving them if possible
- loosen any tight clothing
- give them a warm drink

reassure them constantly

keep them warm

avoid moving them if possible

loosen any tight clothing

The effects of trauma may not be immediately obvious. Prompt treatment can help to minimise the effects of shock. Lay the casualty down, loosen tight clothing, call an ambulance, check their breathing and pulse.

7.29 *Mark **one** answer*

Which of the following should you not do at the scene of an accident?

- Warn other traffic by switching on your hazard warning lights
- Call the emergency services immediately
- Offer someone a cigarette to calm them down
- Ask drivers to switch off their engines

Offer someone a cigarette to calm them down

Keeping casualties or witnesses calm is important, but never offer a cigarette because of the risk of fire. Check for any signs of shock, such as, sweating or clammy skin, giddiness, rapid or shallow breathing, a weak pulse.

7.30 *Mark **two** answers*

When treating someone for shock you should

- reassure them
- loosen tight clothes
- walk them around
- give them a hot drink
- offer them an alcoholic drink

reassure them

loosen tight clothes

Keep talking to the casualty to help them stay calm. Don't leave them alone.

7.31 Mark **two** answers

There has been an accident. The driver is suffering from shock. You should

- give them a drink
- reassure them
- not leave them alone
- offer them a cigarette
- ask who caused the accident

reassure them

not leave them alone

They could have an injury that is not immediately obvious. Loosen any tight clothing and check that their breathing is not rapid or shallow.

7.32 Mark **one** answer

You have to treat someone for shock at the scene of an accident. You should

- reassure them constantly
- walk them around to calm them down
- give them something cold to drink
- cool them down as soon as possible

reassure them constantly

You should lay the casualty down and speak to them reassuringly. If possible, get someone else to call an ambulance to avoid leaving the casualty alone.

7.33 Mark **one** answer

You arrive at the scene of a motorcycle accident. No other vehicle is involved. The rider is unconscious, lying in the middle of the road. The first thing you should do is

- move the rider out of the road
- warn other traffic
- clear the road of debris
- give the rider reassurance

warn other traffic

The motorcyclist is in an extremely vulnerable position, exposed to further danger from traffic. The traffic needs to slow right down and be aware of the hazard in good time.

7.34 *Mark **one** answer*

You are giving mouth to mouth to a casualty. They are still not breathing on their own. You should

- give up if you think they are dead
- only keep trying for up to two minutes
- carry on until an ambulance arrives
- only keep trying for up to four minutes

carry on until an ambulance arrives

Make sure that someone has called the emergency services. They have the expertise and equipment to deal with the situation.

7.35 *Mark **one** answer*

When you are giving mouth to mouth you should only stop when

- you think the casualty is dead
- the casualty can breathe without help
- the casualty has turned blue
- you think the ambulance is coming

the casualty can breathe without help

Don't give up and never assume someone is dead. Look for signs of recovery and check the casualty's pulse.

7.36 *Mark **one** answer*

You arrive at an accident where someone is suffering from severe burns. You should

- apply lotions to the injury
- burst any blisters
- remove anything stuck to the burns
- douse the burns with cool liquid

douse the burns with cool liquid

Try to find fluid that is clean, cold and non-toxic. It will help to cool the burn and relieve the pain. Keep the wound doused for at least ten minutes. If blisters appear, don't attempt to burst them, as this could lead to infection.

7.37 Mark **two** answers

You arrive at the scene of an accident. A pedestrian has a severe bleeding wound on their leg, although it is not broken. What should you do?

- Dab the wound to stop bleeding
- Keep both legs flat on the ground
- Apply firm pressure to the wound
- Raise the leg to lessen bleeding
- Fetch them a warm drink

Apply firm pressure to the wound

Raise the leg to lessen bleeding

As soon as you can, check that the limb is not broken and that there is there is nothing in the wound. Then apply a pad to the wound with a bandage or a clean length of cloth. Raising the leg will lessen the flow of blood. Be aware that any restriction of blood circulation for more than a short period of time may result in long-term injury.

7.38 Mark **one** answer

You arrive at the scene of an accident. A passenger is bleeding badly from an arm wound. What should you do?

- Apply pressure over the wound and keep the arm down
- Dab the wound
- Get them a drink
- Apply pressure over the wound and raise the arm

Apply pressure over the wound and raise the arm

If possible, lay the casualty down. Raising the arm above the level of the heart will reduce the flow of blood. Check that the limb is not broken and that there is nothing in the wound before applying pressure over it.

7.39 Mark **one** answer

You arrive at the scene of an accident. A pedestrian is bleeding heavily from a leg wound, but the leg is not broken. What should you do?

- Dab the wound to stop the bleeding
- Keep both legs flat on the ground
- Apply firm pressure to the wound
- Fetch them a warm drink

Apply firm pressure to the wound

Lift the casualty's leg so that the wound is higher than their heart. This should reduce the flow of blood. Check that the limb is not broken and that there is nothing in the wound before applying pressure over it.

7.40 Mark **one** answer

At an accident a casualty is unconscious but still breathing. You should only move them if

- an ambulance is on its way
- bystanders advise you to
- there is further danger
- bystanders will help you to

there is further danger

Moving them could cause further injury. So it's important that this is only done if there is obvious danger to the casualty.

7.41 Mark **one** answer

At an accident you suspect a casualty has back injuries. The area is safe. You should

- offer them a drink
- not move them
- raise their legs
- offer them a cigarette

not move them

Talk to the casualty and keep them calm. If you attempt to move them it could cause further injury. Call an ambulance straight away.

7.42 Mark **one** answer

At an accident it is important to look after the casualty. When the area is safe, you should

- get them out of the vehicle
- give them a drink
- give them something to eat
- keep them in the vehicle

keep them in the vehicle

Don't move casualties who are trapped in vehicles unless they are in danger.

7.43 Mark three answers

You are stopped by a police officer. Which of the following documents are the police most likely to ask you to produce?

- Insurance certificate
- Vehicle registration document
- Road fund licence
- Theory test certificate
- Driving licence
- Test certificate (MOT)

- **Insurance certificate**
- **Driving licence**
- **Test certificate (MOT)**

These documents must be produced at the time when asked for. If you cannot do this you may be asked to take them to a police station within a specified time.

7.44 Mark one answer

At the scene of an accident a person has become hysterical. You should calm them by

- leaving them to quietly recover
- shouting at them loudly
- giving them a hot drink
- talking quietly and firmly to them

- **talking quietly and firmly to them**

Try to calm somebody who is hysterical by talking quietly and firmly to them.

7.45 Mark one answer

You are at an accident. Why may it be unwise to move a casualty?

- You could damage your back
- You could get blood on your hands
- You could be accused of an assault
- You could cause more injury

- **You could cause more injury**

Be especially careful about moving casualties at the scene of an accident. Inexperienced handling of a casualty could cause more injury, or even prove to be fatal.

7.46   *Mark **one** answer*

There has been an accident. The driver is in contact with live electrical cables. Do not touch the driver unless you can use

- a metal pole
- your bare hands
- a damp piece of cloth
- a length of wood

a length of wood

If you arrive at the scene of an accident, don't touch any casualties who are in contact with live electricity. You should use a dry non-conducting item, such as a wooden sweeping brush or plastic spade. You must not give first aid until you are sure the electrical contact has been broken.

7.47   *Mark **two** answers*

You are at the scene of an accident and someone's arm is bleeding heavily. How could you help stop the bleeding?

- Raise the arm
- Lower the arm
- Place firm pressure on the wound
- Keep the wound free from pressure

Raise the arm

Place firm pressure on the wound

If you notice the limb bleeding heavily, raise it to reduce the flow of blood. Put firm pressure on the wound without pressing on anything that may be caught in it.

7.48 *Mark **one** answer*

When using an emergency telephone on a motorway where should you stand?

- In front of the barrier
- Facing the oncoming traffic
- With your back to the traffic
- Looking towards the grass verge

Facing the oncoming traffic

Motorway phones are free and easily located. You should face the oncoming traffic while using them, so that you can see what is coming.

7.49 Mark **one** answer

Which type of fire extinguisher should NOT be used on flammable liquids?

- Water (red)
- Foam (cream)
- Dry powder (blue)
- Carbon Dioxide (black)

Water (red)

It's very important to know the correct fire extinguisher to use. They are usually painted red but will have a coloured label or badge relevant to their content. Make sure you learn which is which. Using the wrong one could be dangerous and may spread the fire further.

7.50 Mark **one** answer

You have a breakdown on a motorway. You cannot get fully onto the hard shoulder. What should you do?

- Stand at the edge of the carriageway to warn others
- Place a warning triangle in the lane behind your vehicle
- Wear a bright jacket and stand in the lane behind your vehicle
- Go straight to the nearest emergency telephone

Go straight to the nearest emergency telephone

Standing on or near the edge of the carriageway is very dangerous. Your first priority is to alert the emergency services by using an emergency roadside telephone. This connects directly to the police or the Highways Agency control centre. In most cases this is preferable to using a mobile as it will show your precise location.

7.51 Mark **one** answer

Your engine catches fire. Before attempting to put the fire out you should

- shut off the fuel supply
- open the engine housing wide
- drive to the nearest fire station
- empty the air tanks

shut off the fuel supply

An engine fire is serious enough, but if this reached the fuel tank the results would be disastrous. You should ensure that the fuel supply is cut off as your first priority.

7.52 Mark **one** answer

Before driving through a tunnel what should you do?

- Switch your radio off
- Remove your sunglasses
- Close your sunroof
- Switch on windscreen wipers

Remove your sunglasses

Before driving into a tunnel you should remove any sunglasses that you are wearing. If you don't, you'll find that your vision is restricted, even in tunnels that appear to be well lit.

7.53 Mark **one** answer

You are driving through a tunnel and the traffic is flowing freely. What should you do?

- Use parking lights
- Use front spot lights
- Use dipped headlights
- Use rear fog lights

Use dipped headlights

Before entering a tunnel you should switch on your dipped headlights, this will allow you to see and be seen. In many tunnels it is a legal requirement. Other precautions you can take before driving through a tunnel are to remove any sunglasses you are wearing and to tune your radio into a local channel.

7.54 Mark **one** answer

Before entering a tunnel it is good advice to

- put on your sunglasses
- check tyre pressures
- change to a lower gear
- tune your radio to a local channel

tune your radio to a local channel

On the approach to many tunnels a board will indicate a local channel or radio frequency that you should tune into. This should give a warning of any accidents or congestion in the tunnel ahead. Severe loss of life has occurred in recent tunnel fires. Getting advanced warning of problems ahead will help you to be prepared and to take appropriate action.

7.55 *Mark **one** answer*

You are driving through a congested tunnel and have to stop. What should you do?

- Pull up very close to the vehicle in front to save space
- Ignore any message signs as they're never up to date
- Keep a safe distance from the vehicle in front
- Do not switch on your hazard warning lights

Keep a safe distance from the vehicle in front

It's important to keep a safe distance from the vehicle in front at all times. This still applies in congested tunnels even if you are moving very slowly or have stopped. If the vehicle in front breaks down you may need room to manoeuvre past it.

7.56 *Mark **one** answer*

You are driving through a tunnel. Your vehicle breaks down. What should you do?

- Switch on hazard warning lights
- Remain in your vehicle
- Wait for the police to find you
- Rely on CCTV cameras seeing you

Switch on hazard warning lights

If your vehicle breaks down in a tunnel it could present a danger to other traffic. First switch on your hazard warning lights. If there are passengers in your vehicle take them to the nearest exit point. You should then call for help from an emergency telephone point. Don't rely on being found by the police or being seen by a CCTV camera. The longer a vehicle stays in an exposed position the more danger it poses to other traffic.

7.57 *Mark **one** answer*

Your vehicle catches fire while driving through a tunnel. It is still driveable. What should you do?

- Leave it where it is with the engine running
- Pull up, then walk to an emergency telephone point
- Park it away from the carriageway
- Drive it out of the tunnel if you can do so

Drive it out of the tunnel if you can do so

If it's possible, and you can do so without causing further danger, it's safer to drive a vehicle that's on fire out of a tunnel. The greatest danger in a tunnel fire is smoke and suffocation.

7.58 *Mark **one** answer*

You are driving through a tunnel in heavy traffic and it is very busy. What should you do?

- stay close to the vehicle in front to reduce congestion
- switch off your dipped headlights to reduce dazzle
- closely follow the tail lights of other vehicles
- follow instructions given by variable message signs

- **follow instructions given by variable message signs**

In congested tunnels you should always obey the instructions given by variable message signs and tunnel officials. Listen out for radio announcements and observe the road signs and signals. KEEP YOUR DISTANCE!

7.59 *Mark **one** answer*

A vehicle has rolled over and caught fire. The driver's hands and arms have been burned. You should NOT

- douse the burns with cold water
- lay the casualty down
- remove smouldering clothing
- remove anything sticking to the burns

- **remove anything sticking to the burns**

Do not remove anything sticking to a burn. You may cause further damage and introduce infection into the wound.

7.60 *Mark **two** answers*

At an accident a casualty has stopped breathing. You should

- remove anything that is blocking the mouth
- keep the head tilted forwards as far as possible
- raise the legs to help with circulation
- try to give the casualty something to drink
- tilt the head back very gently

- **remove anything that is blocking the mouth**
- **tilt the head back very gently**

These actions will ensure that the casualty has clear airways and is in the correct position if mouth-to-mouth resuscitation is required.

7.61 Mark **three** answers

To start mouth to mouth on a casualty you should

- tilt the head forward
- clear the airway
- turn them on their side
- tilt their head back very gently
- pinch the nostrils together
- put their arms across their chest

clear the airway

tilt their head back very gently

pinch the nostrils together

Use your finger to check for and move any obvious obstruction in the mouth. It's important to ensure that the airway is clear.

7.62 Mark **one** answer

You arrive at the scene of an accident. There has been an engine fire and someone's hands and arms have been burnt. You should NOT

- douse the burn thoroughly with cool liquid
- lay the casualty down
- remove anything sticking to the burn
- remove smouldering clothing

remove anything sticking to the burn

This could cause further damage and introduce infection to the wound. Your first priorities are to cool the burn and check the patient for shock.

7.63 Mark **one** answer NI EXEMPT

You have been involved in an accident and damaged some property. Your vehicle is still roadworthy. Nobody else is present. What should you do?

- Stop, then report the accident to the police within 24 hours
- Leave the scene. Do not report the accident if there are no witnesses
- Stop, then report the accident to the police after 48 hours
- Leave the scene. Do not report the accident if there were no injuries

Stop, then report the accident to the police within 24 hours

If you are involved in an accident that causes damage or injury to a person or property, you must stop. You are also obliged to give your details to anyone who has reasonable grounds to ask for them. If you don't do this, you must inform the police as soon as possible and in any case within 24 hours.

7.64 Mark **one** answer

You have an accident while driving through a tunnel. You are not injured but your vehicle cannot be driven. What should you do first?

- Rely on other drivers phoning for the police
- Switch off the engine and switch on hazard lights
- Take the names of witnesses and other drivers
- Sweep up any debris that is in the road

Switch off the engine and switch on hazard lights

If you are involved in an accident in a tunnel be aware of the danger this can cause to other traffic. You should immediately switch on your hazard lights and switch off your engine.

7.65 Mark **one** answer

While driving through a tunnel your vehicle catches fire. It cannot be driven. What should you do first?

- Wait for the police, tunnels are regularly patrolled
- Stay with your vehicle, you will be seen by the CCTV cameras
- Pull over to the side and switch off the engine
- Do not put out the fire, wait for the emergency services

Pull over to the side and switch off the engine

If your vehicle catches fire pull over to the side and as far away from other vehicles as possible. Warn other traffic by switching on your hazard warning lights.

7.66 Mark **one** answer

You are at the scene of an accident. Which of these is a symptom of shock?

- Flushed complexion
- Alertness
- Rapid pulse
- Slow breathing

Rapid pulse

The effects of shock may not be immediately obvious. Try to recognise the warning signs early. Prompt treatment can help to deal with it. Symptoms include, rapid pulse, pale grey skin, sweating and rapid shallow breathing.

7.67 *Mark **one** answer*

You are driving in a tunnel and your vehicle catches fire. What should you try to do FIRST?

- Drive out of the tunnel
- Pull over to the side of the tunnel
- Stop and extinguish the fire
- Stop and leave the vehicle immediately

Drive out of the tunnel

If your vehicle catches fire in a tunnel you should try to drive it out. Only attempt this if you can do so safely without endangering your passengers, others or yourself.

7.68 *Mark **one** answer*

What will be the likely result of incidents at work?

- More vehicles off the road
- Lower running costs
- Fewer missed customer orders
- Fewer workdays lost

More vehicles off the road

You should do all you can to avoid incidents at work. Otherwise companies suffer substantial lengths of downtime, as staff will need time off to recover. This leads to more vehicles off the road and lost business.

7.69 *Mark **one** answer*

You arrive at the scene of an incident, someone is hysterical. What should you do?

- Talk to them quietly and firmly
- Let them wander off to calm down
- Restrain them physically
- Shout loudly to get their attention

Talk to them quietly and firmly

A person who is hysterical may do things that you would not expect. Try to keep yourself and the casualty calm. Do not allow them to put themselves in any danger.

7.70 *Mark **one** answer*

You are at the scene of a traffic incident. Someone seems to be in shock. What are the symptoms?

- Rapid pulse and sweating
- Flushed complexion and deep breathing
- Slow pulse and dry skin
- Muscle spasms and an itchy rash

- **Rapid pulse and sweating**

Prompt treatment can help to deal with shock. Warning signs to look for include, rapid pulse, sweating, pale grey skin, and rapid shallow breathing.

7.71 *Mark **one** answer*

Your vehicle breaks down in a tunnel. What should you do?

- Stay in your vehicle and wait for the police
- Stand in the lane behind your vehicle to warn others
- Stand in front of your vehicle to warn oncoming drivers
- Switch on hazard lights then go and call for help immediately

- **Switch on hazard lights then go and call for help immediately**

A broken down vehicle in a tunnel can cause serious congestion and danger to other traffic and drivers. If your vehicle breaks down you should get help without delay. Switch on your hazard warning lights and then go to an emergency telephone point to call for help.

7.72 *Mark **three** answers*

At a traffic incident a casualty is unconscious. Which THREE of the following should you check urgently?

- Circulation
- Airway
- Shock
- Breathing
- Broken bones

- **Circulation**
- **Airway**
- **Breathing**

An unconscious casualty may have difficulty breathing. Check that their tongue has not fallen back, blocking their airway. Do this by gently tilting the head back. Check their airway, check for breathing and check their circulation. Compressions may then need to be given.

7.73 Mark **two** answers

You are at the scene of a collision. Some people are injured. Which TWO should you do IMMEDIATELY?

- Pull people who are hurt out of their vehicles
- Check the casualties for signs of bleeding
- Make sure the emergency services have been called
- Get the casualties to drink something sweet
- Clear a parking area for the emergency services

- **Check the casualties for signs of bleeding**
- **Make sure the emergency services have been called**

Always make sure that the emergency services have been called. If you have any first-aid skills use them, if not ask if any bystanders can help. Ask anyone who can't help to stand well back.

7.74 Mark **two** answers

There is a fire in your engine compartment. Which TWO of the following should you do?

- Open all windows
- Disconnect electrical leads
- Flag down a passing motorist
- Cut off the fuel supply
- Try to remove the load

- **Disconnect electrical leads**
- **Cut off the fuel supply**

If you suspect a fire, try to isolate the source. If at all possible, disconnect leads and cut off the fuel supply.

7.75 Mark **one** answer

Before driving a lorry loaded with toxic substances you MUST take training in

- using fire-fighting equipment
- operating a fork lift truck
- operating a lorry mounted crane
- using breathing apparatus

- **using fire-fighting equipment**

Vehicles carrying dangerous goods and other materials which may pose a hazard are subject to detailed emergency procedures. These must be followed. Appropriate firefighting equipment must be available and the driver trained in its use.

section **eight**

VEHICLE CONDITION

This section covers

- Wheels and tyres
- The principles of construction and function of large vehicles
- Vehicle coupling mechanisms
- Breakdowns

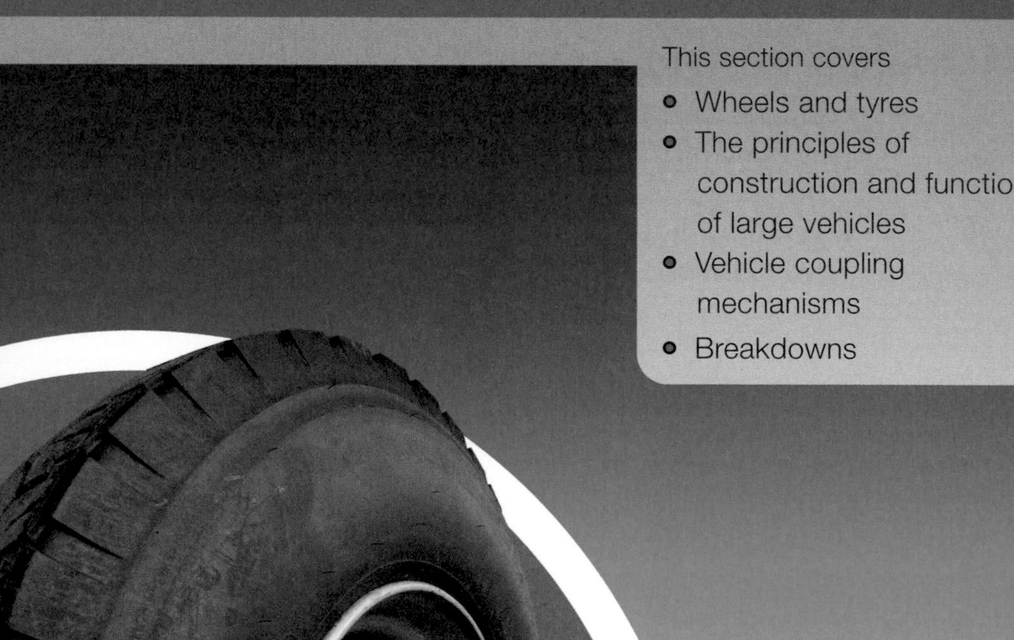

8.1

*Mark **one** answer*

You are driving a three-axle double-deck bus and using full steering lock. Why should you take extra care?

- Passengers might alter the angle of tilt
- The power steering might fail
- You may damage the air suspension
- You may scrub the rear tyres

You may scrub the rear tyres

The course the wheels take on tight corners should be observed and allowed for when driving. Very low speed is advisable when the steering is on full lock.

8.2

*Mark **one** answer*

You are driving a three-axle double-deck bus and using full steering lock. To avoid rear tyre scrub you should use

- the highest gear possible
- a very low speed
- the exhaust brake (retarder)
- a steering ball

a very low speed

When turning tight corners allow for the course the wheels will take. A very low speed is advisable when the steering is on full lock. This is to minimise any scrubbing effect on the rear tyres.

8.3

*Mark **one** answer*

On a double-deck bus, what is the minimum depth of tyre tread required over three-quarters of its width?

- 0.8 mm
- 1 mm
- 1.6 mm
- 2 mm

1 mm

It's essential that the tyres on your vehicle are in good condition. You must never forget that you have passengers on board. Their safety must be your priority. At no time should the depth of the tread be less than 1 mm over three-quarters of the width of the tyre.

8.4 Mark **one** answer

During your journey you notice that your coach's right rear indicator is not working. You should

- continue your journey using arm signals
- get it repaired before continuing
- get it repaired on your return to the depot
- get your passengers to their destination then repair it

- **get it repaired before continuing**

All lights must be in working order, even in daylight. A faulty right rear indicator could cause a serious accident if another motorist attempted to overtake as you changed lanes or turned right.

8.5  Mark **one** answer

Before each journey you should check all warning lights. What should you do if a warning light remains lit?

- Report the fault when you return
- Have the fault checked before setting off
- Have the fault checked at the next service
- Ignore it until the fault shows up

- **Have the fault checked before setting off**

Many buses and coaches have a large panel of warning lights on the dashboard. A system check built into the ignition system will allow you to check that all the warning light bulbs are working before starting your journey. Familiarise yourself with the layout so you know which system is faulty if a warning light becomes illuminated during a journey. Always seek professional help and advice.

8.6 Mark **one** answer

Why should you check your tyres more frequently on a coach with three axles?

- Because punctures can be more difficult to detect
- Because air pressure is more easily lost
- The wheels will need balancing more often
- You have no room for a spare wheel

- **Because punctures can be more difficult to detect**

Tyre checks should be made as a matter of routine. Inspect both the inside and the outside walls and the treads for sign of wear, damage, bulges, separation and exposed cords.

8.7 *Mark* ***one*** *answer*

Some buses have different size wheels on the front and rear. When driving at high speeds on long journeys what do you need to be aware of?

- The larger wheels are more likely to overheat
- The smaller wheels are more likely to overheat
- The larger wheels are more likely to lose pressure
- The smaller wheels are more likely to lose pressure

The smaller wheels are more likely to overheat

Because small wheels will need to rotate faster, they are more likely to overheat on long journeys at speed. Make sure you check them when you take rest stops.

8.8  *Mark* ***one*** *answer*

How frequently should a walk-round check be done?

- Daily
- Weekly
- Every 100 miles
- Every 1,000 miles

Daily

You should carry out a daily walk-round check as a routine. As a driver you have a legal responsibility for taking all reasonable precautions to ensure that legal requirements are met before driving any vehicle. change. Get into the habit of also making a visual check before you move off after rest stops, as well as before you start your journey.

8.9  *Mark* ***one*** *answer*

Your vehicle has a turbo engine. What should you do before switching it off?

- Release the air suspension valve
- Allow the engine to idle
- Select reverse gear
- Rev the engine up sharply

Allow the engine to idle

You should always allow engines fitted with turbos to idle for about a minute before stopping the engine. This prevents the bearings from being starved of oil.

8.10 Mark **one** answer

One of your passengers tells you they have noticed a wheel nut is missing. How often should you check them?

- At the end of every week
- At the start of every week
- Every day before starting out
- Only at every service interval

Every day before starting out

It's essential to make sure that all wheel nuts are tightened with a correctly calibrated torque wrench. The wheel nuts should be checked every day before starting your journey.

However, if one of your passengers tells you they have noticed a wheel nut is missing, check immediately. If there is a problem, don't move off until it has been rectified.

8.11 Mark **one** answer

You are parking your vehicle. It is fitted with a turbo engine. You should

- rev the engine up then switch it off
- switch the engine off immediately
- allow the engine to idle then switch it off
- switch the engine off and on repeatedly

allow the engine to idle then switch it off

Allowing engines fitted with turbos to idle for about a minute before stopping them prevents the turbo bearings from being starved of oil.

8.12 Mark **one** answer

You are on a very busy road and it is dark. Your headlights fail suddenly. The fuse box is on the outside of the bus on the right hand side. What should you do?

- Ask a passenger to watch for traffic
- Drive on without lights
- Fix the problem yourself
- Wait for the breakdown services

Wait for the breakdown services

Fast-moving traffic will be passing close by, so wait for the breakdown services to arrive. Their vehicle will provide safety protection while your vehicle is repaired or recovered.

8.13 Mark **one** answer

Your coach often tows a trailer. How often should you check the trailer tyres for pressure?

- at least once a week when they are cold
- at least once a month when they are hot
- at least once a week when they are hot
- at least once a month when fully laden

at least once a week when they are cold

Just like your bus tyres, your trailer tyres must be in good condition. You may not tow a trailer on every journey you make, but when you do, check the trailer tyres while they are cold and make sure they are suitable for the load they will carry.

8.14 Mark **one** answer

The bus you are driving is fitted with an automatic gearbox. When would you use kickdown?

- When stopping in an emergency
- When changing to a higher gear
- When driving at slow speed
- When needing brisk acceleration

When needing brisk acceleration

The kickdown facility on an automatic gearbox allows a lower gear to be engaged to allow rapid acceleration (for example, when overtaking). This is achieved by pressing the accelerator to the floor.

8.15 Mark **one** answer

Your coach is fully laden. You notice the steering feels heavy. What is the most likely reason?

- An icy road
- A burst rear tyre
- Faulty power steering
- Too many passengers

Faulty power steering

An engine-driven oil pump operates hydraulic rams which assist the movement of steering components. This helps you by reducing the effort required to steer a large vehicle.

8.16  *Mark **one** answer*

Frequent tyre checks are advised on tri-axle double-deck vehicles because

- their tyres are more likely to deflate
- punctures can be difficult to detect
- blow-outs are more common on these vehicles
- their tyre air pressures are difficult to maintain

- **punctures can be difficult to detect**

Frequent tyre checks are advisable on multi-axled vehicles. The inside wheels on the rear twin-axle are the most difficult to check. A deflated tyre will transfer the weight to the second tyre on a twin-axle pair and could cause it to burst as they are not designed to run on their own.

8.17 *Mark **one** answer*

The driver of a coach should always wear gloves when

- loading and stowing passengers' luggage
- operating a disabled passenger lift
- checking the fuel cut-off switch
- topping up the oil or water levels

- **topping up the oil or water levels**

Even the best maintained vehicles accumulate a certain amount of grime around the engine oil filler. By wearing gloves you can keep your hands and cuffs clean to present a smart appearance to your customers.

8.18 *Mark **two** answers*

The driver of a coach should always wear gloves when

- emptying the ticket machines
- emptying waste systems
- driving in cold weather
- driving a vehicle without power steering
- checking the fuel gauge
- checking battery levels

- **emptying waste systems**
- **checking battery levels**

A few simple precautions are necessary when carrying out regular maintenance tasks. Wearing gloves will help eliminate the risk of infections or conditions such as eczema or dermatitis.

8.19 *Mark **one** answer*

On a six-wheel double-deck bus, rear wheel punctures are

- much easier to detect
- more likely to happen
- more difficult to detect
- less likely to happen

more difficult to detect

The handling of a six-wheel bus or coach is not much different from a two-axle vehicle, except that punctures can be more difficult to detect.

8.20 *Mark **four** answers*

You must inspect all tyres on your bus for

- signs of wear
- overheating
- maker's details
- correct pressure
- 'dust cap' in place
- objects between twin tyres

signs of wear

overheating

correct pressure

objects between twin tyres

An unroadworthy vehicle will endanger the lives of your passengers. You should always make these essential checks as a matter of routine.

8.21 *Mark **one** answer*

Tyres which are over-inflated will

- give better acceleration
- wear unevenly and quicker
- give much better grip
- last much longer

wear unevenly and quicker

Your tyres must be in good condition and properly inflated to the manufacturer's recommended pressure. Surveys have shown that the tyres most likely to fail are those which have been over-inflated.

8.22 Mark **two** answers

When you are uncoupling a trailer you should

- disconnect the electrical line first
- unload at least some of the cargo
- choose a well-lit location
- apply the trailer brake first
- choose a firm level surface

- **apply the trailer brake first**
- **choose a firm level surface**

Before uncoupling a trailer always make sure that you have parked on firm, level ground and apply the trailer parking brake. Think SAFETY FIRST.

8.23 Mark **one** answer

It is dark and you are on a very busy road. Your headlights have failed. The fuse box is on the outside of the bus on the right-hand side. What should you do?

- Pull up on the left and call for assistance
- Drive on using sidelights at front and rear
- Try to fix the problem on your own
- Get a passenger to hold a torch for you

- **Pull up on the left and call for assistance**

Don't attempt to work on the right hand side of the vehicle at night without safety protection provided by a breakdown vehicle with flashing amber lights. Many accidents have occurred due to the close proximity of passing traffic.

8.24 Mark **three** answers

You are checking your vehicle's tyres before starting a long motorway drive. Each tyre should be checked for

- air pressure
- tracking
- tread wear
- tread pattern
- bulges
- valve clearance

- **air pressure**
- **tread wear**
- **bulges**

All tyres must be properly inflated and in good condition. Sometimes on motorways you can see the remains of tyres that have disintegrated due to a failure that might have been avoided if the tyre had been checked before the journey started.

8.25 *Mark* ***one*** *answer*

You notice that two wheel nuts are missing from one of the wheels. What should you do?

- Continue your journey
- Drive to the nearest tyre depot
- Use a nut from another wheel
- Park and phone for assistance

- **Park and phone for assistance**

If you notice any missing wheel nuts, park and phone for assistance. It's essential that all wheel fixings are tightened to the torque specified by the manufacturer, with an approved calibrated torque wrench. As a professional driver you must ensure that your vehicle is in serviceable condition at all times. Checks should be made before you leave on any journey, but make a visual check every time you start up again after a rest stop. Don't take risks by driving a defective vehicle.

8.26 *Mark* ***three*** *answers*

Which THREE of the following items would make a tyre illegal for a large vehicle?

- Different makes of tyres on the same axle
- A lump or bulge
- A deep cut more than 25 mm (1 inch) long
- An exposed ply or cord
- Recut tyres
- A tread depth of 1.3 mm

- **A lump or bulge**
- **A deep cut more than 25 mm (1 inch) long**
- **An exposed ply or cord**

You should check your tyres as part of your routine check of the vehicle. A damaged or worn tyre can have a major effect on handling and will make your vehicle a danger to you and other road users. It's also an offence to drive with one or more tyres that have these defects.

8.27 Mark **one** answer

In very cold weather moisture may freeze in your vehicle's air storage tanks. Which of the following would help to prevent this?

- Covering the air tanks with a blanket
- Draining the tanks daily
- Using the brakes frequently
- Pumping the brakes

Draining the tanks daily

In very cold weather moisture can build up in the storage tanks and freeze. Ice can form in the pipes and this will result in loss of pressure or brake failure. Make sure that you drain the tanks daily as part of a routine. Most modern vehicles are fitted with automatic bleed valves. Check that they're working properly and that air-drying systems are effective.

8.28 Mark **one** answer

What does this warning light on the instrument panel mean?

- Low oil pressure
- Battery discharge
- Braking system fault
- Door open

Braking system fault

You should be familiar with all warning lights and buzzers fitted to your vehicle. If you're driving the vehicle for the first time ensure that you know the function of each. If the brake warning light indicates a fault in the system, stop as soon as it's safe to do so. Report the fault, and don't continue until it has been corrected.

8.29 Mark **one** answer

You are driving along a motorway. The brake low-pressure warning device starts to operate. What should you do?

- Stop immediately in the lane you are in
- Continue slowly to the next service area
- Pull up on the hard shoulder as soon as possible
- Leave the motorway at the next exit

Pull up on the hard shoulder as soon as possible

You should never take chances with the braking system. Pull up well to the left on the hard shoulder. Don't even attempt minor repairs on the motorway. Put on the hazard warning lights. Contact the police using the nearest emergency telephone. They will contact a recovery contractor for you.

8.30 Mark one answer

Your vehicle has broken down at night on a two-way road. You should try to park your vehicle

- on the left of the road
- partly on the pavement
- on a grass verge
- on the right of the road

on the left of the road

You must ensure that your vehicle can be seen by other road users. Your reflectors should show red to the rear.

8.31 Mark *one* answer

Whilst driving, your power-assisted steering suddenly fails. What should you do?

- Continue driving to the nearest repair centre
- Return to the depot
- Continue your journey at a slower speed
- Park and seek assistance

Park and seek assistance

Faulty power steering will make your steering wheel very difficult or almost impossible to turn. To continue driving could cause danger to you and other road users. You should park safely and get assistance.

8.32 Mark *two* answers

Whilst driving your steering suddenly becomes heavy to turn. What could this indicate?

- A puncture in a front tyre
- Loss of air brake pressure
- A faulty parking brake
- A failure of power-assisted steering

A puncture in a front tyre

A failure of power-assisted steering

The power-assisted steering may have failed if the steering becomes heavy. It is also possible that your vehicle has a puncture or the load might have shifted. In any case you should stop safely, investigate the cause, then seek assistance.

8.33 Mark *one* answer

What should you do if the brake pedal becomes 'hard'?

- Continue to drive and report it at the end of the day
- Pump the brake pedal continuously
- Drain the air tanks and then continue
- Park and telephone for assistance

Park and telephone for assistance

Don't take risks. As soon as you detect a fault on your vehicle you must take action. Where the brakes are concerned, always park and get assistance. Always report minor faults as soon as you detect them. Minor faults can become major ones if they aren't repaired quickly.

8.34 Mark *one* answer

Air tanks on brake systems require draining because

- excess coolant may collect in them
- rain water can often seep in
- any engine leakages are directed here
- of moisture drawn in from the atmosphere

of moisture drawn in from the atmosphere

This moisture condenses in the air and can be transmitted around a vehicle's braking system. This is especially dangerous in cold weather, as it can lead to ice building up in the valves and pipes.

8.35 Mark *one* answer

Whilst checking your vehicle you discover an air leak in the braking system. What should you do?

- Drive slowly to the nearest garage
- Check the leak from time to time on your journey
- Leave it parked and report it immediately
- Start your journey and report it on your return

Leave it parked and report it immediately

Under no circumstances should you attempt to move or drive a vehicle with an air leak in the braking system. Report the fault immediately, or arrange to have it repaired. Place a warning sign in a prominent position in the cab informing other drivers to prevent them unwittingly moving the vehicle.

8.36 *Mark **one** answer*

You are driving a large vehicle. A loud buzzer sounds in the cab. This is most likely to indicate low

- oil pressure
- air pressure
- tyre pressure
- fuel level

air pressure

Warning buzzers are linked to many systems on modern vehicles. A warning light on the dashboard may help you identify the system that has caused the problem. Under no circumstances should you continue driving until the fault has been identified and rectified. Seek professional assistance if necessary.

8.37 *Mark **one** answer*

How much of the width of a tyre must have the legal limit of tread depth?

- One-quarter
- One-half
- Five-eighths
- Three-quarters

Three-quarters

The condition of the tyres on your vehicle will contribute to its overall stability. Don't leave your tyres until their tread is at the minimum depth. Renew them before they get into that state. Ensuring that the tread is always deep enough will maintain your tyres' grip on the road.

8.38 *Mark **two** answers*

As a professional driver of large vehicles, why should you carry spare bulbs?

- To fix any fault for the safety of yourself
- Because bulbs are more likely to blow when your vehicle is loaded
- To repair the lights for the sake of other road users
- Because bulbs are more likely to blow when your vehicle is empty

To fix any fault for the safety of yourself

To repair the lights for the sake of other road users

Keep a stock of all the various bulbs used on your vehicle. This could save you wasting time trying to locate a spare bulb.

8.39 Mark **one** answer

At very low temperatures diesel fuel will become less effective unless

- ⊙ anti-freeze is added
- ⊙ anti-waxing additives are added
- ⊙ petrol is added
- ⊙ paraffin is added

⊙ **anti-waxing additives are added**

In extremely cold weather, you will have to use diesel fuel with anti-waxing additives to stop fuel lines freezing up. During the winter months this is usually put in by the fuel companies.

8.40 Mark **one** answer

You are about to start a long journey midway through the day. You find that your headlights are not working but you still have sidelights. What should you do?

- ⊙ Don't drive until they are mended
- ⊙ Drive only until light begins to fade
- ⊙ Avoid driving on motorways after dark
- ⊙ Drive only if the weather is good

⊙ **Don't drive until they are mended**

To comply with the law, all lights must be in good working order, even in daylight when they are not being used. Check and make sure that everything is working before you set off. You may need to use your headlights or other lights if you are delayed or find yourself driving in conditions of reduced visibility.

8.41 Mark **one** answer

Before starting a journey you want to check your brake system warning lights. On some vehicles these are not operated by the ignition switch. What else can you do?

- ⊙ Look for a 'check' switch on the dashboard
- ⊙ Get someone behind to check your brake lights
- ⊙ Check them at the end of your journey
- ⊙ Pump the brake pedal a number of times

⊙ **Look for a 'check' switch on the dashboard**

A warning lights system check is sometimes performed automatically when the ignition is switched on, but you may need to do this manually by operating a separate 'check' switch. Never start a journey without doing this. If there is a problem, have it properly checked out before you set off.

8.42 Mark **one** answer

On motorways you are usually driving at higher speeds for long distances. What effect can this have on your tyres?

- They may overheat and disintegrate
- They will be more liable to punctures
- They will lose air pressure more quickly
- They will become very slippery

They may overheat and disintegrate

Driving at higher speeds and for longer periods, such as on motorways, can cause your tyres to overheat and disintegrate. You should make a point of checking them when you stop for a break.

8.43 Mark **one** answer

You notice one of your tyres has a bulge in the side. Why should you not drive the vehicle?

- Your tachograph reading will not be accurate
- Your speedometer will give an incorrect reading
- It will make the vehicle unsteady on corners
- At speed, the tyre could overheat and burst

At speed, the tyre could overheat and burst

Your tyres must all be in good condition before you start any journey. Make sure that you inspect them before setting off and at regular intervals.

8.44 Mark **one** answer

The purpose of a pre-heating device is to heat the

- cab
- gearbox
- engine
- seat

engine

Most diesel engines have pre-heaters which heat the glow plugs in the cylinders to assist in starting when cold. The starter should only be operated when the indicator light goes out.

8.45 Mark **one** answer

A high-pressure fuel injector delivers fuel into the

- carburettors
- cylinders
- camshaft
- crankshaft

cylinders

Most diesel engines use a high-pressure fuel injector system which will deliver pressurised fuel directly into the cylinders of the engine. This system is known as a direct injection engine.

8.46 Mark **one** answer

Why is it most important to avoid overfilling the engine oil level?

- It could leave an oil stain on the road
- It will increase the amount of exhaust gases
- It could increase oil pressure and cause damage
- It will damage the exhaust system

It could increase oil pressure and cause damage

Too much oil in an engine can be just as bad as too little. Overfilling an engine can create excess pressure, cause oil leakage through seals and result in expensive damage.

8.47 Mark **one** answer

Why should you use an approved coolant solution in your engine?

- To prevent the engine freezing
- For easier starting from cold
- To prevent the air tank from freezing
- For effective cab heating

To prevent the engine freezing

Coolant also contains a corrosion inhibitor which prolongs the life of the cooling system. Remember to check the coolant level regularly.

8.48 *Mark **one** answer*

When replacing a tubeless tyre it is good practice to

- fit the same valve
- replace the valve
- have the valve checked
- clean the valve

replace the valve

Always get expert advice when dealing with tyres. It is good practice to have a new valve fitted when replacing a tubeless tyre. Good garages and specialist tyre services know the regulations.

8.49 *Mark **one** answer*

You should check the oil level when your engine is

- running
- cold
- warm
- hot

cold

Oil is vital for lubrication of the engine and should be checked regularly and topped up as necessary. You should always check oil levels when the engine is cold and your vehicle is parked on the level.

8.50 *Mark **one** answer*

When should anti-freeze be used in the cooling system?

- In winter only
- All year round
- In summer only
- When starting from cold

All year round

Today all water cooled vehicles use a mixture of water and anti-freeze to make up the coolant. As well as helping to keep the engine at its correct operating temperature, it also acts as a corrosion inhibitor to prolong the life of the cooling system.

8.51   *Mark **one** answer*

What does this warning light on the instrument panel mean?

- ⊙ Low fuel pressure
- ⊙ Low oil pressure
- ⊙ Low water pressure
- ⊙ Low air pressure

⊙ **Low oil pressure**

You should be familiar with all warning lights fitted to your vehicle. The oil warning light indicates low oil pressure or lack of oil. If it lights up, report the fault and do not continue until it has been corrected.

8.52   *Mark **one** answer*

As you are driving the ignition warning light comes on. What does it warn of?

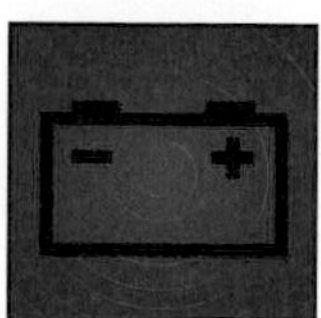

- ⊙ Low oil pressure
- ⊙ An electrical fault
- ⊙ Low air pressure
- ⊙ A hydraulic fault

⊙ **An electrical fault**

The ignition light should go out when the engine has started. If it shows when driving, this indicates an electrical fault of some kind.

8.53    *Mark **one** answer*

Codes are shown on the side walls of bus and lorry tyres. What do these refer to?

- ⊙ Tread pattern
- ⊙ Minimum temperature
- ⊙ Maximum load
- ⊙ Running pressure

⊙ **Maximum load**

Tyres have codes shown on the wall of the tyre. These refer to the maximum load and speed capability of the tyre.

8.54 *Mark **one** answer*

Regular maintenance and servicing will

- prevent unnecessary breakdowns
- increase fuel bills
- allow heavier loads to be carried
- reduce insurance premiums

prevent unnecessary breakdowns

You can reduce the chance of a breakdown with preventive maintenance and regular checks.

8.55 *Mark **one** answer*

Before changing a wheel on your vehicle you should

- leave the parking brake off
- use chocks if available
- dismantle the wheel and tyre
- get someone to check the other tyres

use chocks if available

Always make sure your vehicle is secure and level before a wheel is changed. Apply the parking brake and make sure chocks are used if available. All wheel nuts/studs should be re-tightened to the correct torque. On a motorway, never attempt to change a wheel yourself. Use the emergency phones to call for assistance.

8.56 *Mark **one** answer*

You have had to change a wheel on your vehicle. When should you next check the wheel nuts?

- At the next service interval
- When they are cold
- When they are hot
- Shortly afterwards

Shortly afterwards

When refitting a wheel the nuts/studs should be re-tightened to the correct torque. They should be rechecked after about 30 minutes if the vehicle has remained stationary, or after about 40 to 80 km (25 to 50 miles) of driving.

8.57 Mark **one** answer

A new engine has just been fitted to your vehicle. Why may it be necessary to bleed the fuel system?

- To increase the speed of your vehicle
- To remove any trapped air
- Because it is illegal not to do so
- Because it may cause the tank to freeze

To remove any trapped air

This may be necessary to remove any airlocks that have become trapped in the fuel line.

8.58 Mark **one** answer

When may it become necessary to bleed the fuel system to remove any trapped air?

- When the engine has not been run for some time
- When you intend to carry unusually heavy loads
- When the engine keeps over heating
- When you wish to change the taxation on your vehicle

When the engine has not been run for some time

If your vehicle has been standing for some time it may be necessary to remove any trapped air that has built up. This will prevent any airlocks in the fuel lines.

8.59 Mark **one** answer

Using poor quality diesel fuel may lead to

- better fuel economy
- lower exhaust emissions
- longer service intervals
- early blockage of a fuel injector

early blockage of a fuel injector

Never use poor quality diesel fuel: not only is it likely to cause early blockage of the fuel injector, it may also lead to increased wear of the injector pump.

8.60 Mark **three** answers

Which of these components are generally found in an internal combustion engine?

- crankshaft
- propshaft
- crown wheel
- cylinder
- differential
- piston

- **crankshaft**
- **cylinder**
- **piston**

It can be helpful to understand how your vehicle works. Having some basic mechanical knowledge may help you to identify any faults that develop while you're driving.

8.61 Mark **one** answer

Breakdowns can be reduced by

- driving slowly
- regular servicing
- regular cleaning
- avoiding bad weather

- **regular servicing**

Being aware of components wearing out or requiring replacement will help prevent costly breakdowns. You should follow the manufacturer's guidelines for service intervals.

8.62 Mark **one** answer

Why should your engine oil be changed at the recommended intervals?

- To reduce friction and wear
- For better steering control
- To prevent oil leaks
- To improve clutch wear

- **To reduce friction and wear**

The oil and filter will get dirty in normal use. Following the service interval guidance will ensure that your engine will remain protected and properly lubricated and be less likely to break down.

8.63 Mark **one** answer

Where should you check your engine oil level?

- On sloping ground
- On a steep gradient
- On level ground
- On a downhill slope

On level ground

It's no good checking the engine oil level when your vehicle is standing on a slope. You will not see an accurate reading on the dipstick.

8.64 Mark **one** answer

You overfill your engine with oil. What could this cause?

- Better handling
- Lower emissions
- Damaged gaskets
- Longer service intervals

Damaged gaskets

If you overfill the engine with oil you could cause the engine to build up too much pressure when it is running. This could cause damage to oil seals and gaskets.

8.65 Mark **one** answer

When uncoupling a trailer the very FIRST thing you must do is

- lower the trailer legs to the ground
- apply the parking brake
- release the brake air lines
- uncouple the electrical lines

apply the parking brake

Before leaving the cab it is very important to secure the vehicle by applying the vehicle parking brake. After leaving the cab apply the trailer parking brake.

8.66 Mark **one** answer

You are uncoupling a trailer. Before disconnecting any of the airlines, you MUST

- drain the air tanks
- apply the trailer parking brake
- lower the landing gear
- disconnect the electrical line

apply the trailer parking brake

Whenever you drop or pick up a trailer you must always work through the process methodically to avoid causing danger to yourself or other people.

8.67 *Mark **one** answer*

When should you check the wheel nuts on your vehicle?

- Just before any journey
- Only before long trips
- Only every 1000 miles (1600 km)
- Just before a major service

Just before any journey

Always have a walk round and visually check wheel nuts whenever you take a break. It's important after a wheel has been replaced to recheck the wheel nuts shortly after their initial tightening. Wheel nuts must always be tightened to the torque specified by the manufacturer.

8.68 *Mark **one** answer*

In your vehicle the oil pump is usually driven directly from the

- oil filter
- prop shaft
- piston valves
- engine

engine

The oil pump is driven directly from the engine so that as the engine turns, oil is fed to the bearings quickly. This is important when first starting an engine to prevent damage to the bearings due to insufficient lubrication.

8.69 *Mark **one** answer*

Thick black smoke is coming from the exhaust of your vehicle. You should

- continue on to the nearest garage
- return to your depot and report the problem
- stop in a safe place and get help
- drive slowly with your hazard warning lights on

stop in a safe place and get help

Causing excessive smoke is an offence and could contribute to causing an incident or collision. Mechanical defects could become dangerous if ignored. You could also end up creating traffic chaos if your vehicle breaks down in a difficult location.

8.70 Mark **two** answers

You hit the kerb at speed. You should, as soon as possible, check your vehicle for any damage to the

- exhaust
- brakes
- tyres
- steering
- lights

- **tyres**
- **steering**

Hitting the kerb at speed can split the tyre or put the steering and suspension geometry out of alignment. You should have it checked as soon as possible, as a sudden puncture in a front tyre could result in a loss of steering control and a serious accident.

8.71 Mark **one** answer

Which of the following is most likely to cause a burst tyre when driving?

- Frequent gear changing in varying conditions
- Running at a constant high speed
- Always operating in cool weather
- Mixing tyres with different tread depth

- **Running at a constant high speed**

Tyres can become very hot and disintegrate under sustained high-speed running. Check for excessive heat when you stop for a break.

8.72 Mark **one** answer

When can a 'selective' or 'block' gear change be used?

- To change gear down only
- To change gear up only
- To change gear to a low speed only
- To change gear either up or down

- **To change gear either up or down**

Recognising the opportunities to make selective gear changes can reduce driver effort. Planning ahead will enable you to make the most of any opportunities to put this into practice.

8.73 *Mark **one** answer*

You are driving a vehicle which has a two-speed axle. This

- halves the number of gears
- doubles the number of gears
- engages the diff-lock
- releases the diff-lock

doubles the number of gears

An electrical switch actuates a mechanism in the rear axle which doubles the choice of gear ratios. This can significantly improve the performance of a heavily-laden vehicle.

8.74 *Mark **one** answer*

On a vehicle with automatic transmission you would use 'kickdown' to

- give quicker acceleration
- apply the emergency brakes
- stop more smoothly
- go down a steep hill

give quicker acceleration

Dependent upon road speed, depressing the accelerator pedal firmly to the floor will activate a switch which allows the gearbox to select a lower gear for improved acceleration.

8.75 *Mark **one** answer*

You are driving a modern vehicle. You notice the steering feels heavy. What is the most likely cause?

- Faulty power steering
- An icy road
- A burst rear tyre
- A wet road

Faulty power steering

Many large vehicles are fitted with power-assisted steering. Any fault should be investigated and repaired as soon as possible.

8.76 Mark **one** answer

Your vehicle suffers a tyre blow-out. What is likely to create a hazard for other road users?

- Scattered debris
- Skid marks
- Suspension failure
- Axle damage

Scattered debris

When a tyre explodes, fragments are thrown over a wide area. This can create a serious hazard for other drivers. Always check your tyre pressures and look for cuts or damage to the tyres. Frequent checks and proper maintenance can prevent a blow-out.

8.77 Mark **one** answer NI EXEMPT

The Vehicle and Operator Services Agency (VOSA) and the police carry out spot checks of vehicle condition. If serious defects are found the vehicle is

- impounded until a new driver is found
- restricted to 30 mph for the remainder of the journey
- prohibited from further use until the defects are rectified
- ordered back to the depot to unload goods or passengers

prohibited from further use until the defects are rectified

The Vehicle and Operator Services Agency (VOSA) or police can order an immediate prohibition. Details are always notified to the traffic commissioners. Drivers must NOT use vehicles which they know to be faulty.

8.78 Mark **one** answer NI EXEMPT

A vehicle is found to have serious defects at a Vehicle and Operator Services Agency (VOSA) spot-check. It is prohibited from further use. Who will be notified of the details?

- The Driver and Vehicle Licencing Agency
- The Traffic Commissioner
- The Road Transport Industry Training Body
- The bus coach and commercial vehicle council

The Traffic Commissioner

The Vehicle and Operator Services Agency (VOSA) and the police carry out frequent spot checks of vehicle condition. Where serious defects are found the vehicle is prohibited from further use until the defects are rectified, and details of the prohibition are notified to the Traffic Commissioner.

8.79 Mark **one** answer

You should check your engine oil level regularly. Failure to do this could cause your engine to

- run faster
- break down
- use less fuel
- produce more power

break down

As well as being very expensive to mend, a damaged engine could also cause sudden and unexpected loss of control. This could put you and other road users in danger. If your engine seizes while you are driving you should make every effort to pull up in a safe place.

8.80 Mark **one** answer

While driving, your engine oil warning light comes on. Why could it be dangerous to continue driving?

- The engine will get hot
- The engine may be damaged
- You will need to have the vehicle serviced
- You will need to replace the carburettor

The engine may be damaged

Apart from being very expensive, a seized engine could cause your vehicle to suffer sudden and unexpected loss of control, possibly stopping in a dangerous position and putting you and other road users in danger.

8.81 Mark **one** answer

Bus and lorry tyres have codes on the side wall. What do these refer to?

- Running pressure
- Speed capability
- Minimum temperature
- Tread depth

Speed capability

Codes are shown on the wall of the tyre. These refer to the maximum load and speed capability of the tyre.

8.82 Mark **one** answer

Energy-saving tyres have

- increased tread depth
- reduced rolling resistance
- reduced tread depth
- increased rolling resistance

reduced rolling resistance

When changing or fitting new tyres, consider buying energy-saving tyres. These have a reduced rolling resistance, are more economical and give improved efficiency.

8.83 Mark **two** answers

You have replaced a tyre. What precautions should you take when tightening the wheel nuts?

- Only use a wheel brace
- Fully tighten each wheel nut before going on to the next
- Use a calibrated torque wrench
- Only use an air-operated power tool
- Fit and tighten the wheel nuts gradually and diagonally

Use a calibrated torque wrench

Fit and tighten the wheel nuts gradually and diagonally

After the tyre has been replaced and the wheel is being refitted you should tighten the wheel nuts/studs gradually and diagonally across the wheel using a calibrated torque wrench.

8.84 Mark **one** answer

Using poor-quality diesel fuel may lead to

- better fuel economy
- increased wear of the injection pump
- longer service intervals
- lower exhaust emissions

increased wear of the injection pump

Never use poor quality diesel fuel, it may lead to early failure of the injection pump and could also cause blockage in a fuel injector. It could also lead to additional environmental pollution.

8.85 Mark **three** answers

Energy-saving tyres work because they

- have reduced rolling resistance
- cost less to produce
- have no tread pattern
- never puncture at high speed
- increase fuel efficiency
- improve grip

- **have reduced rolling resistance**
- **increase fuel efficiency**
- **improve grip**

Energy-saving tyres keep fuel costs down because they have lower rolling resistance and better grip than ordinary tyres. You should consider this when replacing your tyres.

8.86 Mark **one** answer

Advice about carrying out minor repairs can be obtained from

- DVLA guidance notes
- EC and UK Directives
- the Health and Safety Executive
- the owner's handbook

- **the owner's handbook**

The handbook for your vehicle will clearly explain what work or maintenance the driver could carry out. Always refer to it and comply with the safety guidance that it contains.

8.87 Mark **one** answer

Where can you get advice about carrying out minor repairs?

- Workshop manuals
- DVLA guidance notes
- EC and UK Directives
- The Health and Safety Executive

- **Workshop manuals**

Workshop manuals are available for detailed technical advice about the servicing, maintenance and repair of your vehicle. They are essential for anyone who intends to service or repair their own vehicle.

8.88 Mark **one** answer

Overfilling your engine with oil could result in

- loss of power
- lower emissions
- better handling
- longer service intervals

loss of power

If the oil level is too high, the moving parts of an engine could hit the oil, causing a loss of power or engine damage. Another problem of overfilling can be excess pressure which may damage oil seals and cause leaks.

8.89 Mark **one** answer

What is the purpose of the oil filter?

- To prevent the engine over-heating
- To give better fuel consumption
- To prevent the engine over-revving
- To collect sediment from the oil

To collect sediment from the oil

As the lubricating oil is pumped around the engine it collects tiny fragments of metal from the moving parts. The oil filter is designed to remove these fragments. Most filters are designed to be replaced at service intervals.

8.90 Mark **one** answer

The oil level in your engine should normally be checked when the engine is

- hot
- revving
- cold
- idling

cold

To get the most accurate reading, manufacturers advise that engine oil levels should be checked when cold.

8.91 Mark **one** answer

When fitting a road wheel which tool is essential?

- Torque wrench
- Ring spanner
- Open-end spanner
- Adjustable wrench

Torque wrench

It's essential that all wheel nuts are tightened to the specified torque, with a calibrated torque wrench. The wheel nuts, fixings, and markers, should be checked every day before starting your journey.

8.92 Mark **one** answer

You are driving a diesel-engined vehicle. The weather conditions suddenly turn very cold. The engine begins to run erratically. What is the most likely cause of this?

- The endurance brake coming on
- The air conditioning not working
- The speed limiter operating
- The fuel partly solidifying

The fuel partly solidifying

In winter if diesel fuel becomes very cold it can partially solidify. During winter additives are used by the fuel companies to try to prevent this. Any solidifying (waxing) of the fuel can prevent it flowing properly and cause the engine to run erratically or even stop.

8.93 Mark **one** answer

Your vehicle is fitted with heated fuel lines. This is especially useful in cold conditions to prevent the

- cab temperature dropping
- radiator from freezing
- windows becoming misty
- diesel from partially solidifying

diesel from partially solidifying

In cold weather the diesel fuel can solidify, this is known as waxing. This prevents the fuel from flowing properly and could cause the engine to run badly or even stop.

8.94 Mark **one** answer

Before setting off you should do a daily walk-round check. What is this for?

- To check your route
- To check for any parking violations
- To check your schedule
- To check for any defects

To check for any defects

You have a legal responsibility to make sure that your vehicle is fully roadworthy. The daily walk-round checks give you the chance to look for any defects.

8.95 Mark **one** answer

What happens to diesel fuel when it gets hot?

- It expands
- It liquefies
- It shrinks
- It waxes

It expands

On a hot day the fuel in your tank will expand. If this happens and the tank is filled to the brim it will spill onto the road. This can be very dangerous or even fatal for other road users especially motorcyclists. DON'T FILL YOUR TANK TO THE BRIM!

8.96 Mark **one** answer

Vehicle operators MUST have an effective system in place for drivers to

- report vehicle defects
- report all motorway hold ups
- inform operators of their progress
- inform operators about traffic delays

report vehicle defects

The operator must have a system in place, so that drivers can report defects and have them repaired properly.

8.97 Mark **one** answer

Your oil pressure warning light comes on while you are driving. What should you do?

- Wait until your next service interval and tell the mechanic
- Ignore the light, it is not the driver's responsibility
- Stop and check the oil level as soon as it is safe to do so
- Continue with your journey but have it checked on your arrival

Stop and check the oil level as soon as it is safe to do so

The oil pressure light gives you a warning that something is wrong with the lubrication system. If it lights up there may be a serious fault which could lead to serious and expensive engine damage. Even if the oil level is correct you should still seek expert help or advice.

8.98 *Mark **one** answer*

What is the main reason for cleaning your wheels and tyres when leaving a building site?

- It helps to keep the tyres in good condition
- So that the tyres will not cause damage to the road surface
- So that air pressure will not leak from the tyre valves
- It is illegal for you to spread mud on the road

- **It is illegal for you to spread mud on the road**

If your wheels leave mud on the road you must arrange for it to be cleared. A slippery, muddy surface could cause danger to other road users.

8.99 *Mark **one** answer*

You should look at the rear wheels before leaving a building site to check that

- the diff-lock is engaged
- the diff-lock is disengaged
- the load-sensing valve is working
- bricks are not wedged between them

- **bricks are not wedged between them**

Bricks will damage the tyres and could be thrown out as you increase your road speed, which could be dangerous to the drivers of following vehicles.

8.100 *Mark **one** answer*

You are driving on a muddy building site. Before driving on normal road surfaces you should

- disengage the diff-lock
- engage the diff-lock
- apply the steering lock
- disengage the twist lock

- **disengage the diff-lock**

Attempting to drive at normal speeds with the diff-lock engaged is dangerous; it will severely affect your steering control. The diff-lock is designed to be used in slippery conditions, at low speed.

8.101 Mark **one** answer

You are driving a lorry along a motorway. You notice that tread is coming away from one of your tyres. What should you do?

- Stop on the hard shoulder and phone for assistance
- Stop on the hard shoulder and change the wheel
- Continue driving to the next service station
- Continue driving and leave by the next exit

Stop on the hard shoulder and phone for assistance

It's dangerous to drive a defective vehicle. Continuous high speeds on the motorway can cause the tyres to become hot and shred. If you notice this in your mirrors you must stop on the hard shoulder as soon as it's safe to do so.

If you're on a motorway and you notice any defect on your vehicle, you must stop on the hard shoulder as soon as it's safe. Use the emergency telephone for assistance.

8.102 Mark **one** answer

What is the MINIMUM depth of tread required over three-quarters of the breadth of a lorry tyre?

- 1 mm
- 1.5 mm
- 2.5 mm
- 5 mm

1 mm

Your tyres are your only contact with the road. It's essential that this contact gives you the grip you need to control your vehicle at all times. If the weather is wet or icy your tyres' grip may be reduced.

8.103 Mark **one** answer

After recoupling a trailer, which of the following should you do LAST?

- Connect the brake lines
- Release the trailer parking brake
- Connect the electrical lines
- Raise the trailer legs

Release the trailer parking brake

It's important to work methodically when uncoupling or recoupling a tractor unit and trailer. After recoupling, check that all connections, systems and lights are working correctly.

8.104 *Mark one answer*

Your lorry coupling system (fifth wheel) should be checked and lubricated

- only prior to an MOT
- every 6 months
- yearly
- regularly

regularly

Maintenance of the fifth wheel should be carried out regularly, ideally monthly or every 10,000 km.

8.105 *Mark **one** answer*

You are driving a new articulated lorry which is fully laden. You notice the steering feels heavy. What is the most likely reason?

- The road is icy
- Faulty power steering
- A tyre on the trailer has burst
- The load on the trailer has shifted

Faulty power steering

Any suspected failure of the power steering should be investigated as soon as possible. Many large vehicles can become undriveable if it fails completely.

8.106 *Mark **one** answer*

Wheel nuts should be checked shortly after

- driving down a steep hill
- initial tightening
- driving on a motorway
- unloading

initial tightening

Always recheck wheel nuts shortly after their initial tightening. Make sure they are tightened to the torque specified by the manufacturer.

8.107 *Mark* ***one*** *answer*

A fifth wheel coupling relies on which of the following connecting devices?

- ⊙ Suzie
- ⊙ Kingpin
- ⊙ D link
- ⊙ Eyelet

⊙ **Kingpin**

It is important to check that the kingpin locking mechanism is secure when recoupling. You should do this by attempting to move forward with the trailer brake applied. Also remember to connect the dog-clip.

8.108 *Mark* ***one*** *answer*

What would you secure with a dog-clip?

- ⊙ Kingpin release handle
- ⊙ Electric cables
- ⊙ Parking brake
- ⊙ Differential lock

⊙ **Kingpin release handle**

When re-coupling you must connect the dog-clip to secure the kingpin release handle.

8.109 *Mark* ***one*** *answer*

How frequently should the components of a fifth wheel coupling be inspected?

- ⊙ Daily
- ⊙ Weekly
- ⊙ Monthly
- ⊙ Yearly

⊙ **Monthly**

A fifth wheel must be maintained properly to ensure safety. It requires regular lubrication and inspection. This should be carried out monthly or every 10,000 km whichever comes first.

8.110 *Mark* ***one*** *answer*

On a draw-bar unit which of these should you check for wear or damage?

- ⊙ Dog-clip
- ⊙ Fifth wheel
- ⊙ Kingpin release handle
- ⊙ Eyelet coupling

⊙ **Eyelet coupling**

The eyelet coupling on draw-bar units, should be regularly checked for damage or wear. It should be lubricated with heavy duty grease.

8.111 *Mark **one** answer*

What is the fifth wheel coupling used for?

- To connect a tractor unit to the trailer
- To support the trailer when detached
- To prevent the trailer from jack-knifing
- To attach air lines to the trailer

To connect a tractor unit to the trailer

The fifth wheel coupling is a device to connect the tractor unit to the trailer. It allows articulation between the tractor and trailer. It should be regularly maintained.

8.112 *Mark **one** answer*

Fifth wheel coupling components should be inspected monthly or every

- 5,000 km
- 10,000 km
- 15,000 km
- 20,000 km

10,000 km

Fifth wheel couplings require regular lubrication and inspection. This should be carried out every 10,000 km or monthly, whichever is the sooner.

8.113 *Mark **one** answer*

When diesel fuel is hot it

- expands
- liquefies
- shrinks
- waxes

expands

When a tank is filled to the brim and then the fuel expands, the only place for it to go is out of the breather and onto the road. This wastes fuel and makes the road surface very dangerous for other road users.

8.114 *Mark **one** answer*

Your vehicle is fitted with a synchromesh gearbox. Double-declutching will have the effect of

- reducing clutch wear
- increasing clutch wear
- increasing the number of gear changes
- reducing the number of gear changes

increasing clutch wear

Double-declutching is not necessary on synchromesh gearboxes. It increases clutch wear and wastes fuel.

section **nine**

LEAVING THE VEHICLE

This section covers

- Passengers
- The driver's cab

9.1 *Mark **one** answer*

When you intend to open your right-hand door you should check

- the mirror
- that all other doors are closed
- the air pressure
- that the interior is clear of passengers

the mirror

When you pull in, other vehicles may be passing on your right-hand side. It's very important to check your mirror, as well as looking round to cover the blind spot, to make sure that it's safe before opening your door.

9.2 *Mark **three** answers*

Many buses have a separate door on the offside for the driver. When leaving the bus by this door you should always

- jump down from the cab
- check for traffic which may be passing
- apply the parking brake
- climb down facing the bus using the footholds
- climb down facing away from the bus using the footholds

check for traffic which may be passing

apply the parking brake

climb down facing the bus using the footholds

Having found a safe place to park your bus, make a final offside check before opening your door. Never jump down from the cab into the road. It's particularly dangerous as you risk injury from landing badly or falling into the path of passing traffic.

9.3 *Mark **two** answers*

When getting out of the driver's door on this bus you should

- look out for overtaking vehicles before opening the door
- climb down facing away from the bus
- climb down facing the bus
- signal your intentions to other traffic
- open the door to get a good view of approaching traffic

look out for overtaking vehicles before opening the door

climb down facing the bus

For your own safety, as well as that of others, you should make sure that it's safe by checking for other vehicles before getting out of the cab. Climbing down facing the bus means that you can make proper use of the footholds to lessen the risk of slipping.

9.4 Mark **two** answers

This bus has a separate door for the driver, opening onto the offside. What should you do when getting out of such a vehicle?

- Climb down facing away from the vehicle
- Check for passing traffic
- Climb down facing towards the vehicle
- Jump down carefully, flexing the knees on landing
- Climb down holding the steering wheel rim tightly

- **Check for passing traffic**
- **Climb down facing towards the vehicle**

If your vehicle has a separate offside driver's door, you must take the precaution of good observation before leaving the vehicle. Don't jump down out of the cab. Leave by climbing down facing towards the vehicle. Consider your own safety as well as that of others and always check for traffic passing closely by before getting out of your vehicle.

9.5  Mark **four** answers

As a bus driver, on which FOUR occasions should you use your hazard warning lights?

- When you are temporarily obstructing traffic
- To thank a driver who has let you pull in
- To warn of an obstruction when driving on the motorway
- When parking in a restricted area
- When you have broken down
- When stationary and children are getting off a school bus

- **When you are temporarily obstructing traffic**
- **To warn of an obstruction when driving on the motorway**
- **When you have broken down**
- **When stationary and children are getting off a school bus**

All drivers may use hazard warning lights to warn other road users of danger on specific occasions. When you are driving a school bus you may also use them when you have stopped and children are getting on or off.

9.6 Mark **one** answer

Damage can be caused when parking close to another vehicle if your coach is fitted with

- air brakes
- hydraulic suspension
- air suspension
- hydraulic brakes

air suspension

Vehicles fitted with air suspension can sometimes move a considerable amount when first started, as the air bags are injected with gas. If you're too close to another vehicle or obstruction, this could result in collision damage.

9.7 Mark **one** answer

You have arrived at your destination. All your passengers want to leave the bus. Ideally their valuables should be

- placed on luggage racks
- taken with them
- placed on the seats
- left with you

taken with them

Ideally passengers should take any personal property and valuables with them, unless they can be locked in secure luggage compartments.

9.8 Mark **three** answers

As a driver, when getting out of your bus you must make sure that

- the parking brake is on
- the vehicle has stopped in a safe place
- the engine is switched off
- the air pressure gauges read full
- you have parked at a bus stop
- you always change the destination board

the parking brake is on

the vehicle has stopped in a safe place

the engine is switched off

Don't park where you will cause obstruction or inconvenience to other road users. It's an offence to leave your bus with the engine running and/or without applying the parking brake.

9.9 Mark **one** answer

When leaving the cab of your bus, which of the following is NOT important?

- Applying the parking brake
- Switching off the engine
- Watching for approaching traffic
- Operating the fuel cut-off switch

Operating the fuel cut-off switch

This is not normally necessary unless the vehicle has been involved in an accident and there is a risk of fire.

9.10 Mark **one** answer

You are going to park your bus. What must you check before leaving it?

- The ticket dispenser
- Litter left under seats
- The parking brake is applied
- The intercom is working

The parking brake is applied

It's an offence to leave any vehicle without applying the parking brake. Make sure that this is firmly applied before you leave the driving position.

9.11 Mark **one** answer

You are unloading luggage from your coach. Which of these should you wear?

- High-visibility vest
- Heat-proof gloves
- Safety goggles
- Ear protectors

High-visibility vest

Very often you will load or unload luggage by the roadside. For your own safety, make yourself visible to other traffic.

9.12 Mark **two** answers

As a driver you should use your mirrors

- as you signal
- to check the blind spot
- when driving along
- before opening your door

when driving along

before opening your door

To be a safe driver, you must always be aware of where other road users are. That way you can plan your driving according to what is going on around you. Before opening your door it's important to check the mirrors, as well as looking round for passing or approaching vehicles.

9.13 Mark **one** answer

Before you get out of your cab, you must

- empty the air tanks
- adjust your mirrors
- apply the parking brake
- check if the warning lights are working

apply the parking brake

The parking brake must always be set whenever you leave the vehicle, it is an offence not to leave it properly secured.

9.14 Mark **one** answer

Before you leave your vehicle you must always

- empty the air tanks
- apply the parking brake
- adjust your mirrors
- switch on your hazard warning lights

apply the parking brake

Whenever you leave the driving seat, you must always make sure that your vehicle is secured by applying the parking brake. Make sure the engine has stopped. It is an offence to leave your vehicle with the engine running.

9.15 Mark **three** answers

Before leaving the cab you should make sure that

- you remove your tachograph chart
- the engine has stopped
- all warning lights are operating
- the parking brake is on
- all documents are safely stowed
- you will not endanger people when opening the door

the engine has stopped

the parking brake is on

you will not endanger people when opening the door

Always make a systematic check of the above before leaving your vehicle. It is your responsibility to make sure your vehicle and load are safe at all times. It is an offence to leave a vehicle unattended with the engine running on a public road.

9.16 Mark **one** answer

Before opening your cab door you should be aware of

- ⊙ vehicles passing close by
- ⊙ the height of your cab from the ground
- ⊙ loose grab rails near the door
- ⊙ people crossing the road behind you

⊙ **vehicles passing close by**

It can be dangerous for vehicles passing close by if you open the door carelessly. Always look properly to make sure that it's safe, using the mirror as well as checking blind spots before you get out of the cab.

9.17 Mark **one** answer

When should you use hazard warning lights?

- ⊙ To warn other drivers that you are towing
- ⊙ Approaching queuing traffic on a motorway
- ⊙ When parked illegally on a busy road
- ⊙ To thank a driver for giving way to you

⊙ **Approaching queuing traffic on a motorway**

You may only use hazard warning lights while driving when you are on an unrestricted dual carriageway or motorway, to warn drivers behind you of a hazard or obstruction ahead. Only use them for just long enough to ensure that your warning has been observed.

9.18 Mark **one** answer

You need to stop and get out of your vehicle. The parking brake should be used

- ⊙ with the service brake
- ⊙ only on uneven ground
- ⊙ at all times when leaving the vehicle
- ⊙ unless the vehicle is in gear

⊙ **at all times when leaving the vehicle**

It is an offence to leave your vehicle unattended at any time without applying the parking brake.

9.19 *Mark **three** answers*

Before leaving your vehicle cab you should make sure that

- the engine is running smoothly
- the engine has stopped
- the parking brake is on
- you have removed your personal things
- the ignition system is switched off

- **the engine has stopped**
- **the parking brake is on**
- **the ignition system is switched off**

The vehicle must always be left safe and secure when you leave the cab.

9.20 *Mark **two** answers*

Before leaving your vehicle cab you should make sure that

- your seat is correctly adjusted
- the ignition system is switched on
- the engine has stopped
- the keys are in the starter switch
- the parking brake is on

- **the engine has stopped**
- **the parking brake is on**

The law requires that the parking brake is set and the engine switched off before leaving the cab of your vehicle.

9.21 *Mark **two** answers*

Hazard warning lights may be used in which TWO of these situations?

- To thank a driver who has let you pull in after overtaking
- As a warning to drivers that you are towing another vehicle
- To show your intention to go ahead at a junction when your position might suggest otherwise
- When driving on motorways or dual carriageways to warn drivers behind you of a hazard ahead
- When your vehicle has stopped to warn others of an obstruction

- **When driving on motorways or dual carriageways to warn drivers behind you of a hazard ahead**
- **When your vehicle has stopped to warn others of an obstruction**

Use your hazard warning lights when approaching a queue of traffic on a motorway or unrestricted dual carriageway. This will alert traffic behind, which may not be able to see the hazard due to the size of your vehicle. Don't use hazard warning lights as an excuse for illegal parking. They should only be used to warn others of an obstruction or hazard ahead.

9.22 Mark *one* answer

You are about to lift a heavy box or suitcase. What should you try to avoid while doing this?

- Bending your knees
- Twisting your back
- Changing your position
- Moving your feet

Twisting your back

Avoid twisting your back when lifting as this may cause injury when you turn. Move your feet and keep your shoulders in the same direction as your hips.

9.23 Mark *one* answer

When lifting a heavy box or suitcase manually, what should you try to do?

- Lift and twist together
- Look down all the time
- Lean sideways and lift
- Look ahead when the load is secure

Look ahead when the load is secure

Once you have a secure hold on the object keep your head up and bend your knees.

9.24 Mark *one* answer

You are lifting a heavy object. What is recognised as good technique?

- Twisting your back while lifting
- Having a stable position
- Holding the load at arm's length
- Lifting the load as quickly as possible

Having a stable position

Your feet should be apart with one leg slightly forward to maintain balance. Place one foot alongside the load if it is on the ground. Be prepared to move your feet to maintain stability.

9.25 *Mark **three** answers*

You are lifting a heavy object. Which THREE things should you do?

- Adopt a stable position
- Get a good hold on the object
- Move smoothly
- Twist your back
- Lean sideways
- Keep your legs straight

- **Adopt a stable position**
- **Get a good hold on the object**
- **Move smoothly**

You should always think before lifting any heavy object. Plan the lift and move any other items out of the way. Decide if you might need any assistance.

9.26 *Mark **one** answer*

When pulling up on the left in busy places you should be careful that

- there is good access to unload
- you have disconnected all air lines
- your nearside mirror does not strike the head of a pedestrian
- you change your tachograph mode

- **your nearside mirror does not strike the head of a pedestrian**

When pulling up on the left you should always be aware of pedestrians, particularly if they are close to the edge of the road. The height of your nearside mirror can vary depending on the size and type of vehicle you are driving. If in doubt, approach these situations with caution and stop if necessary.

9.27 *Mark **one** answer*

You have just parked a lorry at a roadside in very heavy traffic. Before dismounting from the cab you should be particularly careful to do which one of the following?

- Make sure the radio is turned down
- Check the rear view mirrors
- Make sure the hazard warning lights are on
- Check that all windows are closed

- **Check the rear view mirrors**

Getting out of the cab from the offside of a vehicle directly into the road can be hazardous, especially if traffic is travelling at speed. Use your mirrors to check behind and all around the vehicle. Ensure that you use all proper footholds and hand grips. Be responsible for your own health and safety.

9.28 Mark **one** answer

You are driving a long, rigid vehicle. Where must you NOT park?

- On a pedestrian crossing
- In a lay-by
- In a loading bay
- On a service area

On a pedestrian crossing

There are many places where you should not park: it's important to make sure that you always select a place that is both safe and legal. Parking on or too close to a pedestrian crossing can be dangerous as this will restrict the view for drivers and pedestrians.

9.29 Mark **one** answer

You want to park a semi-trailer and leave it unattended. Where should you NOT do this?

- In a lorry park
- On level ground
- In a factory
- In a lay-by

In a lay-by

If you need to park the semi-trailer of your vehicle, find a safe place. Don't park it in a lay-by. Leave these available for drivers who wish to stop and rest. Find a place off the road, preferably a lorry park or somewhere safe which will decrease the risk of theft.

9.30 Mark **one** answer

Which ONE of the following is NOT important when getting out of a lorry cab?

- Watching for approaching traffic
- Using the mirrors
- Applying the parking brake
- Disconnecting the air lines

Disconnecting the air lines

After getting out of your vehicle it's a good idea to walk round and check your tyres, load, lights, brake lines, electrical connections, etc. When you return to your vehicle, or take over a different vehicle, all the safety checks should be carried out.

9.31 Mark **one** answer

About 3000 trucks are stolen every year. For added security, what should you consider having on your vehicle?

- Roof markings
- Diff-locks
- Air horns
- Tinted windows

Roof markings

The Association of Chief Police Officers has approved the wider use of roof markings on lorries to help police air-support units to identify vehicles if they are stolen. Fleet operators, particularly those who regularly carry vulnerable/dangerous loads, are encouraged to use roof markings.

9.32 *Mark **three** answers*

You are the driver of a tanker vehicle. When opening the tank hatches, what dangers should you be aware of?

- Low air pressure
- Speed limiters
- Slippery walkways
- Emergency air lines
- Overhead cables
- Overhead pipeways

- **Slippery walkways**
- **Overhead cables**
- **Overhead pipeways**

Take your time if you're using walkways at high levels. Fuel can make the surface slippery and therefore increase the safety risk.

9.33 *Mark **one** answer*

You are working on the platform of a flat-bed lorry. What is the safest way to get down to the ground?

- Use a suitable set of steps
- Jump down wearing non-slip shoes
- Use ropes to lower yourself down
- Climb down facing away from the vehicle

- **Use a suitable set of steps**

Many people a year are seriously injured by falling from vehicles. Using suitable steps will lessen the chance of falling. Be aware of the dangers, particularly in busy yards or loading bays, when loading or unloading vehicles.

9.34 *Mark **one** answer*

You are transporting a high-value load of cigarettes. What do you need to consider?

- The possibility of a theft or hijack incident
- There will be more Customs and Excise checks
- You will be allowed to take fewer rest breaks
- You will need to maintain your regular route

- **The possibility of a theft or hijack incident**

If you are carrying a high-value load you should consider your personal safety. There is always the possibility of an attempted theft. Watch for anything unusual, such as people taking a special interest in you or your vehicle.

section **ten**

VEHICLE LOADING

This section covers

- Loading
- Safety
- Type of load

10.1 *Mark **one** answer*

Why is it important to distribute the weight evenly over the axles when loading a lorry?

- To ensure easy unloading
- To make it easier to sheet up
- To ensure maximum ground clearance
- To ensure maximum stability

To ensure maximum stability

A vehicle should be loaded so that the weight of a load is evenly distributed over the axles. This will increase the stability of the load. In addition you should brake in good time and when driving in a straight line wherever possible. Look well ahead so that you can avoid harsh braking. Always reduce your speed before you make a turn, so that you aren't braking and turning at the same time.

10.2 *Mark **one** answer*

Which of the following is most important when loading a vehicle?

- Spreading the load evenly
- Loading it towards the rear
- Loading it towards the front
- Easy access for unloading

Spreading the load evenly

It is your responsibility as the driver to make sure that your vehicle load is spread evenly to avoid overloading individual axles. Overloading carries severe penalties for the driver and operator.

10.3 *Mark **one** answer*

You are driving a lorry with an ISO container on a trailer. You must make sure that

- the container is secured by ropes
- all locking levers are secured
- the trailer has a flat-bed platform
- the container is sealed

all locking levers are secured

ISO (International Standards Organisation) cargo containers should only be carried on lorries or trailers with the appropriate securing points. These are designed to lock into the container body.

10.4  *Mark* ***one*** *answer*

You are loading a steel ISO container. Which statement is true?

- Its own weight will hold it in place
- It can be loaded onto any flat-bed lorry
- The locking levers must be secured
- The container should be roped in place

The locking levers must be secured

Container loads use a different type of restraint to secure them to the vehicle. Make sure that you are familiar with all the different kinds of load restraint. The security of the load is your responsibility; don't take chances.

10.5  *Mark* ***one*** *answer*

You are using three sheets to cover your load. Which of the following shows the correct overlap?

Keep a check in your mirrors as you're driving to ensure that the sheets are secure. Air can force itself under the sheets and work them loose.

10.6 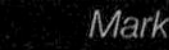 *Mark* ***one*** *answer*

You are covering a load using more than one sheet. You should start with the rearmost sheet first, then work forwards. This will

- stop you tripping over when walking on the load
- stop wind and rain getting under the sheets
- make it much easier to fold up the sheets
- make it easier to carry longer loads

stop wind and rain getting under the sheets

If the load is sheeted incorrectly, when the wind gets underneath the sheet it will lift and flap about. This is dangerous, as it can catch unsuspecting pedestrians or cyclists and also seriously reduce the driver's view of what's happening to the rear.

10.7 *Mark **one** answer*

When roping down a load on your lorry what is the best knot to use?

- A dolly knot
- A reef knot
- A slip knot
- A bow-line knot

A dolly knot

If a load is being secured by ropes you must ensure that they are tied securely to the body of the unit. The most effective method of tying is by 'dolly knots'. These are non-slip knots that hold firmly. You should practise tying these and use them appropriately.

10.8 *Mark **one** answer*

Ropes are unsuitable to tie down a load of scrap metal because they

- are hard to tie
- will loosen in rain
- are hard to untie
- wear and snap

wear and snap

When securing a load, the driver must decide which is the most suitable type of restraint to use. A few extra minutes to make sure that the load is secure gives you peace of mind. It also reduces the risk of the load moving should an emergency situation arise.

10.9 *Mark **one** answer*

You are driving a tipper lorry carrying loose dry sand. Why should you sheet this load?

- To stop handling being affected
- To stop the load from shifting
- To stop the load from blowing away
- To aid your rearward vision

To stop the load from blowing away

If you're carrying a load that consists of loose materials, it must be securely roped and sheeted. You must not risk the chance of losing any part of your load. This could cause damage or injury to other road users, and you would be held responsible.

10.10 Mark **one** answer

The load on a lorry becomes insecure on a journey. The driver should

- continue at a slower speed to ensure the load does not fall off
- attach 'hazard' boards to warn other road users
- park and re-secure the load before continuing
- inform base at the earliest opportunity

park and re-secure the load before continuing

If you become aware that any part of your load is insecure you must stop as soon as it's safe to do so. Re-secure the load before continuing on your journey. If this isn't possible, then you must seek assistance. Don't take risks.

10.11 Mark **one** answer

Which of the following would reduce the 'wave effect' when driving tankers?

- Spray guards
- Harsh braking
- Baffle plates
- Wind deflectors

Baffle plates

Modern tankers are fitted with baffle plates inside the tank compartment. This helps to minimise the movement of liquids and therefore reduce the 'wave effect'.

10.12 Mark **one** answer

You are driving an articulated tanker vehicle on a straight road. When braking to a stop the liquid load will tend to

- push the vehicle forward
- push the vehicle to the side
- make the trailer wheels bounce
- make the trailer wheels skid

push the vehicle forward

When braking with a vehicle carrying a liquid load it's important to apply even pressure on the brake pedal. Do not relax the pedal pressure until the vehicle has stopped. Secure the vehicle with the parking brake before releasing the footbrake. This will minimise the risk of unintentional movement of the vehicle caused by 'surge' from the liquid load.

10.13 Mark **one** answer

You are driving a tanker that is half full. The inside of the tank is not divided into compartments. When braking to a stop you should

- avoid relaxing the footbrake
- relax the footbrake
- pump the footbrake rapidly
- use the footbrake and parking brake together

avoid relaxing the footbrake

Baffle plates help prevent liquids 'surging' around, but extra care is still necessary when driving a tanker vehicle. When braking, always maintain steady pressure on the brake pedal until after the vehicle has stopped. This helps reduce the 'wave' effect which can build up as the liquid load surges back and forth when the vehicle changes speed.

10.14 Mark **one** answer

Which type of load would most benefit from being carried on a lorry fitted with road-friendly suspension?

- Steel
- Timber
- Glass
- Cables

Glass

Fragile loads need extra care in loading and handling. The load must be secured using the most appropriate form of restraint. Air suspension reduces the vibration caused by the impact of the lorry wheels on road surfaces. This also reduces damage to the road, bridges and adjacent structures.

10.15 Mark **one** answer

An attendant must accompany you when your load is wider than

- 2.6 metres (8 feet 5 inches)
- 3.0 metres (9 feet 9 inches)
- 3.3 metres (10 feet 9 inches)
- 3.5 metres (11 feet 5 inches)

3.5 metres (11 feet 5 inches)

Wide loads are a hazard to other road users. In addition to having an attendant with you, you must also notify the police. Side markers must also be used to show other road users that your load overhangs the limits of your vehicle.

10.16 Mark **one** answer

Jack-knifing of an articulated lorry is more likely to occur when the trailer is

- loaded at the front
- loaded at the rear
- unloaded
- fully loaded

unloaded

Severe braking can result in jack-knifing as the tractor unit is pushed by the semi-trailer pivoting around the coupling (fifth wheel). This is more likely to occur when the brakes are applied on a bend.

10.17 Mark **one** answer

After recoupling, how should you make sure that the tractor and trailer are secure?

- Try to move forward with the trailer parking brake on
- Reverse with the trailer parking brake on
- Try to move forward with the trailer parking brake off
- Reverse with the trailer parking brake off

Try to move forward with the trailer parking brake on

Ensure the locking mechanism is secure by selecting a low gear and attempting to move forward. Apply the parking brake before leaving the cab. Connect the 'dog-clip' to secure the kingpin release handle.

10.18 Mark **one** answer

When uncoupling or recoupling your trailer, what must you check first?

- The lights are working
- The tilt cab mechanism is secure
- The trailer brake is applied
- The air lines are safely stowed

The trailer brake is applied

If the trailer begins moving while you're working on it, you could put yourself and others in great danger. You must make sure that it's properly secured using the brake before you start work.

10.19 Mark **one** answer

You are uncoupling a lorry and trailer. After disconnecting the electric line you should

- stow it away safely
- drive forward slowly
- lower the landing gear
- apply the trailer brake

stow it away safely

It's important to stow away all your electric cables and air lines safely to avoid causing injury to others. Connectors left lying around can get damaged if run over by another vehicle. It's your responsibility as the driver to make sure that this does not happen.

10.20 Mark **one** answer

Your lorry has a demountable body. Before demounting the body you should ensure that

- the rear doors are open
- the legs are up
- the body is unloaded and empty
- the surface is firm and level

the surface is firm and level

If you demount the body on a poor or soft surface there is a danger of it sinking and becoming difficult to handle. Always think carefully before you demount the body and be sure that the site is suitable.

10.21 Mark **one** answer

After recoupling your trailer you should adjust your mirrors to enable you to see

- the full view of your load
- both pairs of rear wheels
- down each side of the trailer
- the road on the other side

down each side of the trailer

The view you get in your mirrors may vary depending on the size of the trailer and the load it carries. Always adjust your mirrors to make sure that you have the best possible view down each side of the trailer before you drive away.

10.22 *Mark **one** answer*

Which one of the following vehicles is most likely to be affected by 'vehicle bounce'?

- A long wheel-base empty vehicle
- A short wheel-base laden vehicle
- A short wheel-base empty vehicle
- A long wheel-base laden vehicle

A short wheel-base empty vehicle

A short wheel-base empty vehicle will bounce more noticeably than some long wheel-base vehicles. This can affect braking efficiency and all round control. Don't be tempted to push this type of vehicle into bends or corners simply because the vehicle appears to be easier to drive.

10.23 *Mark **one** answer*

Ropes should NOT be used to tie down a load of

- timber planks
- hay bales
- steel plates
- canvas sacks

steel plates

Ropes are totally unsuitable for loads such as steel plates. If there is danger of sharp edges shearing ropes then chains must be used with a suitable tensioning device.

10.24 *Mark **one** answer*

Which of the following loads is most likely to move forward with some force if you brake sharply?

- Heavy material in canvas sacks
- Loose sand
- Timber secured with dolly knots
- Tubular metal

Tubular metal

When deciding which type of restraint to use consider what may happen if you have to brake sharply. Tubular loads may move forward with some force if you have to brake sharply in an emergency. In such cases the headboard of the vehicle can be demolished with fatal results.

10.25 *Mark* ***one*** *answer*

When part loading a lorry with an empty ISO container you should position it

- close to the fifth wheel
- over the front axle
- close to the trailer edge
- over the rear axles

over the rear axles

To increase stability and reduce the risk of the trailer wheels lifting when turning, it is preferable to locate part loads over the rear axle.

10.26 *Mark* ***one*** *answer*

When carrying spare sheets and ropes on your trailer you MUST make sure that they are

- laid out flat
- visible from the cab
- tied down securely
- stacked loosely

tied down securely

All spare sheets and ropes must be tied down securely to prevent them falling into the path of other vehicles.

10.27 *Mark* ***one*** *answer*

Jack-knifing is more likely to occur when driving

- a flat-bed lorry
- a laden lorry
- a high-sided lorry
- an unladen lorry

an unladen lorry

Jack-knifing occurs when the tractor unit is pushed by the semi-trailer pivoting around the coupling (fifth wheel). This is more likely to occur with an unladen vehicle.

10.28 *Mark* ***one*** *answer*

Short wheel-base vehicles will bounce more noticeably than some long wheel-base vehicles particularly when

- laden
- turning
- empty
- unloading

empty

Short wheel-base vehicles will bounce more noticeably than some long wheel-base vehicles when empty. This can affect braking efficiency and all-round control.

10.29 *Mark **four** answers*

What are the main causes of a lorry shedding its load?

- Driving on motorways
- Sudden change of direction
- Driving over a level crossing
- Harsh use of brakes
- Driving too fast
- Sudden change of speed

Sudden change of direction

Harsh use of brakes

Driving too fast

Sudden change of speed

The main causes of shed loads are driver errors such as sudden changes of speed or direction, driving too fast for the conditions and skidding.

10.30 *Mark **one** answer*

You are driving a double-deck bodied lorry. What could happen if the top deck is loaded and the lower deck is empty?

- The lorry will become unstable under normal braking
- The brakes will be less effective
- The lorry may overturn when cornering
- You will need to change gear more often

The lorry may overturn when cornering

Your lorry is more likely to overturn with only the top deck loaded. If you are only carrying half a load, this should be carried on the lower deck whenever possible.

10.31 *Mark **one** answer*

Your lorry has a double-deck body. The top tier is loaded and the lower deck is empty. When will this cause the most danger?

- In heavy fog
- In high winds
- In hot weather
- In heavy rain

In high winds

A lorry loaded like this will be more likely to overturn in high winds or when cornering. If only carrying half a load you should try to put this on the lower deck.

10.32 *Mark **one** answer*

You are carrying another vehicle piggy-back on your lorry. Chocks should be used to secure the wheels. What else should you use?

- A trolley jack
- Axle stands
- Restraining straps
- A scaffolding bar

Restraining straps

You should use a suitable restraint and chock the wheels when another vehicle is being carried piggy-back. Don't just rely on the parking brake.

10.33 *Mark **one** answer*

The lorry you are driving is heavily laden. Approaching a bend too fast may cause the load to

- push your lorry to the left
- pull your lorry to the right
- push your lorry straight on
- pull your lorry back

push your lorry straight on

Forces acting on your lorry will continue to move it in a straight line as you enter a bend. The grip of your tyres will normally overcome this unless you are going too fast. There is a danger that you could lose your load or even tip over. REDUCE YOUR SPEED IN GOOD TIME.

10.34 *Mark **one** answer*

You are driving a vehicle with an unladen trailer. You change into a low gear while travelling at speed. What could happen?

- Your vehicle may suddenly accelerate
- The endurance brake will come on
- You will not be able to brake
- Your vehicle could go out of control

Your vehicle could go out of control

Changing down at too high a speed will cause your vehicle to slow down suddenly. With no separate braking for the trailer the tractor could be pushed to the point where it turns over.

10.35 Mark **one** answer

Your lorry has a crane fitted. You are loading very heavy items. You feel that the ropes or straps may break. You should

- reposition the load
- use chains and tensioners
- tie two straps together
- continue loading carefully

use chains and tensioners

If there is any danger that the load you are lifting with a crane is too great for the ropes or straps, or that sharp edges on the load may damage them, chains with compatible tensioners should be used.

10.36  Mark **one** answer

You are carrying other vehicles piggy-back. You should use restraints and the parking brake on each. What else should you do?

- Make sure the vehicles are sheeted
- Place chocks under the wheels
- Put the heavy vehicles at the top
- Rope the vehicles together

Place chocks under the wheels

Vehicles being carried piggy-back must always have some form of chocks applied to their wheels, in addition to a restraint. Never rely on just the parking brake.

10.37 Mark **one** answer

An articulated car transporter will be least stable when

- only the lower deck is loaded
- only the top deck is loaded
- it is fully laden
- it is unladen

only the top deck is loaded

Keeping the centre of gravity as low as possible will improve the handling of your lorry. Top-heavy loads are more unstable and require more care when turning and cornering.

10.38 Mark **one** answer

What do the legs on a demountable body allow you to do?

- Load and unload the body without stopping
- Stack one body on top of another
- Drive under and out from the body
- Alter the overall height of the vehicle

Drive under and out from the body

Always make sure that the legs on the demountable body are properly secured before moving the vehicle.

10.39 Mark **one** answer

The legs on a demountable body allow you to

- load and unload the body without stopping
- stack one body on top of another
- alter the overall height of the vehicle
- demount the body without a crane or lift

demount the body without a crane or lift

The legs can be lowered to allow the carrier vehicle to drive out from underneath the demountable body.

10.40 Mark **one** answer

What shape are hazardous cargo labels?

- Diamond
- Triangle
- Circle
- Oval

Diamond

Hazardous substances in transit are readily identified by a diamond-shaped warning label. This label carries other information to identify the type of hazard more specifically, such as

- flammable gas
- toxic gas
- corrosive agents

These are just some of the types of hazard encountered. Strict regulations apply to the storage and carriage of these goods. All drivers of this type of load must receive specific certificated training.

10.41 Mark **one** answer

Baffle plates help reduce the load movement in lorries that are carrying

- containers
- cars
- animals
- liquids

liquids

If the drivers of certain tanker vehicles relax the footbrake when braking to a stop there's a danger that the motion in the fluid load could force their vehicles forward. This is due to the wave effect created in the tank contents and is more likely to happen where baffle plates have not been fitted.

10.42 Mark **one** answer

Baffle plates are fitted to tankers to help

- reduce wind resistance
- reduce the 'wave effect'
- stop the brakes from locking
- make the steering lighter

reduce the 'wave effect'

Fluids carried in tanks can move in 'waves' as the vehicle's speed changes, particularly when braking and then easing off the pedal. This shift of weight could cause the vehicle to surge forward. Baffle plates are designed to reduce the wave effect in the liquid.

10.43 Mark **one** answer

Which of these vehicles will be most at risk of 'roll-over' when laden?

'Roll-over' usually occurs as a result of the inside rear wheels of an articulated vehicle starting to lift when negotiating a curve, such as exiting a roundabout. Changes of direction can create a situation where the vehicle is unstable due to movement of the load. The problem frequently involves vehicles carrying fluids in bulk.

10.44 *Mark one answer*

You are unloading an end-tipper lorry. Before tipping the body what should you do?

- Ensure the vehicle is on a firm level surface
- Park facing uphill to make unloading easy
- Ensure the vehicle is on a soft sloping surface
- Park downhill for easier unloading

- **Ensure the vehicle is on a firm level surface**

Unless you are on firm, level ground there is a risk of your lorry overturning. Before raising the body, check that you are well clear of overhead power lines and other obstructions.

10.45 *Mark two answers* NI EXEMPT

The load on your trailer hits a railway bridge. You must report it to

- The police
- The Transport Police
- The Highways Agency
- The railway authority
- The local authority

- **The police**
- **The railway authority**

If your vehicle hits a bridge you must report it to the police. If a railway bridge is involved you must also report it to the railway authority. The phone number is usually shown on or near the bridge.

10.46 *Mark one answer*

When loading you should NOT exceed axle weight limits. Overloading an axle can result in

- reduced fuel consumption
- increased service intervals
- a shorter stopping distance
- prosecution

- **prosecution**

This is a serious offence that is liable to result in prosecution. It is dangerous as your stopping distance will increase. Your vehicle could also become unstable and difficult to control.

10.47 Mark one answer

Which of these best describes the vehicle's payload?

- ⊙ The maximum load the vehicle can carry
- ⊙ The maximum load over each axle
- ⊙ The maximum load plus the weight of the vehicle
- ⊙ The maximum load each tyre can take

⊙ **The maximum load the vehicle can carry**

The formula used for calculating the maximum payload of a vehicle is the maximum authorised mass (MAM) minus the tare weight. Tare weight is the total weight of the vehicle including the crew and extra equipment.

10.48 Mark one answer

You are transporting frozen foods. What important additional training do you need specific to the food industry?

- ⊙ Packaging procedures
- ⊙ Weight distribution procedures
- ⊙ Waste handling procedures
- ⊙ Hygiene procedures

⊙ **Hygiene procedures**

When transporting frozen food you need to know how to operate your refrigeration unit correctly. It's also essential that you are aware of correct hygiene procedures when handling food.

10.49 Mark one answer

You are delivering a load of building materials on pallets. Before unloading what should you ensure FIRST?

- ⊙ The engine is switched off
- ⊙ You are parked on firm level ground
- ⊙ The stabilising legs are lowered
- ⊙ You have warning cones set out

⊙ **You are parked on firm level ground**

Some vehicles are fitted with equipment for lifting and removing heavy loads. Before lifting it's vital to ensure the vehicle is parked on level ground. This will help eliminate the possibility of the load becoming unstable during lifting.

10.50 Mark one answer

You are loading goods of varying weights. How should these be distributed over the width of the vehicle?

- Heavy items at the front, light items at the rear
- Light items near the centre line, heavy items towards the sides
- Heavy items near the centre line, light items towards the sides
- Light items at the front, heavy items at the rear

Heavy items near the centre line, light items towards the sides

To achieve maximum stability the load should be placed to keep the centre of gravity as low as possible. To do this heavy items should be placed close to the centre line and spread over the full length. Lighter items being placed along the sides.

10.51 *Mark **one** answer*

You are working on a vehicle platform. What should you NOT do?

- Wear brightly coloured clothing
- Walk forward near the edges
- Wear non-slip footwear
- Walk backwards near the edges

Walk backwards near the edges

When working on a flat-bed or open curtain-sided vehicle you should always be aware of your proximity to the edge of the platform. It's too easy to concentrate on moving and positioning the load, and lose sight of your own position. Stepping backwards could be fatal.

10.52 *Mark **three** answers*

Which THREE may need to be transported at controlled temperatures?

- Frozen foods
- Chemicals
- Chilled foods
- Cement
- Bulk grain
- Timber

Frozen foods

Chemicals

Chilled foods

Drivers transporting chilled or frozen foods need to be trained to operate refrigeration units. They also need relevant training in hygiene procedures. Specific training is also essential for drivers who have to carry highly dangerous chemicals.

10.53 *Mark* ***one*** *answer*

You are about to transport livestock. You will need

- to have practical experience to care for animals
- to be a member of the R.S.P.C.A.
- to have no driving convictions
- to drive for long periods without a break

to have practical experience to care for animals

When transporting animals you should have all necessary information regarding their care during transportation. You should have all the practical experience needed to look after the animals. When animals are being transported they may be stressed, avoid ill-treating them.

10.54 *Mark* ***one*** *answer*

You need to transport a small herd of pigs. They will only partially fill the vehicle. What should you do?

- Allow no direct access to the animals
- Check them for disease before you load
- Give the animals plenty of space
- Create compartments using moveable panels

Create compartments using moveable panels

When transporting livestock it is important to limit the amount of space they have to move around. If you allow them to move around freely this could affect the stability of the vehicle when braking and cornering. A sudden shift in weight could cause the vehicle to tip over.

10.55 *Mark* ***one*** *answer*

You have to transport a flock of sheep. The journey will take longer than eight hours. You MUST make sure

- you only use a vehicle with air conditioning
- there is no loose bedding on the floor
- you only drive during daylight hours
- there is direct access to the animals

there is direct access to the animals

Consideration must be given to the welfare and condition of the animals you are transporting. For this reason you will need to have good access to the animals in order to check their condition.

10.56 Mark **one** answer

You have to transport a flock of sheep. The journey will take longer than eight hours. You MUST make sure

- there is sufficient bedding material on the floor
- there is no direct access to the animals
- you do not take your normal rest breaks
- you do not drive through the night

there is sufficient bedding material on the floor

When you are transporting animals for long periods you need to make special provisions. The legislation governing the transport of animals is known as 'The Welfare of Animals (Transport) Order 1997'. Remember, the well-being of the animals during transportation is your responsibility.

10.57 Mark **one** answer

Your vehicle has a maximum authorised mass (MAM) of 40 tonnes. The kerbside weight is 15 tonnes. What would your maximum payload be?

- 15 tonnes
- 25 tonnes
- 35 tonnes
- 45 tonnes

25 tonnes

Overloading a vehicle is dangerous. Your stopping distance will increase, and your vehicle could become unstable and difficult to control. You will need to work out the payload. Do this by taking the kerbside weight from the maximum authorised mass (MAM). This will give you the maximum weight you can carry.

10.58 Mark **one** answer

You are making several deliveries. What problems may this increasingly smaller payload cause?

- You might overload an axle
- You will always have heavy items remaining
- You might exceed your kerbside weight
- You will damage the rest of the load

You might overload an axle

As items are unloaded from the rear of the vehicle weight will be transferred to the front axle. Take care that this axle does not become overloaded. You may need to redistribute the load.

10.59 Mark **one** answer

Axle weight limits should NOT be exceeded. Overloading an axle can result in

- reduced braking efficiency
- reduced braking distance
- increased kerbside weight
- increased fuel efficiency

reduced braking efficiency

Never exceed the permitted axle weight limits. Too much weight can reduce braking efficiency and cause brake fade. As well as being dangerous, you will also be committing an offence that can result in prosecution.

10.60 Mark **one** answer

You are loading a lorry. What could be the result of overloading an axle?

- Reduced tyre temperature
- Damage to the road surface
- Damage to the tachograph
- Increased tyre life

Damage to the road surface

Too much weight over an axle impacts on the environment, causing damage to road surfaces. You also risk a fine and driving penalties.

10.61 Mark **one** answer

You are transporting a skip carrying loose waste. The material should be

- covered
- shrink-wrapped
- visible
- kept dry

covered

Make sure you use a suitable cover for the type of load you are carrying. Any part of your load blowing away could cause danger to other road users and possible environmental damage.

10.62 Mark **one** answer

You are securing a very heavy load with a ratchet strap. What type of anchorage point should NOT be used?

- Rope hook
- Eye bolt
- Shackle
- 'D' link

Rope hook

Rope hooks are NOT designed to withstand high forces. They are usually just welded or bolted to the underside of the platform. Many are so weak they can easily be distorted by a ratchet buckle when a webbing strap is tightened. Anchorage points should be built into the main frame or chassis of the vehicle.

10.63 *Mark **one** answer*

You are securing a load using wire ropes. What is the minimum diameter of rope that should be used?

- 4 mm
- 8 mm
- 12 mm
- 16 mm

8 mm

When using wire ropes to secure a load it's recommended that the rope should be no less than 8 mm in diameter, and free from rust. If there are broken wires or strands DON'T USE THEM.

10.64 *Mark **one** answer*

You are securing a load using chains. What type of chain should NOT be used?

- Short link
- Round link
- Oval link
- Split link

Split link

It is recommended that split link and iron chains should NOT be used to secure a load. These types are less reliable than solid link and steel chains. For more information on the suitability of various sized steel chains consult the relevant British Standard (BS) leaflets.

10.65 *Mark **one** answer*

You are using chains to secure a load. What type of chain should NOT be used?

- Square link
- Round link
- Iron
- Steel

Iron

Chains made of iron, and other unsuitable materials, should NOT be used. They are less reliable than steel. Safety information on the suitability of chains can be found in relevant British Standard (BS) leaflets.

10.66 *Mark **one** answer*

You are securing a load using ropes. What is the minimum diameter that should be used?

- 5 mm
- 10 mm
- 15 mm
- 20 mm

10 mm

When using ropes the ends should be spliced or otherwise treated to prevent fraying. The rope should be of at least three strand construction with a minimum normal diameter of at least 10 mm.

10.67 Mark **one** answer

You are loading timber onto a flat-bed lorry. You want to cover it with sheets. Which sheet should be positioned first?

- Front
- Middle
- Rear
- Side

Rear

When more than one sheet is used to cover and protect a load, the rear sheet should be positioned first. This ensures that the overlaps do not face forward, this prevents wind and rain from getting between the sheets.

10.68 Mark **one** answer

You are driving a loaded skip lorry. The skip should be covered. What is the main reason for this?

- To prevent spillages
- To stop children climbing in
- To keep the contents dry
- To prevent theft

To prevent spillages

Debris falling from vehicles can be very dangerous to other road users. It may also cause environmental damage.

10.69 Mark **one** answer

Which may need to be transported at controlled temperatures?

- Perishable foods
- Barrels of beer
- Cement
- Silage

Perishable foods

Some foods need to be transported at controlled temperatures. Drivers will need to be trained in the use of refrigeration units, and correct hygiene procedures.

10.70 Mark one answer

Which of these may need to be transported at controlled temperatures?

- Chemicals
- Bulk grain
- Sugar
- Beer barrels

Chemicals

Some highly dangerous chemicals have to be transported at prescribed temperatures. Drivers must be fully trained in the use of these specially designed temperature-controlled vehicle's.

10.71 Mark one answer

Which symbol on a lorry means it is likely to be carrying compressed gases?

Vehicles carrying dangerous or hazardous goods need to have markings on them, which will clearly identify the items. This could, for example, help the emergency services to deal with any accident quickly and safely.

10.72 Mark one answer

You see this symbol on a lorry. What is it carrying?

- Corrosive materials
- Compressed gases
- Oxidising agents
- Radioactive materials

Oxidising agents

The symbols on the back or sides of lorries should relate to the type of material that the vehicle is, or will normally be, carrying.

10.73 — *Mark **one** answer*

Which symbol on the back of a lorry means it is carrying corrosives?

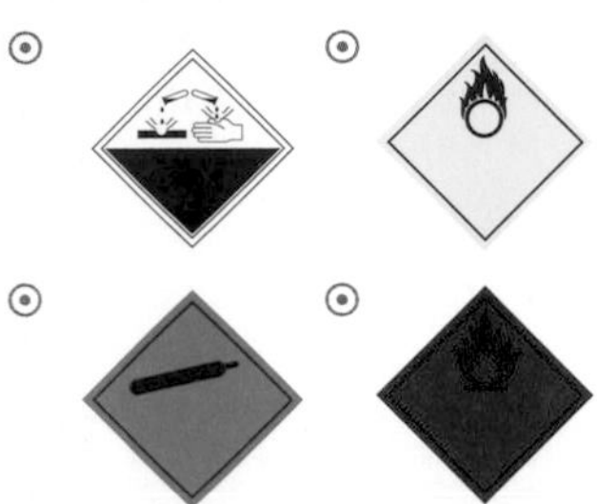

If you drive a vehicle carrying dangerous or hazardous material, you must make sure the correct symbol or mark is clearly visible.

10.74  — *Mark **one** answer*

Which symbol on a lorry shows its load is dangerous when wet?

If any vehicle displaying a warning symbol is involved in an accident, serious consequences could result. You should be aware of what each symbol means.

10.75 Mark **one** answer

You are driving a loaded lorry with curtain sides. You can see the curtain bulging on one side. What should you do?

- Check the load by carefully entering by the rear door or opposite curtain
- Check the load by carefully opening the curtain in the affected area
- Continue driving as this is normal for these types of vehicles
- Continue driving at a much reduced speed

- **Check the load by carefully entering by the rear door or opposite curtain**

You must stop as soon as possible in a safe place. There is a fine line between safety and disaster. The curtain might be the only support to a slipped load so don't open it before checking. Check the load by carefully opening the rear door or opposite curtain, if it shows no sign of bulging.

10.76 Mark **one** answer

You are loading a curtain-sided vehicle. What should you NOT use the curtains for?

- Restraint
- Protection from the weather
- Security
- Advertising the company name

- **Restraint**

Unless the curtains are specifically designed, they must not be used to restrain the load. They should be used to contain it, protect it from the weather and provide a level of security. Most companies also use this as a mobile advertisement.

10.77 Mark **one** answer

You are using a lorry-mounted crane to unload building materials. What safety features should you use?

- Wheel-clamps
- Kingpin locks
- Jockey wheels
- Vehicle stabilisers

- **Vehicle stabilisers**

All drivers should be fully trained and regularly tested to ensure their competence. When using a lorry-mounted crane, stabilisers should always be used.

10.78 Mark **one** answer

You intend to move a heavy object using a barrow or trolley. What is the best position for the handle height?

- Between the shoulder and waist
- As high as you can reach
- Between the knee and waist
- As low as possible for comfort

Between the shoulder and waist

When moving a load, try to push rather than pull. Make sure you can see ahead and that you can stay in control.

10.79 Mark **one** answer

Your vehicle has a maximum authorised mass (MAM) of 40 tonnes. The tare weight is 10 tonnes. What would your maximum payload be?

- 20 tonnes
- 30 tonnes
- 40 tonnes
- 50 tonnes

30 tonnes

To work out your vehicle's payload use the formula, maximum authorised mass (MAM), minus tare weight, equals payload. This is the maximum weight your vehicle can carry.

section eleven

RESTRICTED VIEW

This section covers:

- mirrors
- signals
- parking
- moving off
- blind spots
- observation at junctions

11.1 Mark **two** answers

Some coaches have a mirror on their nearside angled down to show the front nearside wheel. This should be used when you are

- pulling in after overtaking
- pulling up to park at the kerb
- moving close to the left in normal driving
- changing lanes on a motorway

- **pulling up to park at the kerb**
- **moving close to the left in normal driving**

This mirror offers the most benefit when manoeuvring in confined spaces.

11.2 Mark **one** answer

In a bus with a high driving position you may have to look out for

- cyclists close in front
- cyclists close behind
- large vehicles close in front
- large vehicles close behind

- **cyclists close in front**

It's essential that you're constantly aware of other road users and pedestrians around you. A routine of effective mirror checking should be established. You must also know when it's essential to make checks in the blind spots, such as just below the nearside front of the vehicle. A cyclist in that space could be out of your normal vision. Constant awareness should ensure that you've seen any riders getting into that position.

11.3 Mark **one** answer

On a coach with high side windows it can be difficult to see either side. What should you do before you pull away?

- Get out of your vehicle and stop the traffic
- Ask a passenger to make sure it is safe to move off
- Indicate before checking all of your mirrors
- Open the window and look down and round to the right

- **Open the window and look down and round to the right**

High-sided coaches can create extra blind spots and you should be aware of where these are. You will need to make additional checks on this type of vehicle but don't forget your usual observations and mirror checks to make sure it is safe to move off.

11.4 *Mark **one** answer*

Your bus has a high seating position. Which of these may be out of sight below the windscreen line?

- Following vehicles
- Overtaking vehicles
- Cyclists and pedestrians
- Other buses

Cyclists and pedestrians

Always take all-round observations before manoeuvring whether you're moving away, parking or reversing. Cyclists and pedestrians, especially children, can enter your blind spots. If you have been stopped for some time at a bus stop or in a bus station be aware that shoppers may be out of sight below the windscreen line of your bus.

11.5 *Mark **one** answer*

What should you first check before moving to the LEFT?

- The nearside mirror
- The offside mirror
- Behind, over your right shoulder
- Behind, over your left shoulder

The nearside mirror

Before you make a turn or a change of direction, however slight, you should always check the mirrors. If you intend to turn left, check your left-hand (nearside) mirror first.

11.6 *Mark **one** answer*

What should you first check before moving to the RIGHT?

- The nearside mirror
- Behind, over your left shoulder
- Behind, over your right shoulder
- The offside mirror

The offside mirror

If you intend to turn right, check your right-hand (offside) mirror first. You should ensure that all your mirrors are properly adjusted to give a clear view around and behind your vehicle. They should be kept clean at all times and not cracked or broken.

11.7 Mark **one** answer

You are about to move off. You should always

- extend your right arm as far as you can out of the window
- use only the offside mirror and move away quickly
- signal right with indicator and arm together
- use your mirrors and look behind

- **use your mirrors and look behind**

You must use the mirrors well before you signal your intention to make any manoeuvre. Situations when you need to use them include, moving away, changing direction, turning, overtaking, changing lanes, slowing or stopping, changing speed, opening a door.

11.8 Mark **three** answers

In which THREE of the following situations would you FIRST need to check your nearside mirror?

- Before moving out to pass a car parked on your left
- After passing cars on your left
- Before moving to the left
- After passing pedestrians standing on the nearside kerb
- Before moving out to the right

- **After passing cars on your left**
- **Before moving to the left**
- **After passing pedestrians standing on the nearside kerb**

On a large vehicle the nearside mirror is very important and it's essential to use it before moving off. You must check for pedestrians and cyclists along the nearside of your vehicle. Cyclists may ride up on your nearside while you're stationary. If you're driving a bus, passengers may be running for your bus or waiting very close to the kerbside.

As you pass pedestrians or vehicles on your left you should use your nearside mirror and check that you are passing them safely. Leave a safety margin before you move back to the left.

11.9 *Mark **one** answer*

The MSM routine is used to negotiate a hazard. What do the initials MSM stand for?

- Mirror, signal, manoeuvre
- Manoeuvre, speed, mirror
- Mirror, speed, manoeuvre
- Manoeuvre, signal, mirror

Mirror, signal, manoeuvre

Always use the MSM routine when you're approaching a hazard.

M – Mirror: check the position of the traffic behind you.

S – Signal: signal your intention to slow down or change course in good time.

M – Manoeuvre: a manoeuvre is any change in position, from slowing or stopping the vehicle to turning off a busy road.

11.10 *Mark **one** answer*

What does this sign mean?

- Contraflow bus and cycle lane
- With-flow bus and cycle lane
- No buses or cycles
- Priority to buses or cycles

With-flow bus and cycle lane

In some towns there are special lanes set aside for certain types of vehicle. These lanes show a picture of, or state, the authorised road users, and there's usually a sign showing the time that the lane is in operation. Some lanes might only be in operation for a short time. Check the sign and use the lane only if it's permitted.

11.11 *Mark **one** answer*

To have good all-round vision you should make sure that

- windows are open
- a sun visor is fitted
- your seat is properly adjusted
- all lights are clean

your seat is properly adjusted

Large vehicles are designed for their specific function, and this often means the shape and size can impair all-round visibility for the driver. You must make sure that you adjust the seat so that you're able to reach all the controls and see in all the mirrors. You should be seated in such a way that you're able to lean out of the window and check all offside blind spots.

11.12 Mark **one** answer

Some large vehicles with restricted vision to the rear may be fitted with an audible warning device for reversing. In areas with a 30 mph restriction the device may be used

- between 7 am and 11.30 pm only
- between 11.30 pm and 7 am only
- during hours of daylight only
- at any time

between 7 am and 11.30 pm only

Some vehicles are fitted with an audible warning device that sounds when the vehicle is being reversed. As these devices make a loud noise they shouldn't be used between 11.30 pm and 7 am.

These devices are an effective safety feature, but don't take away the need to use good, effective observation around the vehicle before and while reversing.

11.13 Mark **one** answer

Driving too close to the vehicle in front will

- decrease your view ahead
- increase your view ahead
- increase the view of following drivers
- decrease the view of following drivers

decrease your view ahead

Don't get into a position where you reduce your vision unnecessarily, such as driving too close to the vehicle in front. At all times you must be aware that, as a driver of a large vehicle, you won't be able to see all around the vehicle. This is why you must have an excellent mirror routine and be constantly updating your information on what's going on around you.

11.14 Mark **two** answers

At junctions it is difficult to see motorcyclists because they

- are easily hidden in blind spots
- always ride in the gutter
- always wear black leathers
- are smaller than other vehicles

are easily hidden in blind spots

are smaller than other vehicles

When driving large vehicles, windscreen pillars and large mirrors can easily create large blind spots as you look left and right at junctions. Altering your body position slightly while taking observation can give you a much improved view of the traffic. If in doubt, look again. Reassess the situation. DON'T TAKE CHANCES.

11.15 Mark **one** answer

Just before turning right from a main road to a side road, you should check your right-hand mirror. This is because

- there may be pedestrians stepping off the kerb
- you need to check your position
- a motorcyclist may be overtaking you
- your rear view to the left is blocked

- **a motorcyclist may be overtaking you**

Looking and acting sensibly on what you see in your mirrors before you change speed or direction are essential. Driving a large vehicle will sometimes require you to position your vehicle well to the left before making a tight right turn. Inexperienced drivers or riders may not realise your intentions. Make sure you signal in good time. Make a final mirror check before committing yourself to the turn.

11.16 Mark **one** answer

Before turning left you should have a final look into the

- left-hand mirror
- interior mirror
- right-hand mirror
- overtaking mirror

- **left-hand mirror**

When making a left turn with a long vehicle you may have to adopt an unusual position well over to the centre of the road. Always signal your intentions in good time, and make good use of the nearside mirror. Be alert for less experienced road users putting themselves in danger by coming up along your nearside.

11.17 Mark **two** answers

You are driving a long vehicle. Before turning left onto a main road you should be ESPECIALLY careful of

- cyclists alongside you on the left
- motorcyclists alongside you on the left
- motorcyclists coming from your left
- cyclists coming from your left

- **cyclists alongside you on the left**
- **motorcyclists alongside you on the left**

You should always check your nearside mirror before any change of direction. Be alert for cyclists and motorcyclists who don't realise the potential danger involved in trying to squeeze through on your nearside when you are waiting at a junction. Always check for pedestrians and cyclists on the nearside of your vehicle before moving away.

11.18 *Mark **one** answer*

You want to turn right at a roundabout marked with two right-turn lanes. There is ample room for your vehicle in either lane. You should

- use the right-hand of the two lanes
- use the left-hand of the two lanes
- use the left-hand lane then move to the right as you enter the roundabout
- use the right-hand lane then move to the left as you enter the roundabout

- **use the left-hand of the two lanes**

By doing this it will make it easier for you when you leave the roundabout. If you use the right lane there could be traffic on your left and in your blind spot when you exit and try to move back to the left.

11.19 *Mark **one** answer*

Your vehicle is fitted with a reverse warning bleeper. When driving backwards you

- do not need to look round
- should only use the offside mirror
- still need to take all-round observation
- should only use the nearside mirror

- **still need to take all-round observation**

Get someone to guide you if you cannot see all around when reversing.

11.20 *Mark **one** answer*

Large vehicles have many blind spots. What does 'blind spot' mean?

- An area of road covered by your right-hand mirror
- An area of road covered by your left-hand mirror
- An area of road that cannot be seen in your mirrors
- An area of road that is not lit by your headlights

- **An area of road that cannot be seen in your mirrors**

Blind spots can occur when bodywork restricts your view through the mirrors. You should be aware that different types of vehicles have different blind spots.

11.21 Mark **one** answer

Because of its size and design a large vehicle will have

- less blind spots than smaller vehicles
- more blind spots than smaller vehicles
- the same blind spots as smaller vehicles
- no blind spots at all

more blind spots than smaller vehicles

Always take the time to check where your blind spots are at the earliest opportunity when driving a vehicle that is unfamiliar to you. If you are aware of the point when a vehicle disappears from view in your mirrors, then you can take steps to prevent an accident by checking that blind spot area before changes of direction. Good use of the mirrors when driving will help you to be aware of a vehicle in your blind spot areas.

11.22 Mark **one** answer

You are turning right at a T-junction. Your view to the right and left is blocked due to parked vehicles. You should

- lean forward to get a better view without crossing the 'give way' lines
- edge out until you are about 1 metre (3 feet 3 inches) over the 'give way' lines
- ease forward until you can see clearly past the vehicles
- ask a passenger to assist by waving you out when clear

ease forward until you can see clearly past the vehicles

When emerging, if you can't see, then don't go. There could be an approaching cyclist or motorcyclist hidden by parked vehicles.

11.23 Mark **one** answer

Before reversing you MUST always

- remove your seat belt
- look all around
- use an audible warning device
- change the tachograph setting

look all around

Large or long vehicles can have many blind spots when reversing. It's very important to check all angles before starting to reverse and then make sure you keep checking all round while completing the manoeuvre.

11.24 *Mark* ***one*** *answer*

The audible warning device is operating as you reverse. You should be

- relying on a clear path behind
- expecting others to be aware of your course
- taking continuous, all-round observation
- concentrating solely on your blind areas

- **taking continuous, all-round observation**

Don't rely on an audible warning device to claim a right of way. It is your responsibility to be cautious and take all-round observation all the time you are reversing.

11.25 *Mark* ***one*** *answer*

Many modern vehicles are fitted with an additional near-side mirror. This is positioned so that the driver can see

- the front wheel in relation to the kerb
- the exhaust to check for excessive emissions
- the rear of the vehicle when reversing
- the distance the following vehicle is behind

- **the front wheel in relation to the kerb**

This mirror is specifically positioned, so that the driver can see the position of the front near side wheel in relation to the kerb. Use it when pulling in to park alongside the kerb or when you have to move close to the left in normal driving.

11.26 *Mark* ***two*** *answers*

Some lorries have an extra mirror angled down towards the nearside front wheel. This mirror is ESPECIALLY useful when

- moving off
- parking
- checking your trailer
- turning right
- overtaking

- **moving off**
- **parking**

Sitting in a high cab doesn't always give you all-round visibility. Other road users might assume that you can see them and position themselves out of sight close to your vehicle. Making good use of any extra mirrors can help prevent dangerous incidents with less experienced road users, especially when turning left.

11.27 *Mark **three** answers*

You wish to park your trailer. The site you choose should be

- firm
- downhill
- uphill
- legal
- grassed
- level

- **firm**
- **legal**
- **level**

Check that the ground is firm and level before you uncouple the trailer. If you need to, place a heavy plank under the legs to distribute the weight and stop the legs sinking into the ground. Don't park illegally. Make sure that your untended trailer is not blocking access for others.

11.28 *Mark **three** answers*

You are driving a lorry. You are about to move off from behind a stationary car. What should you do?

- Start to signal when moving
- Signal before moving, if necessary
- Check the blind spot before moving
- Use both mirrors before moving
- Use both mirrors only after moving

- **Signal before moving, if necessary**
- **Check the blind spot before moving**
- **Use both mirrors before moving**

Because the body of your vehicle is designed to take loads, your view around it will be restricted. Take extra care to look well out of the window to check the blind spots. Don't forget to check all the mirrors. Check ahead and signal, if necessary, before moving off.

11.29 *Mark **one** answer*

You are driving this lorry. Emerging at this junction needs extra care because of the

- bollards in the middle of the road
- traffic from the right
- motorcycle on the left
- grass verge on the left

motorcycle on the left

Make sure that you signal in good time so that the motorcyclist behind you knows your intention. You may have to position yourself wide in order to negotiate the junction. Be aware that the motorcyclist may see this as an opportunity to filter through on your nearside. Check your left-hand mirror carefully before you start to turn.

11.30 *Mark **one** answer*

You are driving this lorry (arrowed). An emergency vehicle is trying to emerge from the side road. You should

- brake hard to a stop and wave it out
- brake smoothly and allow it to emerge
- drive on, you are on the major road
- turn left quickly to give it a clear view

brake smoothly and allow it to emerge

Good forward planning will allow you to deal safely with this situation. Good intentions are only 'good' if they are achieved safely. Reacting late to this situation may cause danger to other road users. Good forward planning to deal with any situation involves having an all round awareness of other road users. You need to assess how your actions will affect these other road users. Acting on impulse can have disastrous consequences. Be professional and be safe at all times.

11.31 Mark **one** answer

You are unable to see clearly when reversing into a loading bay. You should

- get someone to guide you
- use an audible warning signal
- back into the bay until your bumper touches
- open your door and lean well out.

get someone to guide you

Don't take chances when reversing in a confined space. It is too easy to crush or kill someone without knowing they are in danger. Always double-check, and if in doubt get help from a reliable person.

11.32  Mark **one** answer

You are driving this lorry and turning right from this minor road. What should you be ESPECIALLY aware of?

- Motorcyclist from the right passing the parked van
- Vehicles coming from the left along the main road
- Pedestrians on the footpath on the main road
- Vehicles coming from the rear on the minor road

Motorcyclist from the right passing the parked van

Parked vehicles near junctions can hide smaller road users such as cyclists and motorcyclists. Double-check before emerging with a large vehicle. If in doubt, move forward slowly into a position where you can safely have another look.

11.33 Mark **one** answer

You are parking your lorry at night. In which of these places must you use parking lights?

- On the road
- In a motorway service area
- In a factory entrance
- In dock authority areas

On the road

If you stop in a lay-by you should always leave your lorry's side lights on. The lay-by might be away from street lighting, and other vehicles entering the lay-by must be able to see your vehicle. You must always leave your side lights on when parked on the road.

11.34 *Mark **two** answers*

Your lorry has a sleeper cab. A quick sideways glance would be helpful especially

- after driving over a pedestrian crossing
- when traffic is merging from the right or left
- before climbing a steep hill
- when driving round sharp bends
- before changing lanes on a motorway

- **when traffic is merging from the right or left**
- **before changing lanes on a motorway**

The size and design of some cabs, especially a sleeper cab, can cause blind spots. A quick sideways glance might show up something you cannot see in your mirrors.

11.35 *Mark **two** answers*

You are turning right in this lorry (arrowed). The main dangers to be aware of are

- the pedestrian stepping out
- the following motorcyclist
- the oncoming car
- the 'give way' lines

- **the pedestrian stepping out**
- **the following motorcyclist**

Make sure that you indicate in good time to ensure other road users know your intentions. Always check your mirrors and blind spots before turning. Make sure the following motorcyclist is not about to overtake you. Keep an eye on the pedestrian who may step out unexpectedly.

11.36 *Mark **one** answer*

You have a sleeper cab fitted to your lorry. This could make your driving more difficult because it

- increases your blind spots
- increases your view of the road ahead
- reduces your view in the right-hand mirror
- reduces your view in the left-hand mirror

- **increases your blind spots**

A sleeper cab can cause extra blind spots. Make sure that you are aware of all your blind spot areas. Be alert for vehicles just to the rear offside and nearside of your cab – they could soon become 'invisible', hidden in your blind spot.

11.37 Mark **two** answers

You are waiting to turn right in this lorry (arrowed). What dangers should you be most aware of?

- The oncoming car
- The pedestrians
- The hazard line
- The motorcycle
- The car waiting to emerge
- The 'give way' lines

The pedestrians

The motorcycle

Indicate your intentions in good time so that both the motorcyclist and pedestrians know your intention is to turn right. You should note all potential hazards and keep checking as you turn.

section **twelve**

DOCUMENTS

This section covers

- Documentation
- Driver's responsibility

12.1 Mark **one** answer

Which category licence do you need to drive a tri-axle double-deck coach?

- D1
- D
- D1+E
- C

D

A category D licence allows you to drive any size coach or bus. This also allows you to tow a trailer up to 750 kg. If you want to tow a trailer over 750 kg, with a bus or coach, you will need to have category D+E.

12.2 Mark **one** answer

At international ports, why may coaches be subject to a search by immigration authorities?

- For national security
- To check for red diesel
- For tachograph regulations
- To check vehicle condition

For national security

Because of the threat to national security coaches may be searched at ports and the Channel Tunnel. If the authorities are not satisfied they may refuse to let you continue.

12.3 Mark **one** answer

You are returning from Europe with a coach. Why should you search the vehicle at the port?

- To look for missing property
- To ensure duty-free limits are not exceeded
- To prevent the carriage of illegal immigrants
- To ensure the vehicle has the correct documentation

To prevent the carriage of illegal immigrants

A coach driver can be fined up to £2000 for each illegal immigrant carried. The owner and hirer may also be fined the same amount.

12.4  *Mark **one** answer*

You are making a journey which crosses international borders. Which document should you produce at immigration control?

- A list of passengers
- A breakdown insurance certificate
- A route plan
- A list of alcohol on board

A list of passengers

When passing through immigration control you should have a list of all your passengers. They must all be accounted for.

12.5 *Mark **one** answer*

What licence category do you need to drive an articulated bus ('bendi-bus')?

- D1+E
- D
- D+E
- D1

D

An articulated bus, commonly known as a 'bendi-bus', isn't considered to be a bus towing a trailer. Therefore it can be driven on a category D licence.

12.6 *Mark **one** answer*

The holder of a full category D licence can tow a trailer with a maximum authorised mass (MAM) NOT exceeding

- 750 kg
- 1000 kg
- 1250 kg
- 1500 kg

750 kg

A full category D licence entitles you to tow a trailer up to 750 kg.

12.7 *Mark **one** answer*

You hold a full category D licence. This means you

- cannot tow a trailer at all
- can tow a trailer not exceeding 750 kg
- can tow a trailer of any weight
- cannot tow a trailer with more than one axle

- **can tow a trailer not exceeding 750 kg**

If you wish to tow a trailer over 750 kg, an additional test must be taken.

12.8 *Mark **one** answer*

You are the driver of a coach. You are loading luggage before a long continental tour. In the interests of security and passenger confidence, what should you do?

- Load the luggage before allowing any passengers on board
- Make sure all passengers are seated and then load the luggage
- Make sure the passengers load their luggage as they arrive
- Allow passengers to load their luggage in accordance with the seating plan

- **Load the luggage before allowing any passengers on board**

Passengers should only be allowed to board the coach if a member of the crew is present. No one should be allowed to board without a valid ticket or pass for that particular trip. You should be aware of security issues at all times.

12.9 *Mark **one** answer*

You intend to drive a midibus for hire or reward. It will have more than 16 passenger seats. What is the minimum licence entitlement you need?

- C
- C1
- D
- D1

- **D**

Drivers of buses and coaches with more than 16 passenger seats require a category D licence. Make sure your licence has the correct entitlement for the vehicle you will be driving.

12.10 *Mark **one** answer*

Which licence category do you need to drive a bus with 25 passenger seats?

- D
- D1
- D+E
- D1+E

D

Drivers of coaches or buses with more than 16 passenger seats will require a category D licence.

12.11 *Mark **one** answer* NI EXEMPT

Which authority has the power to impose conditions on a passenger carrying vehicle (PCV) operators licence?

- The Traffic Commissioner
- DVLA
- VOSA
- The Highways Agency

The Traffic Commissioner

Traffic Commissioners are responsible for administering the regulations governing a passenger carrying vehicle (PCV) operators licence. They can take disciplinary action against an operator who falls foul of the legislative requirements.

12.12 *Mark **one** answer*

You will be driving your vehicle in Europe. Which of these documents MUST you carry?

- The vehicle service record
- Your medical examination form
- Your national driving licence
- The vehicle workshop manual

Your national driving licence

You also need to carry the insurance certificate and vehicle registration document. Other documentation may also be required for some countries; check this before starting your journey.

12.13 *Mark **one** answer*

You may be prevented from obtaining a lorry or bus licence if you have

- dyslexia
- partial blindness
- skin problems
- stomach problems

partial blindness

Other factors such as heart and mental disorders can also prevent you from obtaining a lorry or bus licence. For enquiries about medical standards you should contact the Drivers Medical Branch, DVLA, Swansea.

12.14 *Mark **one** answer*

You have been convicted of a drink-drive offence while driving your car, and banned from driving. This ban will affect

- all your driving entitlements
- only your car entitlement
- only your lorry entitlement
- only your bus entitlement

all your driving entitlements

The dangers of drink-driving are well publicised. Anyone convicted of this serious offence will lose their entitlement to drive any motor vehicle on the road.

12.15 *Mark **one** answer* NI EXEMPT

You are two and a half times over the legal alcohol limit. You are disqualified from driving. Before regaining your licence who will you have to satisfy that you do NOT have an alcohol problem?

- The local hospital
- Drivers' Medical Branch, DVLA
- Alcoholics Anonymous
- Vehicle and Operator Services Agency

Drivers' Medical Branch, DVLA

If you are disqualified because you are two and a half times over the legal limit, you will have to satisfy the Driver and Vehicle Licensing Agency's Medical Branch that you do NOT have an alcohol problem, before your licence is returned.

12.16 Mark **one** answer

How long will a Statutory Off Road Notification (SORN) last for?

- 12 months
- 24 months
- 3 years
- 10 years

12 months

A SORN declaration allows you to keep a vehicle off road and untaxed for 12 months. If you want to keep your vehicle off road beyond that you must send a further SORN form to DVLA or DVLNI.

12.17 Mark **one** answer NI EXEMPT

What is a Statutory Off Road Notification (SORN) declaration?

- A notification to tell VOSA that a vehicle does not have a current MOT
- Information kept by the police about the owner of the vehicle
- A notification to tell DVLA that a vehicle is not being used on the road
- Information held by insurance companies to check the vehicle is insured

A notification to tell DVLA that a vehicle is not being used on the road

If you want to keep a vehicle off the public road you must declare SORN. It is an offence not to do so. You then won't have to pay road tax. If you don't renew the SORN declaration or re-license the vehicle, you will incur a penalty.

12.18 Mark **one** answer NI EXEMPT

A Statutory Off Road Notification (SORN) declaration is

- to tell DVLA that your vehicle is being used on the road but the MOT has expired
- to tell DVLA that you no longer own the vehicle
- to tell DVLA that your vehicle is not being used on the road
- to tell DVLA that you are buying a personal number plate

to tell DVLA that your vehicle is not being used on the road

This will enable you to keep a vehicle off the public road for 12 months without having to pay road tax. You must send a further SORN declaration after 12 months.

12.19 Mark **one** answer

A Statutory Off Road Notification (SORN) is valid

- for as long as the vehicle has an MOT
- for 12 months only
- only if the vehicle is more than 3 years old
- provided the vehicle is insured

for 12 months only

If you want to keep a vehicle off the public road you must declare SORN. It is an offence not to do so. You then won't have to pay road tax for that vehicle. You will incur a penalty after 12 months if you don't renew the SORN declaration, or re-license the vehicle. If you sell the vehicle the SORN declaration ends and the new owner should declare SORN or re-license the vehicle.

12.20 Mark **one** answer

A Statutory Off Road Notification (SORN) will last

- for the life of the vehicle
- for as long as you own the vehicle
- for 12 months only
- until the vehicle warranty expires

for 12 months only

If you are keeping a vehicle, or vehicles, off road and don't want to pay road tax you must declare SORN. You must still do this even if the vehicle is incapable of being used, for example it may be under restoration or being stored. After 12 months you must send another SORN declaration or re-license your vehicle. You will be fined if you don't do this. The SORN will end if you sell the vehicle and the new owner will be responsible immediately.

12.21 Mark **one** answer

What is the maximum specified fine for driving without insurance?

- £50
- £500
- £1000
- £5000

£5000

It is a serious offence to drive without insurance. As well as a heavy fine you may be disqualified or incur penalty points.

12.22 Mark **one** answer

It is an offence to bring an illegal immigrant into the UK. The current fine can be up to

- £1000
- £2000
- £3000
- £4000

£2000

The regulations governing the importation of illegal immigrants into the UK carry heavy penalties upon conviction. A fine of up to £2000 can be imposed for each illegal immigrant. This fine can be imposed on each 'responsible person' which includes, the vehicle owner, hirer and driver.

12.23 Mark **two** answers

Drivers can be fined for bringing illegal immigrants into the U.K. Who else can be fined?

- The vehicle repairer
- The vehicle insurer
- The vehicle owner
- The vehicle hirer

The vehicle owner

The vehicle hirer

Bringing illegal immigrants into the UK carries heavy fines if convicted. This can be up to £2000 for each one. The fine can be imposed on each 'responsible person'. This includes, the vehicle owner, hirer and driver.

12.24 Mark **three** answers

Operators should operate an 'effective system' to prevent the carriage of illegal immigrants. What are the three main elements of this?

- Vehicle security
- Vehicle tracking devices
- Vehicle checks
- Mobile communications
- Documentation

Vehicle security

Vehicle checks

Documentation

Current legislation requires all operators to set up an 'effective system' to help prevent the carriage of illegal immigrants. This should include vehicle security and checking, and a checklist. Failure to do this will incur penalties.

12.25 *Mark **one** answer*

You are returning to the UK and about to board a ferry. An immigration officer asks to see your documentation. What must you produce immediately?

- The vehicle registration book
- The driver's hours record
- Operator documentation
- Your driving licence

Operator documentation

Operators must set up an 'effective system' to prevent the carriage of illegal immigrants. This should include documentation with advice on vehicle security and checks, and a checklist. This documentation should be produced immediately if requested by an immigration officer.

12.26 *Mark **one** answer*

For a driver convicted of bringing illegal immigrants into the UK, a fine of up to £2,000 can be imposed for each

- family group they bring in
- court attendance they make
- person they bring in
- journey they made in the last year

person they bring in

Current legislation imposes, on each 'responsible person', if convicted, a fine of up to £2,000 for each illegal immigrant. This includes, the vehicle driver, owner and hirer.

12.27 *Mark **one** answer*

The Driver Certificate of Professional Competence (CPC) requires you to take training every five years. What is the MINIMUM number of hours training required?

- 30 hours
- 35 hours
- 40 hours
- 45 hours

35 hours

To maintain your Driver Certificate of Professional Competence (CPC) you need to take at least 35 hours training every five years. This can be split into sessions of at least seven hours each. One training day a year can be spread over the five years if required. The penalties for non-compliance are the same as driving without a licence.

12.28 Mark **one** answer

You wish to maintain your Driver Certificate of Professional Competence (CPC). To do this you will need to take a minimum of 35 hours training within a period of

- one year
- three years
- five years
- ten years

five years

You must take a minimum of 35 hours training every five years to maintain your Driver Certificate of Professional Competence. This can be done at any time during the five years. It can be done all at once or split into sessions, each of which must be a minimum of seven hours. Penalties for non-compliance are the same as for driving without a licence.

12.29 Mark **one** answer

The holder of a Driver Certificate of Professional Competence (CPC) is required to take 35 hours of training every five years. This training must be taken in blocks of at least

- one hour
- seven hours
- twelve hours
- thirty five hours

seven hours

To maintain your Driver Certificate of Professional Competence, you will need to undergo a minimum of 35 hours training every five years. This must be carried out in sessions of at least seven hours. The penalties for non-compliance are the same as driving without a licence.

12.30 Mark **one** answer

You hold a Driver Certificate of Professional Competence (CPC). Every five years you MUST complete a minimum training period of

- 25 hours
- 30 hours
- 35 hours
- 40 hours

35 hours

Drivers are required to take a minimum of 35 hours training every five years to maintain their Driver Certificate of Professional Competence (CPC). This can be split into shorter sessions of at least seven hours each. These can be spread over the five years so effectively one days training is taken each year. The penalties for non-compliance are the same as driving without a licence.

12.31 *Mark one answer*

A driver is applying for a LGV or PCV licence for the first time. They need UNCORRECTED visual acuity in each eye of at least

- 3/60
- 6/9
- 6/12
- 9/60

3/60

Your doctor will use a standard test card to check this. Further specific eyesight requirement information can be obtained from the relevant medical section at DVLA, or DVA in Northern Ireland. It is your responsibility to inform the authorities if your eyesight changes or you can't meet the requirements.

12.32 *Mark one answer*

You have been asked to drive a fully loaded petrol tanker back to the depot. It has a Maximum Authorised Mass (MAM) of 10 tonnes. What MUST you do?

- Notify the police that you are moving a dangerous load
- Have a fully qualified tanker driver with you for the journey
- Carry a valid DVLA 'approved course' certificate
- Complete the whole journey avoiding built up areas

Carry a valid DVLA 'approved course' certificate

The certificate, valid for five years, is issued by DVLA on receipt of a proof of attending a course and passing a City and Guilds examination.

12.33 *Mark one answer*

As a driver of a goods vehicle it is your responsibility to ensure that

- you are correctly paid for the goods after unloading
- the goods arrive in the same condition as when loaded
- the goods reach their destination ahead of schedule
- your return load is at least as heavy as the outward load

the goods arrive in the same condition as when loaded

As a professional driver you must not allow lack of attention to cause damage to the goods during transit, loading or unloading.

12.34 Mark **one** answer

The CMR consignment note is generally required for carrying goods overseas for hire or reward. How many copies of this note are required?

- Two
- Three
- Four
- Five

- **Four**

Of the four copies required, the consignor, consignee and originator all have a copy, and the fourth one travels with the vehicle.

12.35 Mark **one** answer

You hold a full category C licence. This means that you

- can tow a trailer of any weight
- cannot tow a trailer with more than one axle
- can tow a trailer up to 750 kg
- cannot tow a trailer at all

- **can tow a trailer up to 750 kg**

When you pass a test to drive rigid vehicles only, the regulations allow for trailers up to 750 kg to be towed on a category C or C1 licence. You can do this without taking a further test.

12.36 Mark **one** answer

You are delivering boxes of chilled food to a supermarket. In which area may you require additional specific training?

- Hygiene procedures
- ADR procedures
- Waste-handling procedures
- Eco-safe driving procedures

- **Hygiene procedures**

Chilled foods are transported at temperatures above freezing point. Drivers will need to be trained to operate refrigeration units as well as hygiene procedures.

section **thirteen**

ENVIRONMENTAL ISSUES

This section covers

- Vehicle noise
- Wind resistance
- Fuel consumption
- Refuelling

13.1 *Mark **one** answer*

You are waiting at a terminus for some time. You will reduce pollution by

- revving your engine
- switching off your engine
- leaving your engine on tickover
- keeping your engine at high revs

switching off your engine

If you have to wait for long periods of time you should turn your engine off, as noise and exhaust fumes can cause annoyance as well as pollution.

13.2 *Mark **three** answers*

You are waiting for some time in a stationary traffic queue. Why should you switch your engine off?

- To reduce noise levels
- To save on vehicle air pressure
- To reduce exhaust fumes
- To reduce television interference
- To prevent local annoyance

To reduce noise levels

To reduce exhaust fumes

To prevent local annoyance

When you are delayed in a traffic jam or stationary by the side of a road or in a lay-by, switch off your engine to help protect the environment in which you live. By doing this you will be helping others who are not road users.

13.3 *Mark **one** answer*

You have been waiting in a traffic queue for several minutes. The road in front is blocked. What should you do?

- Keep your engine at tickover speed
- Rev your engine occasionally
- Switch off your engine
- Run the engine at a constant higher speed

Switch off your engine

Switch your engine off when stationary for some time, especially when noise and exhaust fumes cause annoyance and could be harmful.

PROTECT YOUR ENVIRONMENT AND SAVE FUEL.

13.4  *Mark **one** answer*

Using air conditioning systems continuously will usually increase fuel consumption by about

- ⊙ 15%
- ⊙ 30%
- ⊙ 50%
- ⊙ 75%

⊙ **15%**

Avoid using air conditioning systems for long periods as these can increase fuel consumption by about 15%. Try to drive with fuel economy and the environment in mind.

13.5 *Mark **one** answer*

Air pressure should be built up with the

- ⊙ engine switched off
- ⊙ service brake on
- ⊙ engine ticking over
- ⊙ engine revving up

⊙ **engine ticking over**

Vehicle designers and bus drivers have a duty in helping to reduce the effects of pollution on the environment. The most environmentally-friendly way to allow air pressure to build up is with the engine running at tick-over.

13.6 *Mark **one** answer*

The occupants of about how many cars can be carried by one double-deck bus?

- ⊙ 20
- ⊙ 30
- ⊙ 40
- ⊙ 50

⊙ **20**

By being able to carry as many passengers as 20 cars, the bus is helping to reduce pollution. The bus has only one engine and therefore emits less fumes.

13.7 *Mark **one** answer*

After refuelling your bus, what MUST you check before driving?

- ⊙ Your filler caps are securely shut
- ⊙ Your tank is full to the top
- ⊙ The position of the emergency fuel cut-off switch
- ⊙ The low-fuel warning light is working

⊙ **Your filler caps are securely shut**

It is a legal requirement that you check all filler caps are properly closed and secure before driving off.

13.8 Mark **two** answers

Which of the following would be most affected by a vehicle with faulty suspension?

- Underground pipes
- Road surfaces
- Tyre pressures
- Road tunnels
- Overhead gantries

- **Underground pipes**
- **Road surfaces**

If your suspension is damaged, all the weight of the vehicle is compressing the road and anything located below it. The vibrations travel through the ground and can also damage surrounding buildings.

13.9 Mark **three** answers

The pictured vehicle is 'environmentally friendly' because it

- reduces noise pollution
- uses diesel fuel
- uses electricity
- uses unleaded fuel
- reduces parking places
- reduces town traffic

- **reduces noise pollution**
- **uses electricity**
- **reduces town traffic**

This is the sign for a tram. These vehicles are powered by electricity and reduce the emissions released into the environment. As they can carry many people they can help reduce the number of other vehicles on the road.

13.10 Mark **two** answers

Which of the following vehicles are MOST likely to cause severe damage to road surfaces?

- Lorries
- Cars
- Motorcycles
- Bicycles
- Buses

- **Lorries**
- **Buses**

Lorries and buses are much heavier than cars and will have a greater impact on the road surface.

13.11 *Mark **three** answers*

Air suspension can reduce damage to

- the fuel system
- the road surface
- passengers
- bridges
- the tachograph
- underground services

- **the road surface**
- **bridges**
- **underground services**

Air suspension reduces the pressure of the weight of the vehicle driving on an uneven surface. This in turn reduces the vibrations transmitted to buildings along the route.

13.12 *Mark **two** answers*

You can help to reduce the impact of road transport on the environment by

- avoiding high gears
- reducing rest periods
- braking in good time
- increasing your overall speed
- avoiding over-acceleration

- **braking in good time**
- **avoiding over-acceleration**

Good forward planning will reduce the emissions being dispersed into the air and cause less environmental pollution.

13.13 *Mark **one** answer*

As a driver you can help to protect the environment by

- driving faster to reduce travelling time
- avoiding town centres and using bypasses
- filling your fuel tank with red diesel fuel
- leaving your engine running in traffic jams

- **avoiding town centres and using bypasses**

By using bypasses you are less likely to be held up and can travel at a constant speed, thereby reducing the amount of pollution from your vehicle.

13.14 Mark **one** answer

As a professional driver you should

- keep to maximum speeds for shorter journeys
- plan routes to avoid busy times and congestion
- avoid route-planning because of the time it takes
- drive at a faster speed through hazardous areas

plan routes to avoid busy times and congestion

If you plan your journey to avoid busy times you can avoid congestion, and your overall journey time may be reduced.

13.15 Mark **one** answer

You have just refilled your fuel tank. You MUST make sure that the

- tank is completely full up to the filler neck
- filler cap is vented correctly by keeping it loose
- filler cap is properly closed and secure
- tank is nearly full and the filler cap is slightly loose

filler cap is properly closed and secure

Because of the extremely slippery characteristics of diesel fuel, care must be taken at all times to avoid spillages.

13.16 Mark **one** answer

To prevent fuel spillages it is important to

- stop refuelling when half full
- use a filtered system
- close and secure all filler caps
- place the drip tray correctly

close and secure all filler caps

Fuel spilled onto the road causes a serious danger to other road users, especially motorcyclists.

13.17 *Mark **one** answer*

You are following a lorry with a leaking fuel tank. What should you be especially aware of?

- ⊙ The road may be very slippery
- ⊙ The fuel may splash your vehicle
- ⊙ Your brake linings will become slippery
- ⊙ Your spray reducers will not be effective

⊙ **The road may be very slippery**

The leaking fuel can make the road surface extremely slippery. Look out for this, particularly on roundabouts.

13.18 *Mark **one** answer*

The road surface is more likely to be damaged by large vehicles with

- ⊙ a mixture of tyre makes
- ⊙ a mixture of re-cut and new tyres
- ⊙ faulty spray-suppression equipment
- ⊙ faulty suspension

⊙ **faulty suspension**

Suspension faults may result in road damage. Road-friendly suspension is being developed to lessen the impact on the environment, the road surface and under-road services.

13.19 *Mark **three** answers*

How could you save fuel when driving?

- ⊙ By reducing overall speed
- ⊙ By braking as late as you can
- ⊙ By planning routes to avoid congestion
- ⊙ By having properly inflated tyres
- ⊙ By extending vehicles' service times

⊙ **By reducing overall speed**

⊙ **By planning routes to avoid congestion**

⊙ **By having properly inflated tyres**

Your driving skills reflect on the environment. You should consider the impact your attitude will have on the environment every time you drive. By driving sensibly, maintaining your vehicle and planning ahead, you will deserve to be called a professional driver.

13.20 *Mark three answers*

Vehicles have damaged the environment. This has resulted in

- air pollution
- reduced traffic noise
- building deterioration
- less road surface damage
- using up of natural resources

air pollution

building deterioration

using up of natural resources

The increased number of vehicles on the roads has damaged the environment. Transport is an essential part of modern life, but we should not ignore its environmental consequences.

13.21 *Mark one answer*

In a diesel engine which of the following fuels would most improve vehicle emissions?

- High sulphur diesel
- Red diesel
- Low sulphur diesel
- Blue diesel

Low sulphur diesel

This is widely available and has been formulated so that the sulphur content is very low. It makes a considerable improvement to vehicle emissions.

13.22 *Mark one answer*

Using which of the following fuels in a diesel engine would most help the environment?

- Anti-waxing diesel
- Low sulphur diesel
- Red diesel
- Anti-foaming diesel

Low sulphur diesel

Sulphur produces acid gases. Diesel fuels with lower sulphur content have been produced to lessen damage to the environment.

13.23 *Mark **two** answers*

What must you do after filling your fuel tanks?

- Return the pump keys to the office
- Check your tachograph
- Clean up any fuel that has spilled
- Check that the filler caps are closed
- Complete the fuel log sheets
- Check your fuel gauge

Clean up any fuel that has spilled

Check that the filler caps are closed

If fuel has spilled it can be hazardous for anyone stepping onto it. Take care to make certain your filler caps are closed properly so that you don't spill fuel as you drive along the road.

13.24 *Mark **one** answer*

Your vehicle is fitted with a reverse warning bleeper. You MUST switch it off between the hours of 11.30 pm and 7.00 am on a road with a

- 30 mph speed limit
- temporary speed limit
- national speed limit
- 40 mph speed limit

30 mph speed limit

Try to avoid making unnecessary noise. Your vehicle will make more noise than a car, so try to consider others who may be resting.

13.25 *Mark **one** answer*

Your vehicle is fitted with a reverse warning bleeper. You must switch the bleeper off when reversing

- after 11.30 pm at night along a 30 mph road
- after 11.30 pm at night along a 40 mph road
- near a school entrance
- near a hospital entrance

after 11.30 pm at night along a 30 mph road

It is an offence to operate an audible warning system on a road subject to a 30 mph speed limit between 11.30 pm and 7 am. Always remember to reset the alarm outside these times.

13.26 *Mark **one** answer*

Fuel consumption could be made worse by continuous use of

- air suspension
- heated mirrors
- air conditioning
- electrical retarder

air conditioning

Use air conditioning sparingly, running it continuously increases overall fuel consumption by about 15%.

13.27 *Mark **one** answer*

Vehicles are fitted with air suspension to

- reduce wear to roads
- reduce tyre wear
- improve fuel consumption
- help the driver stay awake

reduce wear to roads

Air suspension causes less damage to the road surface than conventional suspension systems. Vehicles transporting glass and fragile loads normally use it and it is considered to be environmentally friendly.

13.28 *Mark **one** answer*

Your vehicle is fitted with a warning device, which sounds when reversing. When should you NOT use it in a built-up area?

- Between 10.30 pm and 6.30 am
- Between 11 pm and 6.30 am
- Between 11.30 pm and 7 am
- Between 12.30 am and 8 am

Between 11.30 pm and 7 am

Some vehicles are fitted with an audible warning that sounds when the vehicle's reversing. This is an effective device to warn pedestrians and other road users of a reversing vehicle, and doesn't take away the need to use effective observation all around your vehicle before and while you're reversing. Don't use the device in built-up areas at night. Have some consideration for the residents and don't disturb them with excessive noise.

13.29 Mark **two** answers

You are driving a vehicle with excessive exhaust smoke. Which of the following is correct?

- You risk being reported
- You risk reducing your vision ahead
- You could cause the brakes to fade
- You are breaking the law

You risk being reported

You are breaking the law

Apart from the fact that excessive smoke causes pollution, it can also make it more difficult for those following you to see properly. If you become aware of excessive smoke you should take steps to have the problem attended to as soon as possible.

13.30 Mark **three** answers

You are driving a vehicle fitted with 'road-friendly' suspension. This helps the environment by reducing damage to

- the driver's seat
- historical buildings
- the road surface
- overhead cables
- river banks
- bridges

historical buildings

the road surface

bridges

Road-friendly suspension reduces the vibration caused by the impact of the wheels on the road surface.

13.31 Mark **one** answer

As a driver you can help to ease traffic congestion by

- planning journeys to avoid the busy times
- planning journeys to avoid driving at quiet times
- driving on motorways for all journeys
- avoiding using motorways for all journeys

planning journeys to avoid the busy times

By planning your journey to avoid busy times you will avoid the build-up of traffic that can often occur.

13.32 *Mark one answer*

You are parked for a short period in a town while you plan a route. You should

- keep the engine running on tickover
- rev the engine occasionally for air pressure
- never turn off the engine for short periods
- switch off the engine

switch off the engine

This will be safer and emit less fumes into the environment. If diesel engines are left idling for any length of time they emit excessive smoke as you drive off. This is unpleasant for any pedestrians who are nearby at the time.

13.33 *Mark three answers*

Which three of the following could cause unnecessary pollution to the environment?

- Excessive exhaust fumes
- Regular servicing
- Vehicles driven poorly
- Poorly maintained vehicles
- High level exhaust systems

Excessive exhaust fumes

Vehicles driven poorly

Poorly maintained vehicles

All drivers on the road should play their part in protecting the environment against pollution. Ensure the vehicle you drive is maintained properly. Immediately report any defects such as unusual exhaust smoke. Consider whether further training could improve your driving skills. CARE FOR THE ENVIRONMENT AS YOU DRIVE.

13.34 *Mark one answer*

Diesel fuel has been spilled on the road. This will be particularly danger for

- lorries
- motorcycles
- horses
- cars

motorcycles

Spilt diesel creates a serious risk to other road users, especially motorcyclists. Take care when refuelling and ensure that all filler caps and tank hatches are properly closed and secure.

13.35 Mark **one** answer

Members of the public are encouraged to report any vehicle with

- ⊙ excessive exhaust fumes
- ⊙ an unsheeted load
- ⊙ different makes of tyres
- ⊙ no contact address visible

⊙ **excessive exhaust fumes**

You should ensure that maintenance schedules are strictly followed, and that filters are changed regularly, exhaust emissions meet current regulations and diesel injectors are operating efficiently.

13.36 Mark **one** answer

You should only sound your horn in a built-up area between 11.30 pm and 7.00 am when

- ⊙ you are parked
- ⊙ your vehicle is moving
- ⊙ you are stationary
- ⊙ another vehicle poses a danger

⊙ **another vehicle poses a danger**

The horn should not be used between 11.30 pm and 7.00 am in built up areas unless another vehicle is unaware of you and poses a danger.

13.37 Mark **one** answer

You should take great care to avoid spilling diesel. It is very slippery and causes a serious risk on the road, particularly to

- ⊙ motorcycles
- ⊙ tractors
- ⊙ buses
- ⊙ lorries

⊙ **motorcycles**

Take care to secure caps and tank hatches – diesel is very slippery and if spilled on the road it is particularly dangerous to motorcyclists.

10.00 *Mark one answer*

A vehicle 'reverse warning bleeper' must NOT be used

- in parking bays
- between 11 pm and 7.30 am
- between 11.30 pm and 7 am in 30 mph limits
- near hospitals

between 11.30 pm and 7 am in 30 mph limits

Transport now operates 24 hours a day. If you are working the 'night shift', show consideration when others are at rest. You must not use your reverse warning bleepers between the hours of 11.30 pm and 7 am, and try to avoid making unnecessary noise.

13.39 *Mark one answer*

You have lost the filler cap to your diesel tank. You should

- get a replacement before driving
- push a rag into the filler pipe
- drive slowly back to your depot
- only fill the tank half-full

get a replacement before driving

Don't drive without a fuel filler cap in place as fuel could spill out onto the carriageway when cornering or turning at roundabouts. Diesel fuel, in particular, will make the road surface extremely slippery, and any spillage should be reported so that the emergency services can make the road safe.

13.40 *Mark one answer*

Why can it be an advantage for traffic speed to stay constant over a longer distance?

- You will do more stop-start driving
- You will use far more fuel
- You will be able to use more direct routes
- Your overall journey time may normally improve

Your overall journey time may normally improve

When traffic travels at a constant speed over a longer distance, journey times normally improve. You may feel that you could travel faster for short periods but this won't generally make your overall time better. Signs will show the maximum safe speed at which you may travel.

13.41 *Mark **one** answer*

Before starting a journey it is wise to plan your route. How can you do this?

- Look at a map
- Contact your local garage
- Look in your vehicle service record
- Check your vehicle registration document

Look at a map

Planning your journey before you set out can help to make it much easier, more pleasant and ease traffic congestion. Look at a map to help you do this. You may need different scale maps depending on where and how far you're going. Printing or writing out the route can also help.

13.42 *Mark **one** answer* NI EXEMPT

It can help to plan your route before starting a journey. You can do this by contacting

- your local filling station
- a motoring organisation
- the Driver Vehicle Licensing Agency
- your vehicle manufacturer

a motoring organisation

Most motoring organisations will give you a detailed plan of your trip showing directions and distance. Some will also include advice on rest and fuel stops. The Highways Agency website will also give you information on roadworks and accidents and gives expected delay times.

13.43 *Mark **one** answer*

How can you plan your route before starting a long journey?

- Check your vehicle's workshop manual
- Ask your local garage
- Use a route planner on the internet
- Consult your travel agents

Use a route planner on the internet

Various route planners are available on the internet. Most of them give you various options allowing you to choose the most direct, quickest or scenic route. They can also include rest and fuel stops and distances. Print them off and take them with you.

13.47 Mark **one** answer

It is a good idea to plan your journey to avoid busy times. This is because

- your vehicle will use more fuel
- you will see less road works
- it will help to ease congestion
- you will travel a much shorter distance

it will help to ease congestion

Avoiding busy times means that you are not adding needlessly to traffic congestion. Other advantages are that you will use less fuel and feel less stressed.

13.48 Mark **one** answer

By avoiding busy times when travelling

- you are more likely to be held up
- your journey time will be longer
- you will travel a much shorter distance
- you are less likely to be delayed

you are less likely to be delayed

If possible, avoid the early morning and late afternoon and early evening 'rush hour'. Doing this should allow you to travel in a more relaxed frame of mind, concentrate solely on what you're doing and arrive at your destination feeling less stressed.

13.49 Mark **one** answer

It can help to plan your route before starting a journey. Why should you also plan an alternative route?

- Your original route may be blocked
- Your maps may have different scales
- You may find you have to pay a congestion charge
- Because you may get held up by a tractor

Your original route may be blocked

It can be frustrating and worrying to find your planned route is blocked by roadworks or diversions. If you have planned an alternative you will feel less stressed and able to concentrate fully on your driving or riding. If your original route is mostly on motorways it's a good idea to plan an alternative using non-motorway roads. Always carry a map with you just in case you need to refer to it.

13.44 Mark **one** answer

Planning your route before setting out can be helpful. How can you do this?

- ⊙ Look in a motoring magazine
- ⊙ Only visit places you know
- ⊙ Try to travel at busy times
- ⊙ Print or write down the route

⊙ **Print or write down the route**

Print or write down your route before setting out. Some places are not well signed so using place names and road numbers may help you avoid problems en route. Try to get an idea of how far you're going before you leave. You can also use it to re-check the next stage at each rest stop.

13.45 Mark **one** answer

Why is it a good idea to plan your journey to avoid busy times?

- ⊙ You will have an easier journey
- ⊙ You will have a more stressful journey
- ⊙ Your journey time will be longer
- ⊙ It will cause more traffic congestion

⊙ **You will have an easier journey**

No one likes to spend time in traffic queues. Try to avoid busy times related to school or work travel. As well as moving vehicles you should also consider congestion caused by parked cars, buses and coaches around schools.

13.46 Mark **one** answer

Planning your journey to avoid busy times has a number of advantages. One of these is

- ⊙ your journey will take longer
- ⊙ you will have a more pleasant journey
- ⊙ you will cause more pollution
- ⊙ your stress level will be greater

⊙ **you will have a more pleasant journey**

Having a pleasant journey can have safety benefits. You will be less tired and stressed and this will allow you to concentrate more on your driving.

13.50 Mark **one** answer

You will find that driving smoothly can

- ⊙ reduce journey times by about 15%
- ⊙ increase fuel consumption by about 15%
- ⊙ reduce fuel consumption by about 15%
- ⊙ increase journey times by about 15%

⊙ **reduce fuel consumption by about 15%**

Not only will you save fuel by about 15%, by driving smoothly, but you will also reduce the amount of wear and tear on your vehicle and reduce pollution. You will also feel more relaxed and have a more pleasant journey.

13.51 Mark **one** answer

You can save fuel when conditions allow by

- ⊙ using lower gears as often as possible
- ⊙ accelerating sharply in each gear
- ⊙ using each gear in turn
- ⊙ missing out some gears

⊙ **missing out some gears**

Missing out intermediate gears when appropriate reduces the amount of time you are accelerating - the time when your vehicle uses most fuel.

13.52 Mark **one** answer

The rev counter on most vehicles has colour-coded bands. For optimum fuel efficiency which band should you try to stay in?

- ⊙ Amber
- ⊙ Blue
- ⊙ Green
- ⊙ Red

⊙ **Green**

Most vehicles have a rev counter (tachometer) that is colour-coded. As a general rule in order to maintain good fuel efficiency you should keep the rev counter within the green band when driving.

13.53 Mark **one** answer

Usually a rev counter is divided into coloured bands. Which band should you stay in for maximum fuel economy?

- ⊙ Blue
- ⊙ Green
- ⊙ Amber
- ⊙ Red

⊙ **Green**

Most large vehicles have a rev counter (tachometer) that is divided into coloured bands. This helps you to drive in the most fuel efficient way and avoid damage to the engine. The green band is the one giving adequate torque and power with the optimum fuel economy.

13.54 Mark **one** answer

Your vehicle is fitted with an engine management system. When starting the engine why should you NOT press the accelerator?

- ⊙ The vehicle will surge forward
- ⊙ It will stall the engine
- ⊙ The endurance brake will be activated
- ⊙ It will waste fuel

⊙ **It will waste fuel**

Pressing the accelerator pedal on these types of vehicles when operating the starter is unnecessary. It causes excessive and wasteful fuel injection which the engine does not need.

13.55 Mark **one** answer

Driving with the rev counter in the red band could

- ⊙ give optimum fuel economy
- ⊙ improve engine efficiency
- ⊙ damage the engine
- ⊙ falsify the tachograph reading

⊙ **damage the engine**

Driving for long periods in the red band will cause the engine to wear prematurely and lead to expensive repairs. This could result in the vehicle being off the road for some time.

13.56 Mark **one** answer

It's expected that a driver who holds a Driver Certificate of Professional Competence (CPC) will drive in a manner that leads to

- increased downtime
- increased fuel consumption
- reduced traffic volume
- reduced emissions

reduced emissions

Better knowledge and use of eco-safe driving techniques can result in lower fuel consumption and emissions. Other benefits are expected to include improved road safety and enhanced professionalism.

13.57 Mark **one** answer

Energy-saving tyres contribute to better fuel economy because they

- have a reduced rolling resistance
- are much easier to manufacture
- allow you to travel at higher speeds
- allow heat to disperse more quickly

have a reduced rolling resistance

You have a part to play in reducing the impact road transport has on the environment. Less fuel will be used to move your vehicle at the same speed if you use a tyre with reduced rolling resistance, compared to one of normal construction.

13.58 Mark **one** answer

Your vehicle is fitted with an engine management system. Pressing the accelerator when starting the engine will

- use an excessive amount of fuel
- cause an excessive build up of air pressure
- decrease exhaust emissions
- decrease oil consumption

use an excessive amount of fuel

When starting most modern engines you do not need to press the accelerator. This wastes fuel, is unnecessary and damages the environment.

13.59 Mark **one** answer

A benefit of the Driver Certificate of Professional Competence (CPC) qualification is expected to be enhanced professionalism. What other adavantage is expected?

- A reduction in fuel consumption
- An exemption from tachograph regulations
- A reduction in road tax charges
- An exemption from all congestion charges

A reduction in fuel consumption

The Driver Certificate of Professional Competence (CPC) qualification and training syllabus is designed to give enhanced professionalism and improvements to road safety. Other expected benefits are a general reduction in fuel consumption and emissions, resulting from a better knowledge of eco-safe driving techniques.

13.60 Mark **one** answer

You have been stopped at a roadside check. What would staff from environmental health departments be looking for?

- Licence entitlement
- Exhaust emissions
- Tachograph changes
- Illegal immigrants

Exhaust emissions

Local authority environmental health departments check the vehicle and its exhaust emissions. They have the power to prosecute the driver and the operator as do enforcement bodies like VOSA.

13.61 Mark **one** answer

What will help you to become an eco-safe driver?

- being aware of hazards
- avoiding block changing
- accelerating rapidly
- using air conditioning

being aware of hazards

Driving in an eco-safe manner means that you plan well ahead for hazards and react in good time. This can save fuel and is good for the environment.

13.62 *Mark **one** answer*

Which of these can help to maximise fuel economy?

- Cruise control
- Air suspension
- Re-grooved tyres
- Diff-lock

Cruise control

Using cruise control can help to make the best use of your vehicle's electronic control system. It should only be used when you can see well ahead in good road conditions. Be prepared to switch it off immediately if the traffic situation change.

13.63 *Mark **one** answer*

What is a benefit of forward planning and early recognition of potential hazards?

- Eco-safe driving
- Increased fuel consumption
- Late braking
- Rapid acceleration

Eco-safe driving

Poor planning leads to late braking and harsh acceleration. This will cause higher fuel consumption, which increases the damage to the environment.

13.64 *Mark **one** answer*

What will help you to achieve eco-safe driving?

- keeping in the lower gears
- planning well ahead
- keeping close to a vehicle ahead
- braking as late as possible

planning well ahead

Increasing your planning, and also hazard perception skills, will help you make the maximum use of your vehicle's, engine, braking and momentum. This can improve fuel consumption and help to reduce damage to the environment.

13.65 Mark **one** answer

Which of these will cause the greatest increase in your vehicles fuel consumption?

- Electric windows
- Manual sun roof
- Air conditioning
- Power steering

- **Air conditioning**

Using air conditioning continuously can increase fuel consumption by about 15%. Think of the environment and only use it when necessary.

13.66 Mark **one** answer

Some ancillary equipment can increase fuel consumption. Which will cause the greatest increase?

- Air suspension
- Air brakes
- Air bags
- Air conditioning

- **Air conditioning**

A number of ancillary systems use power from the engine to operate them. The downside to this is that fuel consumption can be increased. Air conditioning can increase this by up to 15%.

13.67 Mark **two** answers

Your lorry has been fitted with wind deflectors. When driving in windy conditions these will help to

- increase the amount of fuel you will use
- increase the wind resistance on your vehicle
- increase the pressure in the tyres
- reduce the wind resistance on your vehicle
- reduce the amount of fuel you will use

- **reduce the wind resistance on your vehicle**
- **reduce the amount of fuel you will use**

Wind deflectors direct the wind either around or over your vehicle. Your vehicle then requires less power to make progress against the wind. As a result your vehicle will use less fuel.

13.68 *Mark **one** answer*

Cab-mounted wind deflectors can reduce

- journey times
- load capacity
- tyre wear
- fuel consumption

fuel consumption

A wind deflector redirects the air flow around the vehicle. This reduces the amount of fuel required to propel the vehicle forward.

13.69 *Mark **two** answers*

Fuel consumption for lorries can be reduced by fitting

- single axles only
- a high-level exhaust pipe
- side skirts
- wind deflectors

side skirts

wind deflectors

Both of these reduce resistance to wind, which will help the vehicle to use less fuel.

13.70 *Mark **one** answer*

You are a driver who is certified to carry dangerous goods. The certificate is valid for

- one year
- two years
- five years
- ten years

five years

The operator of a UK-registered vehicle engaged in the carriage of dangerous goods should ensure that the driver has a valid vocational training certificate. These certificates are valid for five years.

13.71 *Mark **three** answers*

Which of the following would help to reduce the impact that your lorry has on the environment?

- Driving through town centres
- Braking in good time
- Planning routes to avoid busy times
- Racing to make up time
- Anticipating well ahead

- **Braking in good time**
- **Planning routes to avoid busy times**
- **Anticipating well ahead**

Avoiding town centres will lessen the vibration and pollution caused by your vehicle. Good anticipation and forward planning will always benefit you and the environment, wherever you drive.

13.72 *Mark **one** answer*

The purpose of a fly sheet tightly fastened over a tipper body is to reduce the

- drag effect
- steering effort
- legal load weight
- load capacity

- **drag effect**

The drag effect is caused by wind entering the body of the tipper. If the cavity is covered, then the drag is reduced.

13.73 *Mark **two** answers*

How could you improve the fuel consumption of your lorry?

- Brake late as often as you can
- Fit a cab-mounted wind deflector
- Avoid sheeting any bulky loads
- Try to increase your overall speed
- Make regular checks on tyre pressures

- **Fit a cab-mounted wind deflector**
- **Make regular checks on tyre pressures**

As a professional driver you should consider fuel efficiency and the effect this has on the environment.

Wind deflectors can effectively lower wind resistance.

Correct tyre pressures and proper maintenance also play their part in fuel efficiency.

13.74 Mark *one* answer

Red diesel is

- only used by private cars
- for authorised purposes only
- available at all garages
- very environmentally friendly

for authorised purposes only

Red diesel is subject to less excise duty than standard diesel, so it is considerably cheaper. It should only be used for authorised purposes. Any driver whose vehicle is found to be using this fuel illegally faces severe penalties.

13.75 Mark *one* answer

You are driving a lorry with a loaded skip. The skip should be covered with a net to

- prevent rubbish from falling out of it
- protect the contents from the weather
- make it more visible to other traffic
- stop others from adding to the load

prevent rubbish from falling out of it

If the load is not covered, rubbish can be caught by the wind and blown onto the carriageway. This will create unnecessary hazards for other road users.

13.76 Mark *one* answer

You may park a lorry over 7.5 tonnes on a verge for essential loading, but it must have

- a collection note
- an orange badge
- the owner's permission
- an attendant

an attendant

Goods vehicles with a maximum authorised mass of more than 7.5 tonnes (including any trailer) must not be parked on a verge except where this is essential for loading and unloading. In these cases, the vehicle must not be left unattended.

13.77 Mark *one* answer

You must not park any unattended lorry over 7.5 tonnes on a verge without

- police permission
- warning lights
- the owner's permission
- a loading permit

police permission

If your vehicle has to be left unattended on a verge for any reason, you must inform the police.

13.78  *Mark **one** answer*

Cab-mounted wind deflectors are fitted to

- increase wind buffeting
- increase engine power
- reduce exhaust emissions
- reduce fuel consumption

reduce fuel consumption

Cab mounted wind deflectors can effectively lower wind resistance created by large box bodies. Together with lower side panel skirts, they will help reduce fuel consumption.

13.79  *Mark **one** answer*

All drivers need to consider the environment. Which of these can help to reduce fuel consumption?

- Changing filters regularly
- Keeping tyres under-inflated
- Always using gears in sequence
- Keeping the rev counter in the amber band

Changing filters regularly

Ensure your vehicle is serviced regularly. Poorly-maintained engines use more fuel and emit more exhaust fumes than those that are well maintained. Remember that members of the public are encouraged to report vehicles emitting excessive exhaust fumes.

13.80 *Mark **one** answer*

What will a correctly adjusted air deflector do?

- Save fuel
- Reduce tyre wear
- Reduce road surface wear
- Cut loading time

Save fuel

Correctly adjusted air deflectors will save fuel. These should be adjusted to guide airflow over the highest point at the front of the trailer or load and body.

13.81 *Mark **one** answer*

You are at a roadside check. What would staff from HM Revenue and Customs be looking for?

- Red diesel
- Vehicle defects
- Driver's hours records
- Exhaust emissions

Red diesel

HM Revenue and Customs staff carry out a variety of checks during a roadside stop. These include checking for the correct type of fuel used, and the type and legality of any load being carried.

13.82 *Mark **one** answer*

Why should the height of a load be kept to a minimum?

- To reduce aerodynamic drag
- To increase rolling resistance
- To increase momentum
- To reduce unloading time

To reduce aerodynamic drag

Keeping the height of the load as low as possible will reduce the drag coefficient of the vehicle. This will help to save fuel. It's particularly relevant when using a flat-bodied lorry or trailer.

section **fourteen**
OTHER ROAD USERS

This section covers

- Vulnerable road users
- Other vehicles

14.1 *Mark **one** answer*

When driving through a bus station you should

- ⊙ ensure that your destination boards are correct
- ⊙ drive only in first gear
- ⊙ look out for people leaving the buses
- ⊙ use your mirrors more than usual

⊙ **look out for people leaving the buses**

Bus stations are busy places. If people are in a rush they may not always look properly before getting off the bus. You must always keep your speed down and be aware that danger may suddenly arise when you least expect it.

14.2 *Mark **one** answer*

Your vehicle leaks diesel fuel on a roundabout. This will most affect

- ⊙ three-wheel vehicle drivers
- ⊙ motorcyclists
- ⊙ towed vehicles
- ⊙ car drivers

⊙ **motorcyclists**

When diesel fuel makes contact with most types of road surface it becomes extremely slippery. This can cause danger for all types of vehicle, but particularly those with two wheels, because it reduces the grip between tyres and the road surface.

14.3 *Mark **three** answers*

Which THREE of these vehicles are most likely to be affected by strong winds?

- ⊙ Flat-bed lorries
- ⊙ Double-deck buses
- ⊙ Motorcycles
- ⊙ Horse boxes
- ⊙ Tractors
- ⊙ Estate cars

⊙ **Double-deck buses**

⊙ **Motorcycles**

⊙ **Horse boxes**

Strong winds can force other vehicles into your path. You should be aware of the vehicles which are most likely to be affected. Adjust your speed so that you can stop or take avoiding action safely if necessary. Be vigilant for the more vulnerable road users in these conditions.

14.4 *Mark **one** answer*

The vehicle ahead is being driven by a learner. You should

- ⊙ keep calm and be patient
- ⊙ drive up close behind
- ⊙ put your headlights on full beam
- ⊙ sound your horn and overtake

⊙ **keep calm and be patient**

Learners might take longer to react to traffic situations. Don't unnerve and intimidate them by driving up close behind.

14.5 *Mark **two** answers*

You are about to overtake horse riders. Which TWO of the following could scare the horses?

- ⊙ Sounding your horn
- ⊙ Giving arm signals
- ⊙ Driving slowly
- ⊙ Revving your engine

⊙ **Sounding your horn**

⊙ **Revving your engine**

When passing horses allow plenty of space and slow down. Animals can become frightened by sudden or loud noises so don't sound your horn or rev the engine.

14.6 Mark **two** answers

You have stopped at a pelican crossing. A disabled person is crossing slowly in front of you. The lights have now changed to green. You should

- allow the person to cross
- drive in front of the person
- drive behind the person
- sound your horn
- be patient
- edge forward slowly

- **allow the person to cross**
- **be patient**

At a pelican crossing the green light means you may proceed as long as the crossing is clear. If someone hasn't finished crossing be patient and wait for them.

14.7 Mark **one** answer

Which sign means that there may be people walking along the road?

Always check the road signs. They'll keep you informed of hazards ahead and help you to anticipate any problems. There are a number of different signs showing pedestrians. Learn the meaning of each one. This will help you to be aware of the particular hazard ahead.

14.8 Mark **one** answer

You are turning left at a junction. Pedestrians have started to cross the road. You should

- go on, giving them plenty of room
- stop and wave at them to cross
- sound your horn and proceed
- give way to them

- **give way to them**

If you're turning into a side road you should give way to pedestrians already crossing. They have priority. Don't wave them across the road, sound your horn or flash your lights. If a pedestrian is slow or indecisive be patient and wait. Don't hurry them across by revving the engine.

14.9 Mark one answer

You are turning left from a main road into a side road. People are already crossing the road into which you are turning. You should

- continue, as it is your right of way
- signal to them to continue crossing
- wait and allow them to cross
- sound your horn to warn them of your presence

wait and allow them to cross

Always check the road you're turning into. Approaching at the correct speed will allow you enough time to observe and react.

14.10 Mark one answer

You are at a road junction, turning into a minor road. There are pedestrians crossing the minor road. You should

- stop and wave the pedestrians across
- sound your horn to let the pedestrians know that you are there
- give way to the pedestrians who are already crossing
- carry on, the pedestrians should give way to you

give way to the pedestrians who are already crossing

Always look into the road you're turning into. If there are pedestrians crossing, be considerate, but don't wave or signal to them to cross. Signal your intention to turn as you approach.

14.11 Mark one answer

You intend to turn right into a side road. Just before turning you should check for motorcyclists who might be

- overtaking on your left
- following you closely
- emerging from the side road
- overtaking on your right

overtaking on your right

Never attempt to change direction to the right without checking your right-hand mirror. A motorcyclist might not have seen your signal. This action should become a matter of routine.

14.12 Mark *one* answer

A toucan crossing is different from other crossings because

- moped riders can use it
- it is controlled by a traffic warden
- it is controlled by two flashing lights
- cyclists can use it

- **cyclists can use it**

Pedestrians and cyclists are shown the green light together. The signals are push-button operated and there is no flashing amber phase.

14.13 Mark *two* answers

At toucan crossings

- there is no flashing amber light
- cyclists are not permitted
- there is a continuously flashing amber beacon
- pedestrians and cyclists may cross
- you only stop if someone is waiting to cross

- **there is no flashing amber light**
- **pedestrians and cyclists may cross**

There are some crossings where cycle routes lead the cyclists to cross at the same place as pedestrians. Always look out for cyclists, as they're likely to be approaching faster than pedestrians.

14.14 Mark *one* answer

Where would you see this sign?

- In the window of a car taking children to school
- At the side of the road
- At playground areas
- On the rear of a school bus or coach

- **On the rear of a school bus or coach**

Vehicles that are used to carry children to and from school will be travelling at busy times of the day. Be prepared for a vehicle with this sign to make frequent stops. It might pick up or set down passengers in places other than normal bus stops.

14.15   *Mark* **one** *answer*

What does this sign mean?

- ⊙ No route for pedestrians and cyclists
- ⊙ A route for pedestrians only
- ⊙ A route for cyclists only
- ⊙ A route for pedestrians and cyclists

⊙ **A route for pedestrians and cyclists**

This shared route is for pedestrians and cyclists only. Be aware that when it ends the cyclists will be rejoining the main road.

14.16 *Mark* **one** *answer*

What action would you take when elderly people are crossing the road?

- ⊙ Wave them across so they know that you have seen them
- ⊙ Be patient and allow them to cross in their own time
- ⊙ Rev the engine to let them know that you are waiting
- ⊙ Tap the horn in case they are hard of hearing

⊙ **Be patient and allow them to cross in their own time**

Don't hurry elderly people across the road by getting too close to them or revving the engine. Be aware that they might take longer to cross. They might also be hard of hearing and not able to hear your approach.

14.17 *Mark* **one** *answer*

You see two elderly pedestrians about to cross the road ahead. You should

- ⊙ expect them to wait for you to pass
- ⊙ speed up to get past them quickly
- ⊙ stop and wave them across the road
- ⊙ be careful, they may misjudge your speed

⊙ **be careful, they may misjudge your speed**

Their concentration, judgement, hearing and/or vision could be impaired. Be aware that if they proceed to cross they will take more time to do so.

14.18 Mark **one** answer

You are coming up to a roundabout. A cyclist is signalling to turn right. What should you do?

- Overtake on the right
- Give a horn warning
- Signal the cyclist to move across
- Give the cyclist plenty of room

Give the cyclist plenty of room

Leave plenty of room if you're following a cyclist who's signalling to turn right at a roundabout. Give them space and time to get into the correct lane.

14.19 Mark **one** answer

You are approaching this roundabout and see the cyclist signal right. Why is the cyclist keeping to the left?

- It is a quicker route for the cyclist
- The cyclist is going to turn left instead
- The cyclist thinks The Highway Code does not apply to bicycles
- The cyclist is slower and more vulnerable

The cyclist is slower and more vulnerable

Cycling in today's heavy traffic can be hazardous. Some cyclists may not feel happy about crossing the path of traffic to take up a position in an outside lane. Be aware of this and understand that, although in the left-hand lane, the cyclist might be turning right.

14.20 Mark **one** answer

You are waiting to come out of a side road. Why should you watch carefully for motorcycles?

- Motorcycles are usually faster than cars
- Police patrols often use motorcycles
- Motorcycles are small and hard to see
- Motorcycles have right of way

Motorcycles are small and hard to see

Watch out for motorcyclists if you're waiting to emerge from a side road. They're smaller and more difficult to see. Be especially careful if there are parked vehicles restricting your view, there might be a motorcyclist approaching.

IF YOU CAN'T SEE, DON'T GO.

14.21 Mark **one** answer

In daylight, an approaching motorcyclist is using a dipped headlight. Why?

- So that the rider can be seen more easily
- To stop the battery overcharging
- To improve the rider's vision
- The rider is inviting you to proceed

So that the rider can be seen more easily

A motorcycle can be lost out of sight behind another vehicle. The use of the headlight helps to make it more conspicuous and therefore more easily seen.

14.22 Mark **one** answer

Motorcyclists should wear bright clothing mainly because

- they must do so by law
- it helps keep them cool in summer
- the colours are popular
- drivers often do not see them

drivers often do not see them

Although they're advised to wear clothing that's bright or reflective, motorcyclists often wear black. This means that they're difficult to see. Look out for them.

14.23 Mark **one** answer

Motorcyclists will often look round over their right shoulder just before turning right. This is because

- they need to listen for following traffic
- motorcycles do not have mirrors
- looking around helps them balance as they turn
- they need to check for traffic in their blind area

they need to check for traffic in their blind area

Expect a motorcyclist who makes a quick glance over their shoulder to be changing direction. They should do this before turning. By observing this you'll get an early signal of their intention.

14.24 Mark **two** answers

You are approaching a roundabout. There are horses just ahead of you. You should

- be prepared to stop
- treat them like any other vehicle
- give them plenty of room
- accelerate past as quickly as possible
- sound your horn as a warning

- **be prepared to stop**
- **give them plenty of room**

Horse riders often keep to the outside of the roundabout even if they are turning right. Give them room in case they have to cross lanes of traffic.

14.25 Mark **three** answers

Which THREE should you do when passing sheep on a road?

- Allow plenty of room
- Drive very slowly
- Pass quickly but quietly
- Be ready to stop
- Briefly sound your horn

- **Allow plenty of room**
- **Drive very slowly**
- **Be ready to stop**

Slow down and be ready to stop if you see animals in the road ahead. Animals are easily frightened by noise and vehicles passing too close to them. Stop if signalled to do so by the person in charge.

14.26 Mark **one** answer

At night you see a pedestrian wearing reflective clothing and carrying a bright red light. What does this mean?

- You are approaching roadworks
- You are approaching an organised walk
- You are approaching a slow-moving vehicle
- You are approaching an accident black spot

- **You are approaching an organised walk**

The people involved in the walk should be keeping to the left, but this can't be assumed. Pass slowly, ensuring that you have the time to do so safely. Be aware that the pedestrians have their backs to you and might not know that you're there.

14.27 Mark **one** answer

There are flashing amber lights under a school warning sign. What action should you take?

- Reduce speed until you are clear of the area
- Keep up your speed and sound the horn
- Increase your speed to clear the area quickly
- Wait at the lights until they change to green

- **Reduce speed until you are clear of the area**

The flashing amber lights are switched on to warn you that children may be crossing near a school.

14.28 Mark **one** answer

You are approaching this crossing. You should

- prepare to slow down and stop
- stop and wave the pedestrians across
- speed up and pass by quickly
- drive on unless the pedestrians step out

- **prepare to slow down and stop**

Be courteous and prepare to stop. Do not wave people across as this could be dangerous if another vehicle is approaching the crossing.

14.29 Mark **one** answer

These road markings must be kept clear to allow

- school children to be dropped off
- for teachers to park
- school children to be picked up
- a clear view of the crossing area

a clear view of the crossing area

Keeping the markings clear makes sure that drivers and riders passing and children crossing have a clear, unrestricted view of the crossing area.

14.30 Mark **one** answer

You must not stop on these road markings because you may obstruct

- childrens' view of the crossing area
- teachers' access to the school
- delivery vehicles' access to the school
- emergency vehicles' access to the school

childrens' view of the crossing area

These markings are found on the road outside schools. Do NOT stop (even to set down or pick up children) or park on them. The markings are to make sure that drivers, riders and children have a clear view.

14.31  *Mark one answer*

Stopping on these road markings may obstruct

SCHOOL KEEP CLEAR

- emergency vehicles' access to the school
- drivers' view of the crossing area
- teachers' access to the school
- delivery vehicles' access to the school

drivers' view of the crossing area

You will see these markings outside schools. They must be left clear at all times so that drivers, riders and children have a clear view.

14.32 *Mark one answer*

You are following two cyclists. They approach a roundabout in the left-hand lane. In which direction should you expect the cyclists to go?

- Left
- Right
- Any direction
- Straight ahead

Any direction

If you're following a cyclist onto a roundabout be aware that they might not be taking the exit you anticipate. Cyclists approaching in the left-hand lane may be turning right but may not have been able to get into the correct lane due to the heavy traffic. Give them room.

14.33 *Mark one answer*

You are travelling behind a moped. You want to turn left just ahead. You should

- overtake the moped before the junction
- pull alongside the moped and stay level until just before the junction
- sound your horn as a warning and pull in front of the moped
- stay behind until the moped has passed the junction

stay behind until the moped has passed the junction

Passing the moped and turning into the junction could mean that you cut across in front of the rider. This might force them to slow down, stop or even lose control.

14.34 Mark **one** answer

You see a horse rider as you approach a roundabout. They are signalling right but keeping well to the left. You should

- proceed as normal
- keep close to them
- cut in front of them
- stay well back

stay well back

Allow horse riders to enter and exit the roundabout in their own time. Don't drive up close behind or alongside them, this could disturb the horses.

14.35 Mark **one** answer

How would you react to drivers who appear to be inexperienced?

- Sound your horn to warn them of your presence
- Be patient and prepare for them to react more slowly
- Flash your headlights to indicate that it is safe for them to proceed
- Overtake them as soon as possible

Be patient and prepare for them to react more slowly

Learners might not have confidence when they first start to drive. Allow them plenty of room and don't react adversely to their hesitation. We all learn from experience, and new drivers will have had less practice in dealing with all the situations that might occur.

14.36 Mark **one** answer

You are following a learner driver who stalls at a junction. You should

- be patient as you expect them to make mistakes
- stay very close behind and flash your headlights
- start to rev your engine if they take too long to restart
- immediately steer around them and drive on

be patient as you expect them to make mistakes

Learning is a process of practice and experience. Try to understand this and tolerate others who are at the beginning of this process.

14.37 Mark **one** answer

You are on a country road. What should you expect to see coming towards you on YOUR side of the road?

- Motorcycles
- Bicycles
- Pedestrians
- Horse riders

Pedestrians

On a quiet country road always be aware that there may be a hazard just around the next bend, such as a slow-moving vehicle or pedestrians. There might not be a pavement and people may be walking on your side of the road.

14.38 Mark **one** answer

You are turning left into a side road. Pedestrians are crossing the road near the junction. You should

- wave them on
- sound your horn
- switch on your hazard lights
- wait for them to cross

wait for them to cross

Before you turn into a junction check that it's clear. Check the pavement in each direction. If there are pedestrians crossing let them cross in their own time.

14.39 Mark **one** answer

You are following a car driven by an elderly driver. You should

- expect the driver to drive badly
- flash your lights and overtake
- be aware that the driver's reactions may not be as fast as yours
- stay very close behind but be careful

- **be aware that the driver's reactions may not be as fast as yours**

You must show consideration to other road users. Their reactions may be slower and they might need more time to deal with a situation. Be tolerant and don't lose patience or show your annoyance.

14.40 Mark **one** answer

You are following a cyclist. You wish to turn left just ahead. You should

- overtake the cyclist before the junction
- pull alongside the cyclist and stay level until after the junction
- hold back until the cyclist has passed the junction
- go around the cyclist on the junction

- **hold back until the cyclist has passed the junction**

Make allowances for cyclists. Allow them plenty of room, and be aware that they also have to deal with hazards. They might swerve or change direction suddenly to avoid uneven road surfaces.

14.41 Mark **one** answer

A horse rider is in the left-hand lane approaching a roundabout. You should expect the rider to

- go in any direction
- turn right
- turn left
- go ahead

- **go in any direction**

Horses and their riders will move more slowly than other road users. They might not have time to cut across busy traffic to take up position in the offside lane. If traffic is heavy, it could also be hazardous for them to do so. Therefore a horse and rider may approach a roundabout in the left-hand lane, even though they're turning right.

14.42 Mark **one** answer

You are at the front of a queue of traffic waiting to turn right into a side road. Why is it important to check your right mirror just before turning?

- To look for pedestrians about to cross
- To check for overtaking vehicles
- To make sure the side road is clear
- To check for emerging traffic

To check for overtaking vehicles

There could be another vehicle overtaking you. Motorcyclists often ride along the outside of traffic queues. Keep checking all your mirrors while you are waiting to turn because situations behind you can change quickly. ALWAYS check your right mirror and blind spot just before you make a right turn.

14.43 Mark **one** answer

You are driving past a line of parked cars. You notice a ball bouncing out into the road ahead. What should you do?

- Continue driving at the same speed and sound your horn
- Continue driving at the same speed and flash your headlights
- Slow down and be prepared to stop for children
- Stop and wave the children across to fetch their ball

Slow down and be prepared to stop for children

Beware of children playing in the street and running out into the road. If a ball bounces out from the pavement slow down and stop if necessary. Don't encourage anyone to retrieve it. Other road users may not see your signal and you might lead a child into a dangerous situation.

14.44 Mark **one** answer

You want to turn right from a main road into a side road. Just before turning you should

- cancel your right-turn signal
- select first gear
- check for traffic overtaking on your right
- stop and set the handbrake

check for traffic overtaking on your right

Motorcyclists often overtake queues of vehicles. Always make that last check in the mirror to avoid turning across their path.

14.45 Mark **one** answer

You are driving in town. There is a bus at the bus stop on the other side of the road. Why should you be careful?

- The bus may have broken down
- Pedestrians may come from behind the bus
- The bus may move off suddenly
- The bus may remain stationary

Pedestrians may come from behind the bus

Watch out for pedestrians if you see a bus ahead. They may not be able to see you if they're crossing behind the bus.

14.46 Mark **one** answer

How should you overtake horse riders?

- Drive up close and overtake as soon as possible
- Speed is not important but allow plenty of room
- Use your horn just once to warn them
- Drive slowly and leave plenty of room

Drive slowly and leave plenty of room

Take extra care if you're driving on a country road. Be ready for farm animals, horses, pedestrians and farm vehicles. Always be prepared to slow down or stop.

14.47 Mark **one** answer

Where in particular should you look out for motorcyclists?

- In a filling station
- At a road junction
- Near a service area
- When entering a car park

At a road junction

Always look out for motorcyclists and cyclists, particularly at junctions. They are smaller and usually more difficult to see than other vehicles.

14.48 Mark **one** answer

While driving at night you see a pedestrian wearing reflective clothing and carrying a red light. This means you are approaching

- men at work
- an organised walk
- an accident blackspot
- slow-moving vehicles

an organised walk

Pedestrians who are part of an organised walk using the road at night should wear bright or reflective clothing. The walker in front should display a white light while the one at the back should display a red one. As a driver, though, you need to be aware that they may not always do this. Be particularly careful, slow down and give the walkers plenty of room.

14.49 Mark **one** answer

Which road users are more vulnerable at night in built-up areas?

- Runners
- Drivers of black taxi cabs
- Double-deck vehicle drivers
- Ambulance drivers

Runners

Take extra care. Runners may be difficult to see in the dark.

14.50 *Mark **one** answer*

Which road users are more vulnerable at night in built-up areas?

- Drivers of black taxi cabs
- Pedestrians in dark clothing
- Double-deck vehicle drivers
- Ambulance drivers

Pedestrians in dark clothing

Look out for pedestrians wearing dark clothing.

14.51 *Mark **one** answer*

Which road users are more vulnerable at night in built-up areas?

- Drivers of black taxi cabs
- Double-deck vehicle drivers
- Cyclists
- Ambulance drivers

Cyclists

Look out for cyclists who may not have lights on.

14.52 *Mark **one** answer*

You are about to overtake a motorcyclist. They look over their right shoulder. It is most likely that

- the rider intends moving to the right
- something has fallen from the machine
- the drive chain is slack
- the rear tyre is flat

the rider intends moving to the right

Anticipating the rider's next action in good time could prevent a serious accident, the assessment you make is part of the forward planning of your overtaking manoeuvre.

14.53 Mark **one** answer

You are driving behind a moped. You want to turn left at a junction just ahead. You should

- stay behind until the moped has passed the junction
- overtake the moped before the junction
- pull alongside the moped and stay level until just before the junction
- sound your horn as a warning and pull in front of the moped

stay behind until the moped has passed the junction

Planning your driving will ensure that you anticipate where the moped rider will be in relation to the junction as you arrive to turn left. Overtaking prior to making a left turn is selfish and could result in an avoidable accident, particularly when driving a long vehicle.

14.54 Mark **one** answer

Why should you allow EXTRA room to motorcyclists who are riding through road works?

- There may be a reduced speed limit
- There may be temporary traffic lights
- They may swerve to avoid potholes
- The traffic may be in single file

They may swerve to avoid potholes

Motorcyclists ride through narrow gaps in traffic and generally don't take up as much room as a car. However, other factors, including road surface, can affect their stability. It is wise to give them an extra safety margin when possible.

14.55 Mark **one** answer

At roadworks motorcyclists might swerve to avoid potholes. You should

- give them extra room
- keep alongside them
- try to pass them
- stay close behind them

give them extra room

Always try to anticipate the other road user's next move. Good forward planning by you can help to keep other road users out of trouble. Information to help you do this is available if you look for it. Keep your eyes moving and watch for clues, for example a motorcyclist taking a 'lifesaver' look over their shoulder could show they are going to change direction.

14.56  *Mark **one** answer*

You should be careful NOT to allow your vehicle to spill diesel fuel onto the road. It can be a serious risk ESPECIALLY to

- motorcycles
- empty tankers
- towed vehicles
- fire engines

motorcycles

Those on two wheels don't have the same stability as other vehicles. Where the road surface has been made slippery, for example by spilt diesel fuel, motorcyclists are particularly vulnerable to skidding.

14.57   *Mark **one** answer*

You are driving in a town. Ahead is a stationary bus showing this sign. You should

- accelerate quickly
- stop behind the bus and wait until it moves off
- drive past slowly
- drive normally, the driver will look after the children

drive past slowly

You must be very careful when approaching any hazard where children are concerned, and even more so when the view is restricted. Children getting off the bus will be hidden from your view, and they may not be able to see you. Even if they can see you, they may still suddenly run across the road. It's vitally important that you drive slowly in this situation. Look under the bus, if you can, for signs of feet heading towards the road. Consider sounding the horn, if necessary, to help make the children aware that you're there.

Always be ready to stop.

14.58   *Mark **three** answers*

You are following this scooter on a poor road surface. You should

- overtake without any delay
- stay close behind until you can pass
- make sure you stay well back
- look out as they may wobble
- sound your horn as you get close
- be aware they may suddenly swerve

make sure you stay well back

look out as they may wobble

be aware they may suddenly swerve

On a poor road surface, the rider may need to move out to avoid potholes. You may not get much warning. Look out for signs that the rider may be about to move out – a look to the right or 'lifesaver' check may indicate this. You should also keep a watch on the road surface yourself, to try and predict what path the rider may take. While such road conditions persist, you should stay well back, allowing the rider plenty of room.

14.59  *Mark **one** answer*

You should be extra careful when following riders of scooters as they may suddenly

- look down
- give signals
- swerve
- accelerate

swerve

Scooter riders may suddenly change direction to avoid potholes or raised covers on the road. They can also be blown off course in windy conditions, especially when passing junctions or gaps in buildings, where they may be exposed to sudden gusts.

14.60   *Mark **one** answer*

You are following a scooter. The rider has left it too late to avoid potholes in the road. You should be aware that the rider may suddenly

- accelerate
- slow down
- overtake
- turn left

slow down

A rider on two wheels may need to slow down quickly to avoid a pothole. Wherever the road surface is poor, you should always be prepared for those on two wheels to make sudden movements, and stay well back to allow for this.

14.61 Mark **one** answer

At a toucan crossing you should look out for pedestrians and

- ⊙ horse riders
- ⊙ cyclists
- ⊙ motorcyclists
- ⊙ trams

⊙ **cyclists**

A toucan crossing is signal-controlled, but unlike a pelican crossing it does not have a flashing amber light in the sequence. Cyclists and pedestrians share the crossing and get the green signal together. Cyclists are permitted to ride across. The signals are push-button operated.

14.62 Mark **one** answer

You are driving on a dual carriageway. Ahead you see a vehicle with an amber flashing light. What may this be?

- ⊙ An ambulance
- ⊙ A fire engine
- ⊙ A doctor's car on call
- ⊙ A disabled person's vehicle

⊙ **A disabled person's vehicle**

There is a growing number of small battery-powered vehicles being used by disabled people. On unrestricted dual carriageways they must have a flashing amber light. Be very careful as they can only travel at a maximum speed of 8 mph. You may also see other vehicles on dual carriageways with amber flashing lights such as agricultural or breakdown vehicles.

14.63 Mark **one** answer

You are driving near a school in busy traffic. A group of children are walking close to the kerb on your side of the road. What should you do?

- ⊙ Move to the other side of the road
- ⊙ Wave at them to move back from the kerb
- ⊙ Stop for a moment to see what they do
- ⊙ Drive slowly until you are clear of the area

⊙ **Drive slowly until you are clear of the area**

Children can be unpredictable and should be approached with extreme caution. When they are in groups they may 'fool around' and push each other into the road. You need to take extra care because a large vehicle has many blind spots.

14.64 Mark **one** answer

You are following a scooter on an uneven road. You should

- allow extra room, they may swerve to avoid pot holes
- leave less room so they can see you in their mirrors
- drive closely behind and get ready to overtake
- drive close to shield them

allow extra room, they may swerve to avoid pot holes

Never follow any road user too closely. This is particularly important when you are following scooter or motorcycle riders or cyclists. They might brake or swerve suddenly, for example, due to poor road surface conditions. Don't use the size of your vehicle to intimidate them. Be professional and set an example to others.

14.65 Mark **one** answer

You wish to turn left into a side road. In front of you is a cyclist. You should

- overtake the cyclist before the turning
- wait until the cyclist has passed the turning
- sound your horn, the cyclist will give way to you
- drive alongside and check for the cyclist in the mirrors

wait until the cyclist has passed the turning

Stay back and allow the cyclist to proceed. You must not cut across in front of them. Beware of the cyclist who tries to ride into any blind spot on your nearside.

14.66 Mark **one** answer

You are waiting to turn left at a junction. In your mirror you can see a cyclist moving up between the kerb and nearside of your vehicle. You should

- allow them to move in front of you
- move off and make them wait for you
- steer to the left to make them dismount
- tell them to move out of your way

allow them to move in front of you

You need to be aware of the limited vision you have around your vehicle due to its size and shape. Never move off without checking along the nearside of your vehicle. You should always be aware of the possibility of cyclists between your vehicle and the kerb.

14.67 Mark **one** answer

You are approaching a roundabout. You see a cyclist signal right. Why is the cyclist keeping to the left?

- It is a quicker route for the cyclist
- The cyclist is going to turn left
- The cyclist is more vulnerable
- The Highway Code does not apply to cyclists

The cyclist is more vulnerable

The cyclist may not be able to get into a right-hand lane due to heavy traffic. Give the cyclist room. They may not be taking the exit you expect.

14.68 Mark **one** answer

You are entering a roundabout. A cyclist in front of you is signalling to turn right. What should you do?

- Overtake on the right
- Sound the horn
- Overtake on the left
- Allow plenty of room

Allow plenty of room

Allow the cyclist plenty of room. Give them space to get into the correct lane. Always be prepared for them to change direction without looking or signalling their intentions.

14.69 Mark **one** answer

As you are driving a group of horse riders comes towards you. The leading rider's horse suddenly becomes nervous of your presence. What should you do?

- Brake gently to a stop until they have passed
- Brake quickly to a stop, applying the parking brake
- Continue driving, keeping well in to the nearside
- Increase speed to pass the riders quickly

Brake gently to a stop until they have passed

If any of the animals become unsettled, you should brake gently and come to a stop. A nervous animal is unpredictable, you should wait until the animal is settled or has passed by. Other road users behind you may have limited vision of the hazard, so good mirror work and early signalling will be required.

If you have to pass a group of riders on horseback you must give them plenty of room. Try not to startle the animals, the riders might be learners and have limited control.

14.70 Mark **one** answer

You are emerging from a side road into a queue of traffic. Which of these vehicles are especially hard to see?

- Cycles
- Tractors
- Milk floats
- Cars

Cycles

Cyclists are much narrower than any other vehicle. Always check carefully for cyclists when emerging as they are much more difficult to see than a larger vehicle.

14.71 Mark **one** answer

Motorcycle riders are more at risk from other road users. This is because they

- are easier for other road users to see
- are more likely to break down
- cannot give arm signals
- are more difficult for other road users to see

are more difficult for other road users to see

Always look out for the more vulnerable users on our roads, such as

- motorcyclists
- cyclists
- pedestrians

All need extra consideration. Motorcyclists, in particular, can appear very quickly.

14.72 Mark **one** answer

What is the MAIN cause of motorcycle collisions?

- Other drivers
- Other motorcyclists
- Wet roads
- Icy roads

Other drivers

Motorcyclists are more difficult to see, particularly when the light is poor or it's raining. A bright jacket or single headlight may help you identify an approaching motorcyclist, but you should be aware that not all motorcyclists wear bright clothing or use their headlights during the day.

14.73 Mark **two** answers

Motorcyclists often filter between lines of slow-moving vehicles. Which of the following will cause them particular danger?

- The queuing vehicles
- Vehicles changing lanes
- Vehicles emerging from junctions
- Traffic lights
- Zebra crossings

- **Vehicles changing lanes**
- **Vehicles emerging from junctions**

In slow-moving traffic, particularly on dual carriageways or motorways, always be on the look-out for motorcyclists who approach from behind and filter through narrow gaps between vehicles.

14.74 Mark **three** answers

At road junctions, which of the following are most at risk?

- Motorcyclists
- Pedestrians
- Car drivers
- Cyclists
- Lorry drivers

- **Motorcyclists**
- **Pedestrians**
- **Cyclists**

At busy junctions scan near, middle and far distances to identify all the hazards before emerging with a long vehicle. Be alert for other road users hidden by parked vehicles.

14.75 Mark **three** answers

Drivers should be aware that motorcyclists are more vulnerable ESPECIALLY

- to emerging vehicles
- in gusting winds
- on poor road surfaces
- at traffic lights
- near zebra crossings
- when exiting motorways

- **to emerging vehicles**
- **in gusting winds**
- **on poor road surfaces**

Always be concerned for the safety of yourself and other road users. Be aware of the various factors that create situations where you will sometimes have to take action to keep more vulnerable road users safe.

14.76 Mark **one** answer

You are driving towards a zebra crossing. A person in a wheelchair is waiting to cross. You should

- continue on your way
- wave to the person to cross
- wave to the person to wait
- be prepared to stop

be prepared to stop

As you would with an able-bodied person, you should prepare to slow down and stop. Don't wave them across as other traffic may not stop.

14.77 Mark **one** answer

How will a school crossing patrol signal you to stop?

- By pointing to children on the opposite pavement
- By displaying a red light
- By displaying a 'stop' sign
- By giving you an arm signal

By displaying a 'stop' sign

If someone steps out into the road with a school crossing sign you must stop. Don't wave anyone across the road or get impatient and rev your engine.

14.78 Mark **one** answer

There is a slow-moving motorcyclist ahead of you. You are unsure what the rider is going to do. What is the first thing you should do?

- Pass on the left
- Pass on the right
- Stay behind
- Move closer

Stay behind

Be patient. The motorcyclist might be turning right, changing direction or unsure of their destination. Stay behind until the rider has made a move or you are sure that you can pass safely.

14.79 Mark three answers

At road junctions, which of the following are most vulnerable?

- Cyclists
- Motorcyclists
- Pedestrians
- Car drivers
- Lorry drivers

Cyclists

Motorcyclists

Pedestrians

Good effective observation, coupled with appropriate action, can save lives.

14.80 Mark one answer

You notice horse riders ahead. What should you do FIRST?

- Pull out to the middle of the road
- Be prepared to slow down
- Accelerate around them
- Signal right

Be prepared to slow down

Always look well ahead and be ready to deal with hazards as they occur.

14.81 Mark one answer

As you approach a pelican crossing the lights change to green. Elderly people are halfway across. You should

- wave at them to cross as quickly as they can
- rev your engine to make them hurry
- flash your lights in case they have not heard you
- wait because they will take longer to cross

wait because they will take longer to cross

Even if the lights turn to green, wait for them to clear the crossing. Allow them to cross the road in their own time.

14.82 Mark **one** answer

Where would you see this sign?

- Near a school crossing
- At a playground entrance
- On a school bus
- In a 'pedestrians only' area

On a school bus

Watch out for children crossing the road from the other side of the bus.

14.83 Mark **one** answer

You are following a motorcyclist on an uneven road. You should

- allow less room so you can be seen in their mirrors
- overtake immediately
- allow extra room in case they swerve to avoid potholes
- allow the same room as normal because road surfaces do not affect motorcyclists

allow extra room in case they swerve to avoid potholes

Potholes in the road can unsteady a motorcyclist. For this reason the rider might swerve to avoid an uneven road surface. Watch out at places where this is likely to occur.

14.84 Mark **three** answers

Which THREE of the following are hazards motorcyclists may present in queues of traffic?

- Cutting in just in front of you
- Riding in single file
- Passing very close to you
- Riding with their headlight on dipped beam
- Filtering between the lanes

Cutting in just in front of you

Passing very close to you

Filtering between the lanes

Where there's more than one lane of queuing traffic, motorcyclists use the opportunity to make progress by riding between the lanes. Be aware that they may be passing on either side and check your mirrors before you move off, change lane, turn or make any other change of direction.

14.85 Mark **one** answer

You are driving past parked cars. You notice a bicycle wheel sticking out between them. What should you do?

- Accelerate past quickly and sound your horn
- Slow down and wave the cyclist across
- Brake sharply and flash your headlights
- Slow down and be prepared to stop for a cyclist

Slow down and be prepared to stop for a cyclist

Scan the road as you drive. Try to anticipate hazards by being aware of the places where they are likely to occur. You'll then be able to react in good time, if necessary.

14.86 Mark **one** answer

Yellow zigzag lines on the road outside schools mean

- sound your horn to alert other road users
- stop to allow children to cross
- you must not wait or park on these lines
- you must not drive over these lines

you must not wait or park on these lines

Parking here will block the view of the crossing area. This will endanger the lives of children on their way to and from school.

14.87 Mark **one** answer

You are driving on a main road. You intend to turn right into a side road. Just before turning you should

- adjust your interior mirror
- flash your headlights
- steer over to the left
- check for traffic overtaking on your right

check for traffic overtaking on your right

A last check in the offside mirror will allow you sight of any cyclist or motorcyclist passing on your offside.

14.88 Mark **one** answer

Where should you take particular care to look out for motorcyclists and cyclists?

- On dual carriageways
- At junctions
- At zebra crossings
- In one-way streets

At junctions

Motorcyclists and cyclists may be more difficult to see on the road. This is especially the case at junctions. You may not be able to see a motorcyclist approaching a junction if your view is blocked by other traffic. A motorcycle may be travelling as fast as a car, or faster. Make sure that you judge speeds correctly before you emerge.

section **fifteen**

TRAFFIC SIGNS

This section covers

- Road signs
- Speed limits
- Regulations

15.1 *Mark **one** answer*

This sign means

- buses only
- bus lane
- no buses
- bus stop

no buses

No buses with over eight passenger seats are permitted past this sign. Exceptions apply for scheduled services, school and works buses.

15.2 *Mark **one** answer*

You are driving a 12 metres long, fully loaded coach. What should you do when you approach this sign?

- Do not proceed past the sign but find another route
- Set down all your passengers at a safe place before the sign
- Stop and check the legal lettering on the side panel
- Proceed as normal, the sign does not apply to you

Proceed as normal, the sign does not apply to you

The sign shows the maximum authorised mass allowed for goods vehicles. This sign is used to restrict heavy lorries, for example in residential areas, but does not apply to buses and coaches.

15.3 *Mark* ***two*** *answers*

Which of the following are most likely to share a bus lane?

- Cyclists
- Lorries
- Orange badge holders
- Cars towing caravans
- Taxis

Cyclists

Taxis

Cyclists can be safer travelling in the bus lane. Taxis are allowed to use these lanes as they provide a clearer route and can be quicker, thereby encouraging people to use public transport and so reducing the amount of traffic congestion.

15.4   *Mark* ***one*** *answer*

What does this sign mean?

- End of restricted speed area
- End of restricted parking area
- End of clearway
- End of cycle route

End of restricted parking area

Even though there are no restrictions, make sure that you park where you won't cause an obstruction or endanger other road users.

15.5  *Mark* ***one*** *answer*

Which sign means 'No stopping'?

Stopping where you see this sign is likely to cause congestion. Allow the traffic to flow by obeying the signs.

15.6 Mark **one** answer

What is the meaning of this traffic sign?

- End of two-way road
- Give priority to vehicles coming towards you
- You have priority over vehicles coming towards you
- Bus lane ahead

You have priority over vehicles coming towards you

Before passing this sign, make sure oncoming traffic is going to give way, even though you have priority.

15.7 Mark **one** answer

What does this sign mean?

- No overtaking
- You are entering a one-way street
- Two-way traffic ahead
- You have priority over vehicles from the opposite direction

You have priority over vehicles from the opposite direction

You have priority, but if a vehicle approaching from the opposite direction is obviously not going to stop, slow down and give way to avoid confrontation or an accident.

15.8 *Mark **one** answer*

At a junction you see this sign partly covered by snow. What does it mean?

- Crossroads
- Give way
- Stop
- Turn right

Stop

The 'Stop' sign is the only sign this shape. This is to give it greater prominence. You can still recognise this sign despite snow covering the wording.

15.9 *Mark **one** answer*

What does this sign mean?

- Service area 30 miles ahead
- Maximum speed 30 mph
- Minimum speed 30 mph
- Lay-by 30 miles ahead

Minimum speed 30 mph

This sign is shown where slow-moving vehicles would impede the flow of traffic. However, if you need to slow down to avoid an incident you should do so.

15.10 *Mark **one** answer*

Which of these signs means turn left ahead?

This sign gives a clear instruction. You should be looking out for signs as you drive. Prepare to negotiate a left-hand turn.

15.11 *Mark **one** answer*

What does this sign mean?

- Route for trams
- Give way to trams
- Route for buses
- Give way to buses

Route for trams

Take extra care when you first encounter trams. Look out for road markings and signs that alert you to them. Modern trams are very quiet and you may not hear them approaching.

15.12 *Mark **one** answer*

Which of these signs means that you are entering a one-way street?

If the road has two lanes you can use either lane and overtake on either side. Use the lane that's more convenient for your destination unless directed by road signs or markings.

15.13  *Mark **one** answer*

What does this sign mean?

- ⊙ Bus station on the right
- ⊙ Contraflow bus lane
- ⊙ With-flow bus lane
- ⊙ Give way to buses

⊙ **Contraflow bus lane**

There will also be markings on the road surface to indicate the bus lane. Don't use this lane for parking or overtaking.

15.14  *Mark **one** answer*

What does a sign with a brown background show?

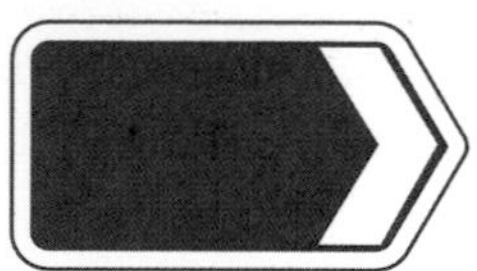

- ⊙ Tourist directions
- ⊙ Primary roads
- ⊙ Motorway routes
- ⊙ Minor routes

⊙ **Tourist directions**

Signs with a brown background give directions to places of interest.

15.15 *Mark **four** answers*

Which FOUR of these would be indicated by a triangular road sign?

- Road narrows
- Ahead only
- Low bridge
- Minimum speed
- Children crossing
- T-junction

- **Road narrows**
- **Low bridge**
- **Children crossing**
- **T-junction**

A triangular sign is a warning sign. Knowing this you can prepare for the hazard ahead.

15.16 *Mark **one** answer*

Which sign means that pedestrians may be walking along the road?

Be cautious, especially if there is a bend in the road and you're unable to see well ahead.

If you have to pass pedestrians, leave plenty of room. Be aware that you might have to use the right-hand side of the road so look well ahead, as well as in your mirrors, before you pull out.

15.17   *Mark **one** answer*

What does this sign mean?

- ⊙ Crosswinds
- ⊙ Road noise
- ⊙ Airport
- ⊙ Adverse camber

⊙ **Crosswinds**

Where weather conditions are frequently bad, signs will give you a warning. A sign with a picture of a wind-sock will indicate there may be strong crosswinds. This sign is often found on exposed roads.

15.18   *Mark **one** answer*

What does this traffic sign mean?

- ⊙ Slippery road ahead
- ⊙ Tyres liable to punctures ahead
- ⊙ Danger ahead
- ⊙ Service area ahead

⊙ **Danger ahead**

A sign showing an exclamation mark (!) will alert you to the likelihood of danger ahead. Be ready for any situation that requires you to reduce your speed.

15.19 Mark **one** answer

You are about to overtake when you see this sign. You should

- overtake the other driver as quickly as possible
- move to the right to get a better view
- switch your headlights on before overtaking
- hold back until you can see clearly ahead

hold back until you can see clearly ahead

You won't be able to see any hazards that might be out of sight in the dip. Imagine there might be

- cyclists
- horse riders
- parked vehicles
- pedestrians.

Oncoming traffic may also present hazards that you need to deal with.

15.20 Mark **one** answer

What does this sign mean?

- Uneven road surface
- Bridge over the road
- Road ahead ends
- Water across the road

Water across the road

This sign is found where a shallow stream crosses the road. Heavy rainfall could increase the flow of water. If the water looks too deep or the stream has swelled over a large distance, stop and find another route.

15.21 Mark **one** answer

You see this traffic light ahead. Which light(s) will come on next?

- Red alone
- Red and amber together
- Green and amber together
- Green alone

Red alone

The amber means stop. You may only go on if the amber appears after you have crossed the stop line or you are so close that to pull up might cause a collision. This is followed by the red light.

You must remain behind the stop line until the green light shows.

15.22 Mark **three** answers

These flashing red lights mean STOP. In which THREE of the following places could you find them?

- Pelican crossings
- Lifting bridges
- Zebra crossings
- Level crossings
- Motorway exits
- Fire stations

Lifting bridges

Level crossings

Fire stations

You must stop if the red lights are flashing. A steady amber light shows before the red lights start flashing; this means stop unless it is unsafe to do so. Don't take risks by trying to beat the amber light even if you think your way is clear.

15.23 Mark **one** answer

You see this sign when driving through roadworks. What does it tell you?

- Large vehicles must go straight ahead
- Traffic is joining from the left
- All traffic must leave at the next exit
- The distance to the next exit

The distance to the next exit

This sign gives you advance warning of a junction where the permanent sign is obscured by roadworks.

15.24 Mark **one** answer

What does this sign mean?

- Stop only to pick up passengers
- No stopping at any time
- Stop only to set down passengers
- No stopping at peak times

No stopping at any time

This traffic sign means no stopping on the main carriageway at any time – not even to set down passengers – unless in a lay-by.

15.25 Mark **one** answer

You are driving on a motorway and there is no traffic ahead. You see this sign. Where should you be driving?

- In the right-hand lane
- Along the hard shoulder
- In the left-hand lane
- Along the middle lane

In the left-hand lane

When there is no traffic ahead of you, you should always drive in the left-hand lane.

15.26 Mark **one** answer

Which of these signs shows an uphill gradient?

You will need to identify the sign in time so that you can select an appropriate gear.

15.27 Mark **one** answer

Which of these signs means uneven road?

Some signs can look similar to others but each one has a different meaning. You should learn the meaning of every sign.

15.28 Mark **one** answer

Some junctions are marked with advanced stop lines. What are these for?

- To allow room for pedestrians to cross the road
- To allow space for large vehicles to turn
- To allow cyclists to position in front of other traffic
- To allow you to select where to stop

To allow cyclists to position in front of other traffic

Advanced stop lines are to allow cyclists and also buses to be positioned ahead of other traffic. When the green signal shows it allows them time and space to move off in front of the following traffic.

15.29 Mark **one** answer

The driver of the car in front is giving this arm signal. This means the driver

- intends to turn left
- is slowing down
- wants you to keep back
- wants you to go past

intends to turn left

Sometimes it may be necessary to reinforce direction indicator signals and brake lights with an arm signal, for example in bright sunshine.

15.30   *Mark **one** answer*

This motorway sign means

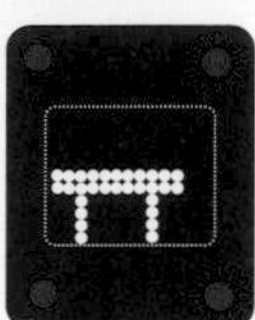

- use the hard shoulder
- contraflow system ahead
- overhead bridge repairs
- all lanes ahead closed

all lanes ahead closed

When the red lights are flashing do not go beyond this signal. This sign shows that all lanes ahead are closed and you must not enter the motorway. Motorway signals are located on the central reservation, to the left of the hard shoulder, on overhead gantries and at the entrance.

15.31   *Mark **one** answer*

This sign warns of

- a slippery road
- a double bend
- an overhead electric cable
- a series of bends

an overhead electric cable

This sign is used to warn of overhead electric cables and is usually accompanied by a plate indicating the safe height limit.

15.32 Mark **one** answer

You are approaching this sign. Who has priority?

- Larger vehicles
- Oncoming traffic
- Smaller vehicles
- You have right of way

Oncoming traffic

When you see this sign you must give way to traffic from the opposite direction, regardless of the size of your lorry or bus.

15.33 Mark **one** answer

What does this sign mean?

- Car lane only
- Single file only
- Queues likely
- Keep your distance

Queues likely

When you see this sign beware of traffic queues ahead, check your mirrors and reduce your speed. Exercise patience when you are delayed. Understand that annoyance and frustration lead to a poor attitude on the road and ultimately may lead to a collision or incident.

15.34   *Mark **one** answer*

What does this sign mean?

- Road flooded
- Risk of punctures
- Loose chippings
- Uneven surface

Loose chippings

This is a warning sign to indicate loose chippings ahead. The sign is usually accompanied by an advisory speed limit. Vehicles travelling too fast for the conditions can throw up chippings or stones. Avoid causing damage to paintwork and windscreens by showing consideration.

15.35  *Mark **one** answer*

What does this sign mean?

- You are allowed to carry on but only with a police escort
- You should continue very slowly if your weight is above the limit
- Do not cross unless the bridge is clear of other vehicles
- Do not cross the bridge if your weight exceeds the limit

Do not cross the bridge if your weight exceeds the limit

Vehicles over the weight advised are prohibited from using the bridge ahead. An alternative route must be found. Plan your route in advance to avoid delays and congestion. This will save time, fuel and frustration.

You must know the weight of your vehicle, including any load.

15.36 *Mark **one** answer*

This is the first countdown marker to a

- motorway slip road
- primary road junction
- concealed level crossing
- roadside rest area

concealed level crossing

Reduce your speed, you may well have to stop. Be sure that you can stop within the distance you can see to be clear.

15.37 *Mark **one** answer*

What do DOUBLE red lines at the edge of a road mean?

- Limited loading
- No stopping
- Bus route
- Short term parking

No stopping

Red route signs and red road markings have replaced some yellow line restrictions.

15.38 *Mark **one** answer*

Where would you expect to see these road markings?

- At the entrance to a car park
- On the approach to an arched bridge
- At the start of a cycle lane
- On the approach to a lifting barrier

On the approach to an arched bridge

High vehicles are often directed to the centre of the road to go under an arched bridge. Check that your vehicle does not exceed the height restriction indicated.

15.39 *Mark **one** answer*

You are approaching a red traffic light. What signal or signals will show next?

- red and amber, then green
- green, then amber
- amber, then green
- green and amber, then green

red and amber, then green

If you know which light is going to show next you can plan your approach. This will help prevent excessive braking or hesitation at the junction.

15.40 Mark **two** answers

The double white line along the centre of the road is continuous on your side. You may cross the line to

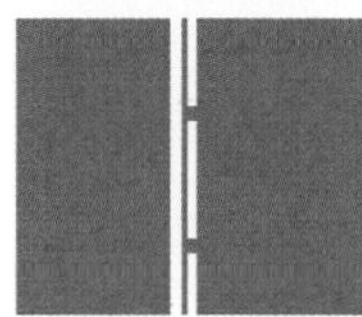

- overtake any slower moving vehicle
- pass a stationary vehicle
- see if it is safe to overtake
- overtake a learner driver travelling at 20 mph or less
- pass a pedal cycle travelling at 10 mph or less

pass a stationary vehicle

pass a pedal cycle travelling at 10 mph or less

Solid white lines are placed where it would be dangerous to overtake. If the solid line is on your side of the road you may cross it to pass a stationary vehicle, or to overtake a pedal cycle, horse or road maintenance vehicle if they are travelling at 10 mph or less. You may also cross the solid line to enter premises or a side road.

15.41 Mark **one** answer

You see this sign ahead. What should you do?

- Accelerate because you have priority
- Slow down, the road may be narrow ahead
- Stop and give way to oncoming traffic
- Maintain your speed, it's just an information sign

Slow down, the road may be narrow ahead

Even when you have priority at a 'road narrowing', you should still slow down and approach with caution. There will be less room than normal. You should be aware that others may not obey the rules.

15.42 *Mark **one** answer*

Why should you slow down when you see this sign?

- ⊙ Because pedestrians have right of way
- ⊙ There is a 'road race' in progress
- ⊙ There are pedestrian crossings ahead
- ⊙ Because children may be crossing

⊙ **Because children may be crossing**

Whenever you see this sign take extra care with these very vulnerable road users.

15.43 *Mark **one** answer*

What does this sign mean?

- ⊙ Vehicle carrying dangerous goods in packages
- ⊙ Vehicle broken down ahead
- ⊙ Holiday route
- ⊙ Emergency diversion route for motorway traffic

⊙ **Emergency diversion route for motorway traffic**

Major roadworks often cause complicated diversions for large vehicles. Drivers may be advised to follow a special symbol until the original road is rejoined. Look for the yellow and black

- square
- triangle
- diamond
- circle

symbols combined with additional information, to help you rejoin your route.

15.44 Mark **one** answer

You are driving on a three-lane motorway. There are red reflective studs on your left and white reflective studs on your right. Which lane are you in?

- Hard shoulder
- Middle lane
- Right-hand lane
- Left-hand lane

Left-hand lane

White reflective studs separate each of the lanes. Red studs mark the left-hand edge of the carriageway where the hard shoulder begins.

15.45 Mark **one** answer

Diamond-shaped signs give instructions to drivers of

- lorries
- trams
- buses
- tractors

trams

You need to show caution when driving in areas where trams operate. You may not hear their approach and they cannot change direction to avoid you. There may also be crossing points where you will need to give way to them, or areas specifically reserved for trams which you are not allowed to enter.

15.46 Mark **one** answer

On which of the following pedestrian crossings can a cyclist ride across without dismounting, as well as pedestrians crossing over?

- Toucan
- Pelican
- Puffin
- Zebra

Toucan

Toucans are shared crossings, where cyclists may ride across the road alongside pedestrians. Look out for them where you see signs and markings for cycle tracks.

15.47 Mark **one** answer

Certain types of crossings are shared by pedestrians and cyclists. Which one of these may a cyclist ride across at?

- Puffin
- Zebra
- Pelican
- Toucan

Toucan

Where a cycle track meets a busy road you may also find a toucan crossing. They're similar to other types of crossing, but have no flashing amber signal.

15.48 Mark **one** answer

'Red Routes' tell you that

- special waiting restrictions apply
- part-time traffic lights operate
- drivers have to pay a toll
- night-time and weekend weight limits apply

special waiting restrictions apply

The main types of 'Red Route' controls are

- double red lines
- single red lines
- parking boxes
- loading boxes (red and white).

Red loading boxes allow up to 20 minutes for loading outside of rush hours. White loading boxes allow up to 20 minutes for loading at any time during the day.

15.49 Mark **one** answer

On a motorway the colour of reflective studs on the right-hand edge of the carriageway is

- amber
- green
- red
- blue

amber

Reflective studs on motorways and dual carriageways are provided to help drivers in bad visibility. Reflective studs are coloured

- red on the left-hand edge of the carriageway
- white to indicate lane markings
- green at slip roads and lay-bys
- amber on the right-hand edge of the carriageways marking the central reservation.

15.50 Mark **one** answer

On a motorway, green–yellow fluorescent studs

- mark the lanes in a contraflow system
- separate the slip road from the motorway
- mark access points for emergency services
- separate the edge of the hard shoulder from the grass verge

mark the lanes in a contraflow system

Roadworks can involve complex lane layouts. To make it easier for you as a driver, reflective green-yellow fluorescent studs are used to separate the lanes in a contraflow traffic system.

Always look well ahead for traffic signs giving you advance information which may relate to the size or type of vehicle you are driving.

15.51 Mark **one** answer

This sign means

- tramway speed limit
- distance to level crossing
- maximum passenger capacity
- goods vehicle weight limit

tramway speed limit

Tramways are becoming increasingly common in large towns and cities, as the move to more environmentally-friendly transport continues. They may either cross the road you're driving on, or share it with you. Always be aware of their virtually silent approach, and look out for places where you may be required to give way to them.

15.52 Mark **one** answer

At puffin crossings which light will not show to a driver?

- Flashing amber
- Red
- Steady amber
- Green

Flashing amber

A flashing amber light is shown at pelican crossings, but not at puffin crossings. These are controlled electronically and automatically detect when pedestrians are on the crossing. The red phase for traffic is shortened or lengthened according to the position of the pedestrians.

15.53 Mark **one** answer

You are approaching a red light at a puffin crossing. Pedestrians are on the crossing. The red light will stay on until

- you start to edge forward onto the crossing
- the pedestrians have reached a safe position
- the pedestrians are clear of the front of your vehicle
- a driver from the opposite direction reaches the crossing

- **the pedestrians have reached a safe position**

The electronic device will automatically detect that the pedestrians have reached a safe position. Don't proceed until the green light shows and it's safe to do so.

15.54 Mark **one** answer

A bus lane on your left shows no times of operation. This means it is

- not in operation at all
- only in operation at peak times
- in operation 24 hours a day
- only in operation in daylight hours

- **in operation 24 hours a day**

You should always be aware of the times when bus lanes are operating. If there is no plate indicating any times of operation, this means that the bus lane operates all the time.

15.55 Mark **one** answer

At a puffin crossing what colour follows the green signal?

- Steady red
- Flashing amber
- Steady amber
- Flashing green

- **Steady amber**

Puffin crossings have infra-red sensors which detect when pedestrians are crossing and hold the red traffic signal until the crossing is clear. This means there is no flashing amber phase as there is with a pelican crossing.

15.56 *Mark* ***one*** *answer*

You are approaching a pelican crossing. The amber light is flashing. You MUST

- give way to pedestrians who are crossing
- encourage pedestrians to cross
- not move until the green light appears
- stop even if the crossing is clear

give way to pedestrians who are crossing

When the amber light is flashing, you must give way to any pedestrians on the crossing.

DON'T encourage pedestrians to cross by waving or flashing your headlights; they or other road users may misunderstand your signal.

DON'T rev your engine impatiently or edge forward.

15.57 *Mark* ***one*** *answer*

On the motorway the hard shoulder should be used

- to answer a mobile phone
- when an emergency arises
- for a short rest when tired
- to check a road atlas

when an emergency arises

Pull onto the hard shoulder and use the emergency telephone to report your problem. You'll be connected to the police or Highways Agency control centre. They will put you through to a breakdown service. Never cross the carriageway or a slip road to use a telephone on the other side.

15.58 *Mark* ***one*** *answer*

You are allowed to stop on a motorway when you

- need to walk and get fresh air
- wish to pick up hitch hikers
- are told to do so by flashing red lights
- need to use a mobile phone

are told to do so by flashing red lights

If red lights flash on the overhead signals above your lane you must NOT go past the signal in that lane. If other lanes are not displaying flashing red lights you may go ahead in those lanes if it's clear and you can move into them safely. If red lights flash on a signal in the central reservation or at the side of the road you must NOT go past the signal in any lane.

15.59   *Mark **one** answer*

Usually, on a motorway, how far from the exit is the first sign showing the junction number?

- Half a mile
- One mile
- Two miles
- Three miles

One mile

Motorway traffic travels at higher speeds, and advance signs warning of junctions are vital to enable you to be in the correct lane in good time to take your exit. In most cases, one mile before the exit you will see a junction sign with road numbers. Half a mile before the exit the sign will also include the names of places accessible from that junction.

15.60   *Mark **one** answer*

Which sign means 'No overtaking'?

This sign is placed on sections of road where overtaking would be dangerous. There will often be a plate underneath this sign telling you how far the restriction extends. You must not overtake where you see this sign until you pass another sign cancelling the restriction.

15.61  *Mark **one** answer*

You might see this sign on a motorway. What does it mean?

- Right hand lane closed ahead
- One tonne weight limit ahead
- Left hand lane closed ahead
- T-junction one mile ahead

Right hand lane closed ahead

Four amber lights flash in alternate horizontal pairs to provide a warning and to draw the driver's attention to the message displayed.

15.62 *Mark **one** answer*

What does this sign mean?

- Accident blackspot ahead
- Ancient monument ahead
- Humpback bridge ahead
- Tunnel ahead

Tunnel ahead

Check any height limits that may accompany this sign.

15.63 *Mark **one** answer*

What does this sign mean?

- No U-turns
- Two-way traffic
- One-way system
- End of one-way system

No U-turns

You must not make a U-turn on roads where this sign is displayed.

15.64   *Mark **one** answer*

What does this sign mean?

- Low bridge
- Tunnel ahead
- Accident blackspot
- Speed camera

Tunnel ahead

A tunnel can present a number of dangers to large vehicles. Look out for height or width limits. Always be aware of your vehicle's size. Reduce speed; as you enter the tunnel your eyes may need to adjust to the sudden darkness. Turn on your headlights before entering the tunnel; this is compulsory in many tunnels.

15.65   *Mark **one** answer*

What does this sign mean?

- Rumble strips
- Road humps
- Uneven road
- Double hump-back bridge

Uneven road

Prepare to slow down especially if carrying passengers, livestock or fragile items.

15.66 Mark **one** answer

Why should you slow down when you see this sign?

- Your tyres may suffer a blow-out
- To avoid splashing others with water
- To avoid throwing up loose chippings
- There is a road gritter ahead

To avoid throwing up loose chippings

This sign will usually be accompanied by a reduced speed limit. When chippings fly out from your tyres they can cause a lot of damage to other vehicles, or injury to pedestrians, cyclists and motorcyclists. Slowing down will lessen the risk.

15.67 Mark **one** answer

You are in an Active Traffic Management area on a motorway. When the hard shoulder is in use as a running lane

- all speed limits are only advisory
- the national speed limit will apply
- the appropriate speed limit is displayed
- the speed limit is always 30 mph

the appropriate speed limit is displayed

Within Active Traffic Management areas a red cross without flashing beacons will usually appear above the hard shoulder. When the hard shoulder is being used as a running lane an appropriate speed limit will be displayed instead. This speed limit is mandatory and must be obeyed.

15.68 Mark **one** answer

Motorway emergency telephones are usually linked to the police. In some areas they are now linked to

- a Highways Agency Regional Control Centre
- the Driver Vehicle Licensing Agency
- the Driving Standards Agency
- a local district Vehicle Registration Office

a Highways Agency Regional Control Centre

In some areas motorway telephones are now linked to a Highways Agency regional Control Centre, instead of the police. Highways Agency Traffic Officers work in partnership with the police and assist at motorway emergencies and incidents. They are recognised by a high-visibility orange and yellow jacket and high-visibility vehicle with yellow and black chequered markings.

15.69 Mark **one** answer

An Emergency Refuge Area is an area

- on a motorway for use in cases of emergency or breakdown
- for use if you think you will be involved in a road rage incident
- on a motorway for a police patrol to park and watch traffic
- for construction and road workers to store emergency equipment

- **on a motorway for use in cases of emergency or breakdown**

Emergency Refuge Areas may be found at the side of the hard shoulder about 500 metres apart. If you break down you should use them rather than the hard shoulder if you are able to. When re-joining the motorway you must remember to take extra care especially when the hard shoulder is being used as a running lane within an Active Traffic Management area. Try to match your speed to that of traffic in the lane you are joining.

15.70 Mark **one** answer

What is an Emergency Refuge Area on a motorway for?

- An area to park in when you want to use a mobile phone
- To use in cases of emergency or breakdown
- For an emergency recovery vehicle to park in a contra-flow system
- To drive in when there is queuing traffic ahead

- **To use in cases of emergency or breakdown**

In cases of breakdown or emergency try to get your vehicle into an Emergency Refuge Area. This is safer than just stopping on the hard shoulder as it gives you greater distance from the main carriageway. If you are able to re-join the motorway you must take extra care especially when the hard shoulder is being used as a running lane.

15.71 Mark **one** answer

Highways Agency Traffic Officers

- cannot assist at a breakdown or emergency
- cannot stop and direct anyone on a motorway
- will tow a broken down vehicle and its passengers home
- are able to stop and direct anyone on a motorway

are able to stop and direct anyone on a motorway

Highways Agency Traffic Officers (HATOs) do not have enforcement powers but are able to stop and direct people on motorways. They don't operate in Scotland or Wales. They work in partnership with the police at motorway incidents and provide a highly-trained and visible service. Their role is to help keep traffic moving and make your journey as safe and reliable as possible. They are recognised by an orange and yellow jacket and their vehicle has yellow and black markings.

15.72 Mark **one** answer

You are on a motorway. A red cross is displayed above the hard shoulder. What does this mean?

- Pull up in this lane to answer your mobile phone
- You may use this lane as a running lane
- This lane can be used if you need a rest
- You should not use this lane as a running lane

You should not use this lane as a running lane

Active Traffic Management schemes are being introduced on motorways. Within these areas at certain times the hard shoulder will be used as a running lane. A red cross above the hard shoulder shows that this lane should NOT be used, except for emergencies and breakdowns.

15.73 *Mark **one** answer*

You are on a motorway in an Active Traffic Management (ATM) area. A mandatory speed limit is displayed above the hard shoulder. What does this mean?

- You should not use the hard shoulder as a running lane
- The hard shoulder can be used as a running lane between junctions
- You can park on the hard shoulder if you feel tired
- No service area facilities or fuel are available for fifty miles

- **The hard shoulder can be used as a running lane between junctions**

A mandatory speed limit sign above the hard shoulder shows that it can be used as a running lane between junctions. You must stay within the signed speed limit. Look out for vehicles that may have broken down and are blocking the hard shoulder.

15.74 *Mark **one** answer*

The aim of an Active Traffic Management scheme on a motorway is to

- prevent overtaking
- reduce rest stops
- prevent tailgating
- reduce congestion

- **reduce congestion**

Active Traffic Management schemes are intended to reduce congestion and make journey times more reliable. In these areas the hard shoulder may be used as a running lane to ease congestion at peak times or when an incident occurs. It may seem that you could travel faster for a short distance, but keeping traffic flow at a constant speed may improve journey times.

15.75 Mark **one** answer

You are in an Active Traffic Management area on a motorway. When the Actively Managed mode is operating

- speed limits are only advisory
- the national speed limit will apply
- the speed limit is always 30 mph
- all speed limit signals are set

all speed limit signals are set

When an Active Traffic Management (ATM) scheme is operating on a motorway you must follow the mandatory instructions shown on the gantries above each lane. This includes the hard shoulder.

15.76 Mark **one** answer

You are travelling on a motorway. A red cross is shown above the hard shoulder and mandatory speed limits above all other lanes. This means

- the hard shoulder can be used as a rest area if you feel tired
- the hard shoulder is for emergency or breakdown use only
- the hard shoulder can be used as a normal running lane
- the hard shoulder has a speed limit of 50 mph

the hard shoulder is for emergency or breakdown use only

A red cross above the hard shoulder shows it is closed as a running lane and should only be used for emergencies or breakdowns. At busy times within an Active Traffic Management area the hard shoulder may be used as a running lane. This will be shown by a mandatory speed limit on the gantry above.

15.77 Mark **one** answer

You are travelling on a motorway. A red cross is shown above the hard shoulder. What does this mean?

- Use this lane as a rest area
- Use this as a normal travelling lane
- Do not use this lane as a running lane
- National speed limit applies in this lane

Do not use this lane as a running lane

When a red cross is shown above the hard shoulder it should only be used for breakdowns or emergencies. Within Active Traffic Management (ATM) areas the hard shoulder may sometimes be used as a running lane. Speed limit signs directly above the hard shoulder will show that it's open.

15.78 Mark **one** answer

You see this sign on a motorway in an Active Traffic Management area. You can use

- any lane except the hard shoulder
- the hard shoulder only
- the three right hand lanes only
- all the lanes including the hard shoulder

all the lanes including the hard shoulder

Mandatory speed limit signs above the hard shoulder and all other lanes, show that you are in an Active Traffic Management (ATM) area. In this case you can use the hard shoulder as a running lane. You must stay within the speed limit shown. Look out for any vehicles that may have broken down and be blocking the hard shoulder.

15.79 Mark **one** answer

You should not normally travel on the hard shoulder of a motorway. When can you use it?

- When taking the next exit
- When traffic is stopped
- When signs show that you can
- When traffic is slow moving

When signs show that you can

Normally you should only use the hard shoulder for emergencies and breakdowns, and at roadworks when signs direct you to. Active Traffic Management (ATM) areas are being introduced to ease traffic congestion. In these areas the hard shoulder may be used as a running lane when speed limit signs are shown directly above.

15.80 Mark **one** answer

Why should you NOT park on the verge where you see this sign?

- Your wheels will sink into the mud
- Only cars may park here
- Parking restrictions apply
- Fuel and water tanks will leak

Your wheels will sink into the mud

This sign tells you that the verge is soft, and if you park here there is a danger that your vehicle will become stuck. This can be inconvenient and could be costly if you need to be pulled out. In extreme cases your vehicle may even tip over, endangering yourself and other road users.

15.81 Mark **one** answer

You are driving a 38 tonnes lorry on a single carriageway road. You see this sign. You may drive at up to

- 40 mph
- 50 mph
- 60 mph
- 70 mph

40 mph

The national speed limit for a goods vehicle exceeding 7.5 tonnes on a single carriageway road is 40 mph. A speed limit does not mean it is safe to drive at that speed. Drive according to the road conditions.

15.82 Mark **one** answer

You are driving a 38 tonnes lorry and trailer on a dual carriageway. This sign means you may drive at up to

- 40 mph
- 50 mph
- 60 mph
- 70 mph

50 mph

This may be the legal limit but it does not mean that it is safe to drive at that speed in all conditions. You should always take into account the road and weather conditions and drive accordingly.

15.83 Mark **one** answer

You are driving an articulated lorry. What should you do when you see this sign ahead?

- Turn round and find an alternative route
- Park safely and arrange alternative transport for the goods
- Inform your vehicle operator and await further instructions
- Proceed as normal, the sign does not apply to you

Proceed as normal, the sign does not apply to you

The sign prohibits buses and coaches with more than eight passenger seats.

15.84 — Mark **one** answer

Which sign must you NOT drive your lorry past?

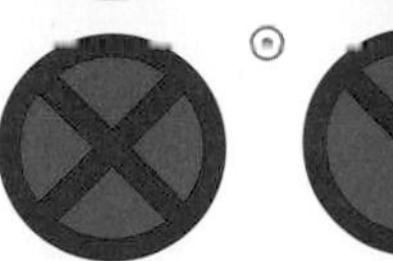

This sign means no motor vehicles. Although a motorcycle and car are shown it applies to all classes of motor vehicle.

15.85 — Mark **one** answer

You are driving a lorry 30 feet long and towing a trailer 15 feet long. You see this sign ahead. What should you do?

- Find an alternative route to your destination
- Stop and wait for a police escort
- Continue past the sign but reduce your speed
- Carry on, as the sign applies to the towing vehicle only

Find an alternative route to your destination

The maximum permitted length of vehicle includes any trailer being towed. Ensure you know the total length of your vehicle.

15.86 Mark **one** answer

You are driving a lorry with a heavy load. You see this sign ahead. What should you be prepared to do?

- Brake to a lower speed
- Change up to a higher gear
- Stop to check your load
- Change down to a lower gear

Change down to a lower gear

A heavy vehicle will lose speed when climbing a steep hill. Changing to a lower gear will help you to maintain an appropriate speed.

15.87 Mark **one** answer

You are on a motorway. Your lorry has a maximum authorised mass of more than 7.5 tonnes. What does this sign mean to you?

- You must not use the right-hand lane
- You can only use the right-hand lane
- You cannot leave the motorway at this junction
- You can use the middle or right-hand lane

You must not use the right-hand lane

At motorway roadworks some lanes may be narrower than normal and large vehicles may not be allowed to use those lanes. Look for weight limit signs to check for any lanes that you can't use. Move to the appropriate lane in good time.

15.88 *Mark **one** answer*

What is the national speed limit for a lorry over 7.5 tonnes on a motorway?

- 50 mph (80 kph)
- 55 mph (88 kph)
- 60 mph (96 kph)
- 70 mph (112 kph)

60 mph (96 kph)

Be aware of, and obey, all speed limits. On a motorway a lorry that is articulated or towing a trailer, or that is over 7.5 tonnes, must not exceed 60 mph (96 kph).

15.89 *Mark **one** answer*

As a lorry driver, when MUST you use these two signs?

- When the load overhangs the front or rear of the vehicle by more than one metre (3 feet 3 inches)
- Whenever your vehicle is being towed
- Whenever a police escort is required
- When the load overhangs the front or rear of the vehicle by more than two metres (6 feet 6 inches)

When the load overhangs the front or rear of the vehicle by more than two metres (6 feet 6 inches)

The law requires you to use projection markers for long or wide loads. It is the driver's responsibility to ensure the markers are clean and secure and also that they are independently lit at night.

15.90 *Mark **one** answer*

You are driving a 14 tonnes lorry on a motorway. What does this sign mean ?

- Maximum speed 40 mph
- Maximum speed 50 mph
- Maximum speed 60 mph
- Maximum speed 70 mph

Maximum speed 60 mph

The maximum speed for lorries over 7.5 tonnes on a motorway is 60 mph. But it may not always be appropriate or possible to drive at this speed.

15.91 *Mark **one** answer*

You are driving a 14 tonnes lorry on a dual carriageway. What does this sign mean?

- Maximum speed 40 mph
- Maximum speed 50 mph
- Maximum speed 60 mph
- Maximum speed 70 mph

Maximum speed 50 mph

Be aware of the speed limits applying to different types of vehicles on particular roads. These are the maximum speeds allowed but it may not always be safe to drive at this speed.

15.92 *Mark **one** answer*

You are driving a 14 tonnes lorry on a single carriageway road. What does this sign mean?

- Maximum speed 30 mph
- Maximum speed 40 mph
- Maximum speed 50 mph
- Maximum speed 60 mph

Maximum speed 40 mph

The national speed limit for lorries over 7.5 tonnes on a single carriageway road is 40 mph.

15.93 *Mark **one** answer*

When a Red Route is in operation you must not

- stop and park
- overtake
- change lanes
- straddle the lines

stop and park

The hours of operation of red routes vary from one area to another. As a rule you must not stop in these areas, but there may be special marked boxes where loading and unloading can be carried out at certain times. Look out for signs giving information regarding the restrictions in place.

annex one
LIST OF TEST CENTRES

England
Aldershot
Barnstaple
Barrow
Basildon
Basingstoke
Bath
Berwick-upon-Tweed
Birkenhead
Birmingham
Blackpool
Bolton
Boston
Bournemouth
Bradford
Brighton
Bristol
Bury St Edmunds
Cambridge
Canterbury
Carlisle
Chatham
Chelmsford
Cheltenham
Chester
Chesterfield
Colchester
Coventry
Crawley
Derby
Doncaster
Dudley
Durham
Eastbourne
Exeter
Fareham
Gloucester
Grantham
Grimsby
Guildford
Harlow
Harrogate
Hastings
Hereford
Huddersfield
Hull
Ipswich
Isle of Wight
Isles of Scilly
King's Lynn
Leeds
Leicester
Lincoln
Liverpool
London
– Croydon
– Ilford
– Kingston
– Southgate
– Southwark
– Staines
– Uxbridge
Lowestoft
Luton
Manchester
Mansfield
Middlesbrough
Milton Keynes
Morpeth
Newcastle
Northampton
Norwich
Nottingham
Oldham
Oxford
Penzance
Peterborough
Plymouth
Portsmouth
Preston
Reading
Redditch
Runcorn
Salford
Salisbury
Scarborough
Scunthorpe
Sheffield
Shrewsbury
Sidcup
Slough
Solihull
Southampton
Southend-on-Sea
Southport
St Helens

Stevenage
Stockport
Stoke-on-Trent
Stratford-upon-Avon
Sunderland
Sutton Coldfield
Swindon
Taunton
Torquay
Truro
Watford
Weymouth
Wigan
Wolverhampton
Worcester
Workington
Worthing
Yeovil
York

Scotland

Aberdeen
Ayr
Dumfries
Dundee
Dunfermline
Edinburgh
Elgin
Fort William
Gairloch
Galashiels
Glasgow
Clydebank
Greenock
Helmsdale
Huntly
Inverness
Isle of Arran
Isle of Barra
Isle of Benbecula
Isle of Islay, Bowmore
Isle of Mull, Salen
Isle of Tiree
Kirkwall
Kyle of Lochalsh
Lerwick
Motherwell
Oban
Pitlochry
Portree
Stirling
Stornoway
Stranraer
Tarbert, Argyllshire
Tongue
Ullapool
Wick

Wales

Aberystwyth
Bangor
Builth Wells
Cardiff
Haverfordwest
Merthyr Tydfil
Newport
Rhyl
Swansea

Northern Ireland

Ballymena
Belfast
Londonderry
Newry
Omagh
Portadown

annex two

SERVICE STANDARDS

We judge our performance against the following standards (printed in our Business Plan) which we review each year

- 95% of calls to booking offices will make contact with our automated call-handling system without receiving an engaged tone
- after a call has gone through our automated call-handling system, we will answer 90% of all incoming calls to booking offices in no more than 20 seconds
- we will give 95% of candidates an appointment at their preferred centre within two weeks of their preferred date
- our online booking service will be available 99% of the time over 24 hours, 7 days a week.
- we will keep 99.5% of all theory test appointments
- we will answer 97% of all letters and e-mails within 10 working days
- we will pay 95% of all refunds within 15 days of receiving a valid claim.

Complaints guide - We aim to give our customers the best possible service. Please tell us when we have done well or you're not satisfied.

Your comments can help us to improve the service we offer.

If you have any questions about your theory test please contact us using the numbers below.

For DSA
Tel 0300 200 1122, fax 0300 200 1177

For new numbers from November, see page 3.

For DVA (in Northern Ireland)
Tel 0845 600 6700, fax 0845 010 4372

If you have any complaints about how your theory test was carried out, or any aspect of our customer service, please call the Customer Enquiry Unit on 0300 200 1188. Alternatively you can write to the Customer Enqiry Unit at the following address:

Customer Enquiry Unit
Driving Theory Test
PO Box 381
Manchester M50 3UW

If you're dissatisfied with the reply you can write to the Managing Director at the same address.

If you're still not satisfied, you can take up your complaint with:

The Chief Executive
Driving Standards Agency
The Axis Building
112 Upper Parliament Street
Nottingham NG1 6LP

In Northern Ireland you should write to

The Chief Executive
Driver and Vehicle Agency (Testing)
Balmoral Road
Belfast BT12 6QL

None of this removes your right to take your complaint to your Member of Parliament, who may decide to raise your case personally with the DSA or DVA Chief Executive, the Minister or the Parliamentary Commissioner for Administration (the Ombudsman). Please refer to our leaflet *Service Standards - putting things right*.

DSA is a Trading Fund and we are required to cover our costs from the driving test fee.

We don't have a quota for test passes or fails and if you demonstrate the standard required, you'll pass your test.

Refunding fees and expenses - DSA will normally refund the test fee, or rearrange another test at no further cost to you, if

- we cancel your test
- you cancel and give us at least three clear working days' notice
- you keep the test appointment but the test doesn't take place, or isn't finished, for a reason that isn't your fault.

We'll also repay you the expenses that you had to pay on the day of the test if we cancelled your test at short notice.

We'll consider reasonable claims for

- the cost of travelling to and from the test centre
- any standard pay or earnings you lost through taking unpaid holiday leave (usually for half a day), after tax and national insurance contributions.

Please write to the address below and send a receipt showing travel costs and an employer's letter, which shows what earnings you lost. If you think you're entitled to fees and expenses write to:

Customer Enquiry Unit
Driving Theory Test
PO Box 381
Manchester M50 3UW

This reimbursement policy doesn't affect your existing legal rights.

DVA has a different reimbursement policy.

Other Official DSA Publications

The Official DSA Theory Test for Drivers of Large Vehicles CD-ROM

Includes new question bank for 2008/09 and is valid for tests taken from 4 August 2008 when the Large Goods Vehicles (LGVs) and Passenger Carrying Vehicles (PCVs) theory test changes to 100 questions. This new edition includes a digital version of the latest edition of The Official Highway Code.

ISBN 9780115529047 £35.00

The Official DSA Guide to Hazard Perception DVD

Contains the official DSA video clips to help you prepare fully for your theory and practical tests. Includes references to the latest edition of The Official Highway Code.

ISBN 9780115528651 £15.99

The Official Highway Code

This latest edition contains new and amended rules of the road and is essential reading for all road users, not just learners. The CD-ROM version is a great interactive alternative to the best-selling book and includes games and quizzes to help bring the Highway Code to life.

Book - ISBN 9780115528149 £2.50

CD-ROM - ISBN 9780115528460 £9.99

Driver CPC – the Official DSA Guide for Professional Bus and Coach Drivers

Brand new title for 2008 – this publication aims to help bus and coach drivers prepare for Modules 2 and 4 of their initial Certificate of Professional Competence, which comes into force in September 2008.

ISBN 9780115529405 £9.99

Published *June 2008*

The Official DSA Guide to Driving Buses and Coaches

This is the only official guide which explains the standards required to pass today's practical PCV test. Packed with expert advice to help all PCV drivers become safer on the road, this latest edition includes a wealth of additional information which will form the basis of the new Driver CPC test to be introduced in September 2008.

ISBN 9780115529009 £15.99

The Official DSA Guide to Driving Goods Vehicles

This is the only official guide which explains the standards required to pass today's practical LGV test. Packed with expert advice to help all LGV drivers become safer on the road, this latest edition includes additional information which will form the basis of the new Driver CPC test to be introduced in September 2009.

ISBN 9780115528996 £15.99